Praise for

Engaging, inspiring, open, honest, and brave, this is a deeply moving and reflective account of Carol's odyssey from non-scientist, non-researcher, non-academic to the successful completion of her PhD, the world's first in Reflexology and pain management. Clear and engaging, the narrative interweaves her personal and academic journey against all the odds, her dogged determination and gutsy refusal to give up even when faced with the most challenging life events, ensuring her final success. In the book, Carol talks the reader through the challenges faced by those undertaking research on holistic therapies from a scientific standpoint, especially when there is limited if any prior existing research/evidence base, as was the case in her chosen specialism. Her story is also interspersed with reflective passages and explanations of the science behind her research specialism which clearly demonstrates her authority on this fascinating and complex topic area. Her honest and unfiltered account of the research process and academia would be invaluable to anyone considering undertaking a higher degree by research. Brilliant!

Roz Gibbs, PhD; BSc (Hons); LicAc; MBAcC; FHEA.

Dr Carol Samuel has broken new ground in this fascinating and extremely readable book. Carol charts her difficult, yet inspiring life journey from her early days as a non-academic to being the first person in the world to achieve a PhD in Reflexology and pain management.

This book will be of great interest to all complementary therapists as it gives worldly and well written insights into the scientific world at a high level of academia in an English university. Its appeal will also reach many laypersons and those readers who will take inspiration themselves to aim high in their own personal lives and goals, and who may aspire to achieve what was once deemed impossible.

Carol takes us through the process of PhD selection to illustrate how research projects are conducted. She belies the idea of fusty academia and breathes life into her descriptions of the challenges involved in getting a reflexology project started that has had limited previous recognition at the highest level of research. She has more than enough memorable experiences of love, loss and the unexpected, to write a full autobiography but she is a pragmatist and a realist who writes without ego or a desire to elicit sympathy. She simply tells it as it is. This approach enables her to describe, very sparingly and honestly, her life history as a backdrop to the book while her main focus is to share her university experiences in the widest sense. She is a highly intelligent, compassionate therapist and author who has brought a scientific, therapeutic benchmark to clinical reflexology. I highly recommend this book that both challenges and invites the reader to join her on a journey of discovery through the chapters, and by the end we are left informed, inspired and touched by her excellent and most unusual achievements.

Lynne Booth, BOOTH VRT LTD

Dr Carol Samuel is a fine example of tenacity and guts. This book showcases her journey through the muddy waters of academia, when she really shouldn't have succeeded at all. Starting on an uphill journey towards a PhD is something nobody takes on lightly. People who do it have trained for years to develop the skills necessary to pull everything together to tight timescales. Carol had none of those skills, and was told often that she couldn't do it, she shouldn't do it, but she did it anyway. This book is an exercise in rolling up your sleeves, and getting the job done. Despite a natural disaster, personal and physical challenges along the way, she picked herself up and just kept going. This book is her story. Read it and be inspired.

Judith Whatley MRes. BSc(Hons). MAR. PRM. FHEA.

'What an extraordinary book! Carol has very cleverly managed to combine her own deeply personal experiences with those of undertaking a difficult PhD journey. Integrating researched articles and explanations based in science whilst explaining the effects of stress (for example) upon the body makes using the information tangible, understandable and accessible. It not only provides access to articles for further reading and research but allows the practitioner to relate this to their own clients much more readily. The book is brave, bold, and courageous and truly shows that Carol was and continues to be a 'Tenacious Student'. I am delighted to have had the opportunity of a 'sneak preview'".

Barbara Scott, Chair Association of Reproductive Reflexologists

Carol highlights the highs and lows of the PhD pathway whilst giving the reader a really personal insight into her journey. This book is a must read for anyone considering or embarking on a PhD, particularly for those coming from a non-conventional background, or with an interest in Complementary and Alternative Medicine research. In fact, everyone should read it to see what can happen with a bit of tenacity and determination. Carol's PhD story is an inspiration.

Samantha Larkin PhD. BSc (Hons)

THE TENACIOUS STUDENT

Non-academic to PhD

Dr Carol A Samuel

Copyright © 2021 by Dr Carol A. Samuel. All rights reserved.

This book or any portion thereof may not be reproduced or used in any manner whatsoever without the express written permission of the publisher except for the use of brief quotations in a book review.

Strenuous attempts have been made to credit all copyrighted materials used in this book. All such materials and trademarks, which are referenced in this book, are the full property of their respective copyright owners. Every effort has been made to obtain copyright permission for material quoted in this book. Any omissions will be rectified in future editions.

Cover image & illustrations by: Tina Signorelli B.A. (Hons) M. A
Book design by: SWATT Books Ltd

Printed in the United Kingdom
First Printing, 2021

ISBN: 978-1-9993798-0-3 (Paperback)
ISBN: 978-1-9993798-1-0 (eBook)

Dr Carol A. Samuel
Havant, Hampshire
PO9 3LU

www.reflexmaster.co.uk

Contents

Foreword 13
Introduction 15

CHAPTER 1: Who am I? 17
Working career 19
Blue 27
Looking Back 31

CHAPTER 2: How it began 33
The Literature Review 36
Control methods 43
The hypothesis 48
The importance of a control arm in research 49
Looking Back 52

CHAPTER 3: Losing my way 55
Inclusions and Exclusions 56
The Transfer Report 60
Tsunami 61
Post-Traumatic Stress Disorder 64
PhD to MPhil 68
Looking Back 69

CHAPTER 4: Not good enough? 71
Compliance of pressure 77
What is it about pressure? 79
Financial setback 82

Confusing results 84
Looking Back 85

CHAPTER 5: Fighting back – the battle is not yet over.   87
Review of Direction of Study 90
BBC documentary 96
Physiological Stress 100
Physiological measurements 101
Looking Back 104

CHAPTER 6: Throwing everything at it   105
A novel idea 106
Pharmacy students 110
Final experiment 111
Scientific writing 114
Looking Back 116

CHAPTER 7: Writing the Thesis   117
New Year, new hope 124
Applying for an extension 127
Looking Back 131

CHAPTER 8: The final hurdles   133
Corrections 138
Life changing news 141
Day of the surgery 144
Looking Back 150

CHAPTER 9: A hopeful road   151
Facing the future 153
Chemo-brain and corrections 155
Setbacks, disappointments, and frustrations 160
Graduation Day 164
Looking Back 168

CHAPTER 10: What future beckons?   169
Who am I? 172
Nerve Reflexology 176

Meeting my peer group...177
Pain in Cancer Survivors..179
Pain, Stress, and the Inflammatory Response.....................................180

Closing voice...183
Acknowledgements..187
About the author..189
Glossary of terms..191
Useful resources..199
Biobliographic references...203

For Mum and Dad

*My world would have been nothing
without your love and direction*

THE TENACIOUS STUDENT | Dr CAROL A. SAMUEL

Foreword

According to a song by the singer-songwriter Paul Simon, "some folks' lives roll easy" while many may stumble and fall and "never catch their stars". In this autobiographical book, Carol Samuel gives an account of the many problems, tragedies, and difficulties she faced in her personal life while she coped with the stresses and frustrations of completing a PhD on the effects of reflexology on pain in human subjects. I suspect that writing this book and telling her story was a cathartic experience for her. Carol did not register for a higher degree at the University of Portsmouth by the traditional route of having a good BSc honours degree in a relevant science subject, but rather had other qualifications that met the criteria for acceptance. However, Carol had extraordinarily little knowledge of the basic scientific principles underpinning her research project when she started and, in addition, her understanding of how to design and carry out scientific research was wanting. She was therefore faced with a steep learning curve with a long and winding path, which was challenging both for Carol and her research supervisors.

Although the writing is largely autobiographical, there is another theme that runs through the book. It is a primer for aspiring practitioners and others who wish to do postgraduate research towards the degrees of Master or Doctor of Philosophy (MPhil or PhD) in complementary therapies. She details the various steps that are normally required in a programme of research that prospective students must undertake together with some of the pitfalls that they may experience. One of the points that Carol emphasises is the importance of carrying out placebo-controlled experiments to test the validity of claims made for the use of complementary therapies for various maladies. Many of these claims are based on anecdotal observations and have not been tested using rigorous scientific methodology, and this results in many mainstream medical practitioners being highly critical of or rejecting the use of complementary therapies. So, this book is also important as it may inspire more people who practice or are interested in complimentary therapies to conduct meticulously controlled scientific studies to validate some of the anecdotal assertions, and make these therapies acceptable so that they may be introduced into mainstream medical practices.

I enjoyed reading the book. Although Carol did stumble and fall many times during the course of her PhD studies, she picked herself up, made lots of sacrifices and changes in her personal life and through sheer determination did "catch her star".

Ivor Ebenezer PhD, FHEA, FBPhS

Introduction

I have been asked over and again, when am I going to write a book, but after completing my PhD I felt like I never wanted to write again; and yet here I am in the midst of the COVID-19 pandemic about to embark on a journey that almost seems inconceivable to me. So, why am I writing it…because people have been pushing me? No, not really, I'm writing it because I feel ready to write it. Lockdown 2020/21 has given me the headspace I need to challenge my feelings, the ones I have been harbouring since I first started my PhD. I am hoping that it will be cathartic and provide me with an outage to get rid of all the stress, anxiety and anger I experienced along the way. Alongside that, I am looking for an opportunity to really reflect on that experience and find the good in it. I am also hoping that it will help me to offload my experiences in a beneficial way for you, the reader, so that you can somehow learn from me and fully appreciate the depth of my education.

I have tried to write this book in a conversational style but because it is also a book about research, I have included the science in my book, not to confuse you, but hopefully to guide you and make clear how involved research in complementary and alternative medical practices can be. You will see numbers like this[1] alongside the text, they indicate a reference which you will find in the bibliography at the back of the book. These references are given so that you may, if you so wish, review the research papers I have used in my text.

I carried out my PhD in a Science Faculty that did not have a dedicated department of complementary medicine. There was extraordinarily little prior research in reflexology from which to draw evidence and I was faced with pulling out all the stops, mentally, emotionally, and physically to secure a science-based qualification at the highest level. I am hoping that it will encourage and excite you, the reader, to think about research in reflexology, research in pain management or just simply research within your own field of study. It isn't just a human story of achievement, but about the challenges of gaining a PhD as a non-academic against the backdrop of life in real terms.

Carol Samuel, PhD. Cert-Ed. FFHT. HMAR

CHAPTER 1
Who am I?

*There is no greater agony than bearing
an untold story inside you.*
Maya Angelou

I can truthfully tell you that I didn't go looking for a PhD. In fact, I didn't even know what a PhD was and if I had known, I would probably have run a million miles. I would most certainly have assumed that I didn't have enough academic knowledge to even begin with something like that. You see, I never really considered myself as an academic and left school at the age of 15 without a single qualification to my name. I was good at sports, especially gymnastics, trampolining and contemporary dance and sure, I could have taken my education further, but it was never at the forefront of my mind. Like many kids of my age back then, all I wanted to do was go to work and earn some money of my own.

I wasn't a bad student, well not at the beginning at least, but after a defining change in my family circumstances at the age of 13, my life was turned upside down, and I lost concentration in academia.

My parents had just separated and after the usual struggles, traumas and battles between couples who go their own way, we found ourselves under the sole care of our father. I have to start by saying that I am extremely proud of both my parents and share with you, just a snippet of who they were.

Mum was a widely respected footballer who played in the first ever women's football team, the famous Dick Kerr Ladies (1946). She then went on to play for Manchester Corinthian ladies who raised more than £43k for charity when they won the European Cup in Berlins Olympic Stadium. She played in front of an 80,000 strong crowd at the Lisbon Stadium of Light and was part of the team that won the first ever women's FA cup final in 1971. As well as playing for her local teams she was also part of the England squad. Mum was never one to let age get in the way of her game and at the age of 64 she was paramount in developing the young girls' teams in the local area and became the coach to the Portsmouth Young Blues football team. As a family, we have all played football across the years, in fact my brother Mick, used to play for Southampton, whilst my eldest sister Janice played alongside mum for Southampton ladies and England. I can happily say that football is in our blood and was a big part of our childhood days.

Dad was an incredible man and an unbelievable role model for us all. After mum and dad split up, he bought up seven children, six of whom are girls. This meant he endured all the teenage angst, flying hormones and relationship issues that goes with having girls. He held for us a loving home in a close and supportive family environment, demonstrated a huge sense of commitment and determination and allowed us to develop into the people we are today.

I am absolutely certain that my tenacity and strength is borne out of these two amazing parents who taught us to face the world as it is, and not through rose-tinted spectacles. The pick yourself up and dust yourself off attitude is, and no doubt will always be, part of our family way.

I didn't know it at the time, but I was a troubled child and would often draw attention to myself through self-harm and fainting episodes. I recall I had to have a cartilage removed in my right knee after a lay-out back somersault on the trampoline went wrong. I soon learned that being in hospital and then on crutches bought me a lot of attention so I would hammer my knees with my fists over and over again, trying to create further damage. To my shame I eventually had all but one of my cartilages removed and whilst the fist-hammering didn't cause the original problem, it most certainly exacerbated it. I also had to undergo an EEG at the age of thirteen for suspected epilepsy because of the fainting episodes; again, an attention seeking opportunity that resulted in a period of taking phenobarbitone a central nervous system drug for the control of seizures. I was taken off the drug when at the age of fourteen I took an overdose of phenobarbitone and paracetamol after falling out with a friend.

It's only as an adult and with life-experience that you become wise as to why you do these things, and for me it was probably all about attention seeking. As the middle child I didn't feel I mattered that much, I wasn't old enough to be part of the decision making, nor young enough to require close supervision. My parents had their own reasons for separating and over the years I was privileged to gain an understanding of that, but to be respectful to them both, I realised that the only two people who truly know what went on in that, or indeed any relationship, are the two people who were in it. I learned not to judge, and not to blame, but to accept that whatever it was that drove them apart, was their business, their journey, and their lesson.

Working career

My first job was as a children's nanny for one of my old school teachers and then I went on to work in a factory, but factory work didn't turn out to be my forte after I crushed my hand, burst a blood vessel in my nose, and had a contusion on my elbow from three different jobs.

As a result of this I took my first foray back into education and signed up to night school at the local college to learn how to type and do shorthand, and it was a good move. I managed to get a job for the Post Office as a punch-card operator followed by a post as a clerical assistant where I was also involved in stock control and marketing.

I got married in 1977 at the age of 19 and settled in administration/secretarial roles for a number of years. I discovered I was pregnant in 1978 and when my daughter was born in 1979, I became a full-time mum. A couple of years later we were hoping to expand our family, but it wasn't to be, so I started up as a child minder for my neighbours and friends. It was a job I loved dearly and continued to do until my daughter went to school. To help with the household finances I took a part-time evening job at IBM as a data control clerk and worked privately as a secretary and bookkeeper for a local builder. I learned a lot about book-keeping and was able to use my shorthand with a mix of speed writing to take dictation over the phone. When my daughter started school, I went back to work as a customer services representative with a credit card registration company, whilst also learning travel and ticketing with British Airways, leading to a qualification in Travel Management. I didn't pass my travel and ticketing exams first time, so had to start again, and the following year I was eventually successful.

It was whilst working at the credit card registration company that I got my first break. My boss at the time recognised that I had good organisation skills, that I could communicate very well with members of the public and that I had an eye for detail. Anyhow, this company decided that my further education was important, so offered me an opportunity, under the 'Investors in People' scheme to go to college to learn a number of new skills that would provide me with a Foundation degree in Purchasing and Supply Management. This included Business Maths and Statistics, Accounting, Economics, Project Management and Purchasing and Supply Management. I recall that I failed the exam for Business Maths and Statistics initially, so just as I had with the British Airways Travel and Ticketing, I sat it again and this time I passed with flying colours; no pun intended.

When I look back at this time in my life, I probably had to do most things twice before achieving my goals. I recognise that I am a slow learner and that it takes me a while to absorb information in the right order. I'm not sure if it's just because I don't listen properly, if I get bored, distracted, or just have difficulty concentrating, but I do know that if you want something badly enough, you find a way that works for you and usually get there in the end. I suspect that half the problem for me is that I get what I call an over analytical brain freeze, often termed as 'paralysis by analysis' and it can be a real pain in the arse at times. It makes me a bit of an overthinker and is something I have had to learn to temper across the years, but when it comes to research, it appears it is quite a good skill to have.

In 1988 I went through the next major divide in my life...divorce! Although necessary for us both, it was, as these things often are, very painful and confusing. I moved into a new home with my eight-year-old daughter only to find out that the house had dry rot, wet rot, and woodworm. After an extremely stressful three years working alongside a builder, and I do mean physically working alongside a builder, trying to remove all the rotted wood, drilling bricks to fumigate and rebuild the house, I finally found myself back on an even keel.

At the time I was purchasing print and design materials for the UK and American branches of the credit card registration company I worked for, and thought I was enjoying the fast-paced life of business. I was travelling across Europe and the length and breadth of the UK but what I had overlooked was that I spent so much time at work, I didn't get to spend as much time with my daughter as perhaps I should have done. I didn't make a conscious decision not to be with her, I just needed to earn as much money as I could in order to pay the bills and rebuild my home. They were difficult days for us and huge adjustments were needed, she hated being in the new house away from her daddy and I completely understood that, but I couldn't turn back the clock for either of us.

In 1989 I met Sam and it was lust at first sight. He was fun to be with, he made me laugh and he liked to live life...it was a hugely different kind of relationship to the one I had experienced with my first husband; that had been all about building a home, security, stability, and family. Everything I thought I wanted, but I was young when we met, just 16 whilst he was 28. Looking back now I can see that the reason I wanted that relationship was because I was looking for someone to love me, to take care of me, to provide for me and make me their priority, and he did. My relationship with Sam on the other hand took me on a wild and sometimes wonderful new journey of discovery but it was often unpredictable and challenging. He had two children, a 5-year-old son with an ex-girlfriend and a 15-year-old daughter from his first marriage. His relationships with these two women were, to say the least, quite tenuous and although he had many opportunities to move away from the area he stayed for the love of his children and a real desire to be part of their lives. I admired that in him, perhaps he reminded of my own father in that way.

I had always wanted a bigger family and saw myself as a real earth mother. I had this picture that my role in life was to take care of a big family, to help them grow and develop and to bring out the best in them. Unfortunately, my body had other ideas. I suffered dreadfully with endometriosis and at the age of 32, after collapsing and being hospitalised on several previous occasions, I underwent a hysterectomy. If I only knew then, what I know now about the benefits of reflexology and the skill and knowledge of my dear friend Barbara Scott.

In 1992 at the age of just seven, my stepson, whom I called Blue, was diagnosed with a life-limiting condition known as Adrenaleukodystrophy (ALD). At the time very little about the clinical pathogenesis of the disease was understood and we were simply told that it was an X-linked genetic disorder, occurring primarily in males and that it causes a build-up of very long chain fatty acids which results in the breakdown of the myelin-sheath around neurons, which causes extensive and widespread damage.[1][2] Children with ALD often develop adrenocortical insufficiency, known as Addison's Disease, which means they don't produce enough of the hormone cortisol and/or aldosterone.[3][4] We were told that Blue had the rapidly progressive form of the disease, causing a rapid inflammatory demyelination in the cerebral hemisphere, and that his life expectancy was somewhere between three months and three years. It was the start of a long and troubled journey for us all, including his birth mother and our respective children.

Blue's birth mother didn't drive, and he needed to be ushered from one hospital to another for an array of different tests. It seemed only natural to me that I take up the role of driver and communicator. I put myself in the middle of two parents who were desperate for answers and in the initial stages it seemed to work out fine, but the more involved I became, the more difficult it was to separate myself from Blue, and instead I ended up being the victim of hatred and jealousy. Despite working full-time and trying to juggle my relationships as well as parenting my own daughter Claire, I would take the eight-hour round trip to Birmingham Children's hospital regularly. My role was to tackle the arduous task of understanding his condition, finding a way to feed back that information to his birth parents and establish some kind of hope to which they may cling. Sam quite naturally wasn't coping well with it and his relationship with Blue's mother became more and more toxic as time went on. Nonetheless we were all desperate to try and find out how we could best help Blue, and I remember at the invitation of a friend, one of the things we did together was go to a Methodist church. I learned that parents of children faced with life limiting conditions fear for the loss of control over their child's health.[5][6] You want to be able to plan things, to control the situation, and religion seems to help you find the patience you need, and somehow seems to give you the time to think things through more holistically.

I am not by nature a particularly religious person, erring more on the side of spiritualism, but you take desperate measures when you are in a desperate situation. I was invited to go forward and stand in front of the priest, but my immediate response was definitely not. You see I had watched as the priest touched people on the head, and they fell to the ground like a ton of bricks. I watched as Blue stood with his mother at the front of the church and both were touched by the priest, but neither fell down. My head was all over the place but the feeling in the church was euphoric and I was beginning to get caught up in it. After further encouragement from our friends, I allowed the priest to lay his hands on my shoulders. As he did so he said *...you will touch a lot of lives...* and in that same moment, he touched my forehead and I, like others before me, fell to the ground. Sadly, it didn't change anything for Blue, and we watched as he slowly deteriorated, first of all losing his sight, then his ability to walk, to talk, to feed, control his muscles and his bowel and bladder functions. It was one of the most painful and distressing experiences I and his family have ever had to endure in our entire lives, and it got progressively worse for everyone involved.

In 1993 Sam and I were married, and life seemed to be moving on, we found ways to manage our emotions with each other and with the dreadful situation we were experiencing with Blue, but life seemed to challenge my every move and I was trying so hard not to upset anyone.

Then in the Spring of 1994 I found I was struggling to hold on to life, to the hope of better things. The weight of running a home, holding down a full-time job, coping in a testing relationship and taking care of a by now, completely dependent nine-year-old and a growing teenager started to engulf me. I struggled to cope with being the target of spite and acting as the 'go between' for Blue's birth mother and my husband. I started crying, a lot, at ridiculous times, for what appeared to be no reason at all. I made a complete idiot of myself at the works annual dinner-dance after being awarded employee of the year by completely falling apart…for what appeared to be absolutely no reason at all. I was so embarrassed and decided to speak with my GP who put me off work for six weeks with stress. I didn't see it coming, Sam didn't see it coming and yet here I was a complete bloody mess, out of control and unable to function but I didn't have a choice because life doesn't stand still.

I have found on many an occasion that when I am really low something happens, I seem to get help from somewhere. I now believe that help comes from spirit. It was on one of my really down days, when I was sitting on the floor of my lounge crying, and I mean really sobbing, that I experienced a real impression that I should call a lady with whom I had previously had a reflexology treatment. She was also a spiritualist medium, gifted from birth. I found an old diary with her telephone number in it and gave her a call. She told me that she wasn't sure she was going to continue working as a reflexologist as she was struggling with shoulder pain, but as I was now the sixth person who had called for an appointment that day, she felt that the universe was telling her that now was not the time for her to stop. It was a visit that was to change the course of my entire life.

I made an appointment and went to see her the very next day. Whilst giving me a treatment she asked me if I had ever thought about therapy myself. I wasn't very quick on the uptake I have to say, because I thought she meant that I needed therapy...as in counselling. She explained that she thought I would make a great therapist and gave me the name of a man who taught the International Therapy Examinations Council (ITEC) body massage diploma. She told me he taught it across the weekends so it would work with my full-time job. She sold it to me as a distraction from my current life events and so I went along and spoke to the tutor who agreed that I could join the course. I completed the course with a credit and got an A++ for my project dissertation on Adrenaleukodystrophy. It was my first real detailed insight into the nervous system, and I was desperate to learn more about how I might use massage to help support the spasticity Blue was experiencing in his limbs. I noticed it made such a tremendous difference to him, so much so, that we were able to reduce the amount of diazepam he was taking to help relax his muscles, and with some passive physiotherapy thrown in, I could help straighten out his curled-up arms, albeit for a short while.

Sam told me once that I was known as the Ice Maiden at work because I wouldn't take any shit from anyone and that I wasn't very approachable. When I think of that now, it absolutely abhors me, particularly as I always felt that I was a good listener and ready to help anyone who needed my support. Following my breakdown, I went back to work, but didn't feel quite as strong as I had been previously. I had been with the company for ten years and for almost eight of those ten years our company director had been my direct line manager, but a short while after my return to work he suddenly changed my reporting line. Instead of reporting to him, I was now having to report to the Finance Director, and it was a further two months before I was to find out why. I was aware that some of the original employees like me, those who were there at the companies' inception, had been made redundant, but I had not expected there to be any further redundancies. I was wrong. I had been responsible for a multi-million-pound spending budget, I was manager of the mail services department, the stock control department and purchasing and design projects but I dropped my guard. Apparently, I had trained my purchasing assistant so well, they decided I was no longer required, and I was made redundant from my position as a Special Projects/Purchasing Manager. I thought the bottom had dropped out of my world.

Once again, I found myself struggling to cope with life's events but what really pissed me off was that our company director didn't have the balls to make me redundant himself. Instead, he changed my reporting line to give the task to someone who did. I had known my director for ten years and he had supported me with my work development and across all of the challenges I had experienced in my personal life, so it was quite a shock that he couldn't talk to me and give his reasons face to face. Not one to let these things go, I asked to speak with him openly and he admitted to me that he couldn't do it because he cared. He was a big bear of a man, married with a family of his own and he was a great boss to everyone in the company. It hurt, but after he explained himself I kind of understood where he was coming from. He didn't have to tell me, but in doing so he earned my further respect. I could see that after my breakdown I was vulnerable, I had a lot happening in my personal life and I had let my work ethic slip to second place. When you are placed in a position of great authority and trust, you need to be on the ball all the time. You need to stay at the top of your game to make sure negotiations come in on budget, that work is managed in a strict fashion under clear guidelines, and clearly, I wasn't doing that anymore. As a growing company they couldn't and wouldn't carry me.

They say that as one door closes, another opens but I was desperately worried about being out of work, wondering how on earth, as the major breadwinner I was going to continue to pay my mortgage and support my family. I continued to study part-time and by the end of 1995 I had completed my training as a Reiki practitioner/master teacher, the ITEC Sport and Remedial Massage and Vocational Training Charitable Trust (VTCT) Aromatherapy qualifications. All of this, whilst also taking care of Blue, managing the emotional roller-coaster from the fall out between Sam and Blue's birth mother, working in temporary positions for a number of different staff agencies in a variety of different jobs, and by now, trying to cope with the emotions of a young teenager whose father had become an alcoholic, struggling to manage his life without me in it. I still cared for my ex-husband, he was, after all the father of my child and I didn't want to see him destroy himself and also our daughter. I tried to help him, I tried to find a way that would ease his pain, but I was the cause of his pain and I couldn't work around that. It's a strange kind of guilt that you carry in these situations and learning to manage that guilt wasn't easy.

By 1996 I felt confident enough in my skills and knowledge as a holistic practitioner that I took on a part-time role at my local further education college teaching the VTCT anatomy & physiology body massage qualification. As part of my continuing professional development (CPD) it was recommended that I do my Further and Adult Education Teaching Certificate (FAETC) together with the VTCT Assessor awards. I passed with a commendation for my one-to-one work with practitioners learning in a third language and the quality of my portfolio evidence was promoted as one of the best seen. I continued at the college for another four years, during which time I also developed a Reiki course and in partnership with a close friend taught Reiki privately. I completed my teacher training with the Certificate in Education (Cert.Ed). and alongside that, it was also a requirement to undertake some Key Skills training so I took the level 4 qualifications in Managing Own Learning and Performance, Communication Skills and Working with Others, all of which would stand me in good stead for my future in teaching. As is usual when teaching in college I was asked to undertake further CPD and my course mentor Jane whom I was shadow-teaching thought that I might like to consider beauty therapy. At the time beauty therapy didn't sit well with me as I'm not really a facials kind of girl, so I asked if there were any 'holistic' therapies I could do, and I was offered Reflexology or Indian Head Massage. I took both and qualified in 1998.

It was during this time that my husband suffered pain in his lower back whilst lifting Blue into the car and I learnt probably one of the biggest lessons of my massage career to date. I didn't know the extent of the damage and so when he said that something had gone in his back, I assumed that he had pulled a muscle. I suggested ice and/or heat and perhaps paracetamol and anti-inflammatory drugs, but after a couple of days and no real improvement I offered him some sport and remedial massage, but it didn't help. He disliked reflexology and would not allow me to work his feet. The normal route for non-specific low back pain in conventional medicine is to offer conservative treatments with medication and/or physiotherapy, so he continued with the medication. He eventually reached a point where he couldn't stand, couldn't sit, and certainly couldn't lie down and although I had been telephoning his GP on an almost daily basis, all they kept telling me was that he was to continue with the medication. Sam hadn't slept in days; he was in dreadful pain and I felt completely powerless to provide the support I had hoped I could. I made another call to the surgery and this time I didn't take no for an answer. I literally wept over the telephone and begged them to do something for him. Our own GP knew about our home situation and so they finally decided to take him into hospital. After two weeks in hospital trying to sort out his pain, they finally had to operate, and he underwent a discectomy for an L4/5 prolapse. I know the treatments I gave him hadn't made the condition worse, I know that the psychological impact of his pain meant that he was unable to provide for his son in the way he had been doing which also changed the context of his pain.[7][8] It was to be many years later and only when I was confident enough in my own level of knowledge and understanding that he would allow me to do any kind of therapy work on him again.

It was also during this time that I took on the role of caring for an elderly neighbour who was struggling with rheumatoid arthritis. Sherry had previously been one of my case-studies for the reflexology qualification and was a special and very dear friend who had given up her career to take care of her invalid mother but had no other close living relatives. She was my confidante, my friend and subsequently my benefactor, without whom I could not even have considered going to university. I found that she benefitted hugely from reflexology treatments and so I took on more elderly clients with arthritis, finding that I had the same positive outcomes. The results varied amongst these clients, some had less pain and more mobility for several days at a time, whilst in others it was short-lived and needed topping up regularly, but there was always some benefit.

At college, the number of students signing up to attend VTCT qualifications dropped, so my role as a part-time tutor was no longer required. I transferred to another college, closer to home where I taught the part-time VTCT Aromatherapy diploma. At some point along the way I decided to start my own school where I could offer training alongside treatments. I developed courses aligned to the VTCT diploma level 3 for anatomy physiology and body massage, aromatherapy, Indian head massage and reiki levels one through to mastery. Rather oddly the one course that I didn't develop was reflexology but there is definitely something to be said for knowing your market. I clearly hadn't done my homework properly or thoroughly enough because during this time, the VTCT courses at college had reduced their costs so much for student intake that I was unable to compete, and after two years I was forced to close the school.

Blue

In January 2001 at the age of just 15 Blue lost his battle with adrenaleukodystrophy and passed away after contracting yet another bout of pneumonia. I had endured many years of his mother's jealousy and rage and at that time I had not been able to visit him at the respite centre for almost a year, as she had taken out a court order banning my attendance. She had become a born-again Christian and unfortunately felt that the treatments I was providing for him were the work of the devil. One day when she came to collect Blue from us, she became abusive to me and my daughter. She wouldn't step aside for me to put him across the threshold in his wheelchair and I caught her leg as I did so. In a letter from her solicitor, she had complained that I was interfering with his medications, that I was dirty and that I had physically harmed her; as a result, she sought to prevent me from seeing him. Fortunately for me, when the case went to court the judge ordered in my favour but told us that if she broke the ruling there was absolutely nothing we could do about it, as they wouldn't put the mother of a dying child in prison for breach of contract.

When he died, I was completely distraught and despite the fact that I wasn't his birth mother, the pain I endured from his loss was unbearable. It was such a deep pain, and I experienced the loss so strongly, but I also felt so dreadfully guilty too, because I didn't think I had the right to feel that way. I was an imposter, I wasn't his real mother, a surrogate if you will, but not really his mum. I told myself I had no right to be like that, so I pushed my feelings away and got on with life. After his death, my life seemed so empty, and I didn't know what to do with myself. He had occupied so much of my time and there was just this emptiness inside me. I needed another focus, so I took another temporary job, this time for the School Improvement Service. I became the administrator for the primary maths lead, but it didn't take up all my time and I needed to fill the hours, especially the weekends when Blue would have been at home with us, so I began a course of study in nutritional medicine. It started well and I was getting straight A's, but it became apparent to me that I wasn't really interested, it didn't give me a buzz or the thirst for knowledge that I was seeking, and I knew I was really only filling time to stop myself from feeling his loss.

The role at the School Improvement Service was going well and when we moved to new offices that were nearer my home, they upgraded me to secretary. As time went on my managers found that I could cope with more work, so they gave me the role of secretary to two of the senior staff. Catherine was the Early Years and Development lead, and Gerry was the Continuing Professional Development lead for all the schools in the area. But once again, as time progressed and I learned more about education, I realised that I needed to do something else for myself. I was still working part-time as a practitioner, so I started looking for courses that might help my progression in the field of complementary & alternative medicine (CAM). I knew that I wanted to learn more about the science behind CAM and gave some serious consideration to undertaking a 3-year degree in Traditional Chinese Acupuncture, but at £17,000 I struggled to justify the expense.

I came across a Bachelor of Science degree in Natural and Complementary therapies at the University of Portsmouth. At the time I didn't have any idea how to apply so Gerry directed me through the application process, but I needed to have two referees who would write a good review for me. I asked my college mentor Jane, and Gerry was happy to write the second reference. Both wrote glowing references which led to an interview with Dr Sheelagh Campbell, who was the Principal Lecturer in Chemistry at Portsmouth and the person who had developed the course. We met at the university in Sheelagh's office where she described the course to me. She explained that since I didn't have any formal science background, I would need to complete an Access course before I would be considered. She suggested I look at the local colleges for this and I duly enrolled (rather late) on Access Chemistry. The course had already been running for six weeks when I started, so I felt a little awkward and got a bit overwhelmed initially with all the new and strange knowledge that I had to learn. I knew that I could apply myself and wasn't shy in asking for help. I completed the remainder of the course and passed with an AS level, equivalent to 40% of an A-level or the first year of an A level, which alongside my CAM background, was sufficient for me to gain access to university.

Sheelagh and I met again, less formally this time and she explained that the course she had written didn't get validated when it was reviewed by the education board, so they had to rewrite a few components before it could start. She said that she hoped to be able to contact me again later in the year with a definite start date. The course was changed to incorporate more biomedical studies but still lacked a practical component, which for me, wasn't really an issue, but I could certainly see that it would a bit of a no-no for anyone who was having to pay for a course of study. What was the point in a course of theory that didn't train anyone in the practical skills that accompanied that knowledge? I think I knew right there and then that it wouldn't take off.

Sheelagh and I discussed this further, and she asked me if I would consider lecturing on the course with a view to also providing the practical tuition. It wasn't what I wanted. I wanted to learn about the biomedicine, the science behind it all, the in-depth physiological processes that occur in the body, and try to fully comprehend the reasons we did the work the way we did, so I refused. She suggested then that perhaps I could do some research...where was this coming from? I couldn't figure out why it was so difficult to actually do what I wanted to do...join the course as an undergraduate student. However, after further discussion she convinced me that my maturity and knowledge of CAM so far was sufficient for me to undertake a Masters' degree. She contacted the academic registry and they suggested that I sign up not for a Masters' degree in research, but for a Master of Philosophy degree (MPhil) which could lead to a Doctor of Philosophy (PhD). I honestly didn't understand it all and just took it as another stage for my development. I was to learn that you don't usually get to do a PhD without having a Bachelor or a Masters' degree first and that your Bachelors' degree should be at least an upper second-class honour's. The alternative route is based on your potential research capability, but I was soon to find out that I could enter for a PhD based on other factors, somewhat unrelated to my previous academic achievements.

I had absolutely no clue what she was talking about, so she explained that it was a research programme and that I needed to look at something to do research on...a specific subject matter. And so, my journey began.

CHAPTER 1 | WHO AM I

Looking Back

Throughout this book you will find sections like this one, where I will be looking back and reflecting on the various parts of my journey and the lessons I learned along the way.

This last section has introduced me to you. It provides you the reader with a small insight into where I came from, who I am and how I became a reflexologist, and subsequently came to enter higher education as a research student.

My relationship experiences have been a factor that have shaped me into the person I am today. I have hurt, I have been betrayed, beaten, demoralised and shamed but I believe these things make me a better, stronger more compassionate woman.

I am not unique in the story I am about to tell, nor am I looking for sympathy or flouting an ego. I am however trying to encourage you to nourish your soul and know that what you make of your future, is your own doing.

My hope is that you will find your own strength of purpose and future in the person you really are, and not in the person others expect you to be.

THE TENACIOUS STUDENT | Dr CAROL A. SAMUEL

CHAPTER 2
How it began

Philosophia from the ancient Greek
– translated 'Love of wisdom'

I joined the Science Faculty of the University of Portsmouth on 23rd September 2002 as a research student ready to undertake a Master of Philosophy (MPhil) degree. My official research tenure was for 3 years full time and funding would come from the university. During the pre-registration meeting I was given an overview of the expectations and informed that one of the first milestones would be a 'transfer report'. This report is a formal assessment document that must be written to prove a student's ability in convincing examiners they can carry out original and significant research at a higher level. If it were successful, I would follow the route to a full PhD.

When you are officially registered for a research programme you are usually told who your supervisor(s) are likely to be and their area of expertise, which of course must correlate with your subject matter. Their role is to ensure you reach all the right milestones, to report on your progress and guide you along the way. Before continuing each year, you must have achieved those milestones, and if you fail to do so, your progression is at risk.

At this point I didn't yet know for sure what my subject matter was going to be and there were many questions still waiting to be answered before I could begin, such as:

- What is my research question (hypothesis)?
- What would I like to look more closely at?
- What results was I getting with my own clients that might require further investigation to prove how I got those results?
- How would I measure it to provide scientific evaluation?
- Why do I need to do it?

During my pre-registration talks with Sheelagh I learned that whatever subject matter I chose, it had to be measurable, and I needed to have a supervisor with whom I could work who had knowledge of the subject.

My first choice for the research was Reiki, particularly as I was getting some wonderful feedback from my clients, but Sheelagh explained that Reiki was far too tenuous and required the skills of a physicist, so she would not be able to support the subject.

She went on to explain that to carry out a research programme I needed to prepare a hypothesis on something that was measurable. Already, I felt that I may be in over my head...what was a hypothesis and how do you work out how to measure it?

A scientific hypothesis is a proposal for research based on observations from something you have done, which can be explained through obtaining measurable scientific evidence.

Once I had this worked out, we also had to find someone who could supervise the research. Sheelagh was my Director of Studies, technically my first supervisor and an electro-chemist. Her only foray into complementary therapies was that she had completed an aromatherapy course at a local college.

I mentioned to Sheelagh that I had been getting great results with reflexology in clients who were experiencing pain from arthritis, and she immediately jumped on the idea of carrying out a research programme on pain, but she had absolutely no idea what reflexology entailed. After giving her a brief explanation, she mentioned there was a neuropharmacologist in the faculty who had done some previous research in acupuncture and pain at the medical school at the University of Newcastle Upon Tyne and so she thought he may be an appropriate supervisor for me.

You may recall that when I joined the university, I didn't have the relevant qualifications, so Sheelagh had made a special case for me based on my non-degree qualifications and considerable practical experience in the field of complementary medicine. The MPhil option, which is an advanced master's degree for research, was the best option based on my lack of research experience, so it meant there would be additional taught courses to take along the way.

Despite having already done an Access Chemistry course to gain my position at university, Sheelagh asked me to do further study in this area and, to revise the electronic structure of atoms. I honestly couldn't figure out why I needed to know this for the programme of study I was going to be doing but I went along with it as she offered to tutor me, so I assumed there was some relevance for my work. The first thing I learned was never to assume anything. The tutoring didn't last as Sheelagh was too busy with other things, and the subject got dropped. I was to discover across the course of my PhD that Sheelagh was not easy to pin down and so any additional tuition from her was going to be very hit and miss.

In the meantime, the course I had originally hoped to be doing as an undergraduate, a 'BSc in Natural and Complementary Medicine' needed lecturers and Sheelagh once again asked me if I would apply for the post. I am by nature a very intuitive person, but despite my inner voice telling me it wasn't a good idea, I still applied for the post and put myself through the interview process. It was like nothing I had experienced before, not only did I have to be interviewed by the head of the Science faculty *and* Sheelagh, but I also had to give a presentation entitled *'Complementary and Alternative Therapies - Theoretical and Clinical Issues involved in its delivery as an academic discipline'* to lecturers and technicians within the faculty. I recall that one particular pharmacy lecturer drove home a very valid point when he asked me *"do you really feel capable enough to manage lecturing, research, your job, home life and the additional learning requirements to fulfil a PhD?"* I remember at that very moment I felt completely out of my depth and replied, rather rudely, *"do you?"* to which he replied, *"no madam I do not"* and that was me told! I didn't get the job and looking back on it, that was most definitely the best outcome. The pharmacy lecturer was right, there was no way I could have managed to lecture, learn some new subject matter, and carry out research all at the same time, although I know many do, it was definitely not my path and I felt that someone was clearly watching my back.

The Literature Review

To obtain your PhD you must carry out 'original and extensive work in a specific topic' so the first and most vital part of any piece of this research work is the 'Literature Review'. The literature review means that you need to look at a wide range of literature on the subject under study with a view to learning from it, being able to critically evaluate it and perhaps use the basis of any previous research to build upon your own. What you don't want to do is repeat what someone else has already done unless it is going to add to the evidence base. In short, it helps you develop your own research question by identifying the extent and quality of work that has already been carried out in your proposed area of study. I had never done anything like this before and had no idea how or where to start. I was directed to my workspace, a shared room at the end of Sheelagh's lab. In the room there were already four other people, one of whom was the lab technician, Steve, and some other PhD students. We each had a section of wall and for most of us, the use of a very antiquated computer, although some were fortunate enough to have their own laptops paid for out of their PhD stipend.

I was told to research the literature, but there was no direction about which databases I should look at and no guidance on how to access those databases to get the papers. Instead, I was told that I should visit the library and ask the librarians to register me for a workshop 'Information Skills for Research Students'. I was rapidly discovering that research was very much self-directed learning and I needed to show I was capable, so off I went.

Whilst there is a plethora of different ways to find research articles, searching the right databases for your subject area is an essential part of the literature review and I was told to search in the following databases as a starting point.

- OVID
- WEB OF SCIENCE
- CAMBRIDGE SCIENTIFIC ABSTRACTS DATABASE
- SCIENCE DIRECT
- PUBMED (Medline)
- EMBASE
- AMED

- CINAHL and,
- COCHRANE

To find what you are looking for in these databases is an art in itself and requires both skill and practice. Generally speaking, you can either use Medical Subject Headings (MeSH) or keywords.

Keywords include the title or subtitle of a piece of literature but when you are unsure of the title you are looking for you can also add something called a wildcard or metacharacter. These consist of either a question mark or an asterisk. So, for example, if you were searching reflexology but were unsure if the research title included the term reflexology, reflex therapy, reflex zone therapy or reflex massage, you might use reflex* and this would yield all terms in the results and then some, thus producing masses of papers.

Unfortunately, not all databases support the use of wildcards. Where the spelling differs, you can use the '?' in the word to get more results, for example, colour *vs* colo?r or perhaps metre *vs* met?r but again, not all databases use the same wildcard characters to truncate words, so it is good to find out what works on each.

Using both methods in your search terms can mean one heck of a lot of references, so you can use something called BOOLEAN logic which helps to reduce the number of references returned from the search. BOOLEAN helps you to identify groups of references by using additional sets that manipulate the data such as AND, OR and NOT. For example, I might have put in 'reflexology AND pain' which would produce results for all references that contained both words. If I used the OR in place of the AND, I would get references that included either one or the other of the terms, reflexology, OR pain but this means that I would have a lot more references to search. The final one, NOT, allows me to remove terms from one set that also occur in the other and this refines my search results and produces fewer articles.

Perhaps you might remember the old BODMAS (brackets, of, division, multiplication, addition, and subtraction) method of calculations from your school days. The BOOLEAN system operates under a similar process, so that using brackets around your search terms you find better results. AND is evaluated before OR, or NOT, so your search term might look something like; reflexology AND (pain OR nociception) rather than reflexology AND pain OR nociception.

The most common use of MeSH terms I have seen has been in the PubMed database and my understanding is that it is used to control the keyword vocabulary used for indexing PubMed articles.

It was a good start and the workshop provided me with the necessary account login to search the databases and download the papers. I didn't fully appreciate how or what search terms I needed to use, nor how to obtain full text papers when sometimes there was only an abstract of the research available to view. It didn't take me long to learn that I could obtain the full paper using the inter-library loan system through the University library system.

Reading a research paper was one thing but understanding it sufficiently to enable me to write a critical evaluation of a paper was something completely different.

Many undergraduates do some research for their dissertation, so may be familiar with the process of critiquing and evaluating a research paper, but never having been an undergraduate it was all new to me. Before being able to write a literature review, I had to learn how to read a research paper effectively and efficiently enough to critique it with some level of knowledge, without becoming too absorbed in the finer detail. Some of the most important things I needed to note in the research included:

- The study topic – what was the subject matter?
- Type of study e.g., randomised controlled trial, case study/series, comparative, exploratory, explanatory etc.
- Number of subjects (patients) included in the trial
- The main measurement methods used
- Statistical methods used for the analysis
- The main conclusions
- Comments and limitations

Most of this information can be obtained from a simple research abstract, but there are a few points you will only be able to find by obtaining the full paper. It is these points that will help determine the real validity of a trial, for example: -

- Did the research focus on a specific issue?
- How were the patients randomized or assigned to their group?
- Do the outcomes account for all those who were initially recruited to the study?

- Was there any blinding within the study (patients/practitioners/assessors)?
- Were participant's baseline scores similar in each group?
- Were each group treated equally?
- What were the methods for the intervention?
- Were the treatment and control arms clearly specified?
- What do the results tell you?
- Are they clinically relevant/precise?
- Can they be applied to the population generically or are there limitations in the outcomes?

A 'systematic review' can be helpful in your literature search because it helps you identify the current evidence for your topic and will give you an indication of who the prime researchers are that may be considered leaders in the field. The process of a systematic review is to systematically summarize the available evidence and to provide empirical evidence of the findings so far. Systematic reviews also highlight any gaps in the research. They will often feature areas of concern in the methods used within a study and all of this will help you to plan your own research more carefully.

When I felt I was able to answer the above questions I chose to produce a summary sheet, a sort of synopsis of the research which I pinned to the front of the paper I had just read and filed it. For me it was a good way of quickly reviewing each paper, which was fine, but filing it this way was a big mistake. You need to have a method so that the reference is picked up easily when you are writing. When you locate a reference through one of the search engines, you can cite the reference which then uses a digital object identifier (DOI) to enter the details into the referencing programme you are using. What I should have done was enter it into a 'reference management programme straight away, but I didn't know about these things until much later on. This meant that I had loads of files full of papers in a fairly reasonable order, but nothing logged anywhere.

There were two systems that would enable me to process these papers efficiently, but the next hurdle was to learn how to use them and then take each of those papers I had read and type them into the database. The library support team directed me to a workbook that I could download and suggested that I follow the technical instructions provided. Now I'm not one for learning technical stuff from a manual, especially if it's related to computer work. I know my learning style is very much on the visual/kinaesthetic side, so it was a slow process and took me quite some time to deal with my references in the correct manner. Not long after that, I found out that the department for learning and development would be offering more formal training and I took up the opportunity as soon as I could.

Reference management software makes it much easier to create bibliographic references in your text and is certainly a necessary and recommended part of scientific writing. Knowing how to enter the details into this type of database can be difficult for someone who doesn't know how to use them correctly, and if like me, you don't do well with technical 'how to guides' enlisting the help of someone else can prove extremely valuable.

When reading a research paper, it's useful to go to the reference section at the back. These references are a valuable resource that can help you identify papers you may have overlooked, but which may be relevant for your own research. I highly recommend that you use these to support any literature review you may do yourself. I had focussed my literature review on reflexology and pain because I thought that was what I needed to do; I was soon to find out that I also needed to research the literature for pain, pain medications, mechanisms of pain, other complementary therapies used for pain, touch based therapies, hypnotherapy, relaxation…and the list went on. It is a long and involved process but an extremely necessary part of any research programme.

Three months after starting my research at the university I had my first official meeting with my supervisor, Dr Ivor Ebenezer. We discussed the experimental project strategy, ethical issues and measurements that might be required. I was also informed that I needed to put together an outline programme of what I wanted to achieve for each year – 'Programme of Events'. That seemed a little weird to me. Why was I having to say what I needed to achieve when surely, they were supposed to tell me what I needed to do? Not so, and that's the difference between a directed learning programme and a self-directed learning programme such as research. You lead the way, you decide what you need to achieve each year to complete your goals, you decide how you are going to do it, what equipment you might need, who needs to be involved, how you are going to get them involved, how much it will cost to carry out the analysis of any tests used and so much more. Of course, there is supposed to be guidance and conversations with your supervisors, but research is primarily self-directed.

In our initial discussions we talked about testing people with acute pain and then following that up to test people experiencing chronic pain. In the acute pain study, I would need to inflict pain on anyone who would offer themselves as part of the study programme and I would do that by using ice or the 'Cold Pressor Test'.

There are a number of different methods you can use to induce acute pain in an experiment, including, but not limited to, pressure, heat and cold. The cold pressor test is commonly used to induce pain because it is scientifically proven and is a valuable method for controlling the impact of any 'confounding variables', these are extra things that you can't easily account for in a study. It has a high degree of 'internal validity' which means the outcomes can't be associated with methodological issues and it has for many years been used as a method for inducing pain. It doesn't cost much to use as you only really need an ice bath, ice or ice slurry and a timer, so it's cost-effective and considered reliable. It also has minimal side-effects. Because the test also mimics the effects of chronic pain conditions[1] I could use it in both the acute and chronic pain studies. My measurements were pain threshold (the time it takes to experience the first sensation of pain) and pain tolerance (the length of time one can tolerate that pain), so it would provide me with the information I needed to get some results. As the test is also used to evaluate cardiac health[2] and gain feedback from the autonomic nervous system e.g. blood pressure and heart rate, I would also be able to use it for this purpose too.[3][4][5]

The idea was to induce pain and see if there were any benefits from the reflexology treatment in terms of improving both pain threshold and tolerance levels in individuals. Whilst we were discussing pain, Ivor told me there was a correlation between cortisol levels in saliva and blood, and that because of this, it's possible we might be able to use cortisol as a marker to obtain measurements for stress levels. At the time I wasn't aware that when people are in pain, stress increases the inflammatory markers in the blood, or that inflammation is often a pre-cursor of pain.[6] When stress levels are high, for example in periods of chronic stress, the hypothalamic-pituitary-adrenal (HPA) axis is activated repeatedly. This means that the negative feedback loop, which is supposed to switch off the release of hormones, fails, and cortisol circulation is maintained. This causes extensive neurochemical changes within the cells, which in turn generates an imbalance in the homeostatic environment.[7][8]

Ivor had also suggested that we should measure heart rate using some ECG equipment but, in neither case, did he, at this stage, explain how, where, or what

I needed to achieve this. We discussed subjective rating tests, sleep patterns and long-term effects, all of which, at the time just seemed to rush over the top of my head.

My next job was to write up the testing protocol which meant deciding how often I would treat, what methods I would use to do so, and where I would carry out the research. I needed to find out whether I should perform a complete reflexology sequence or only use certain points. I sought some advice from others who were more experienced in reflexology - Tony Porter, Nico Pauly and even went to visit Ann Lett the author of Reflex Zone Therapy for Health Professional[9] but again, none had carried out any peer-reviewed published research that I could draw on.

According to the Chinese meridian theory of reflexology, the Liver 2 point is thought to release endorphins, but beyond that there was no specific routine as such, that was known to attenuate pain. I remembered reading an article in the Australian Reflexology journal about pain and reflexology, so I wrote to the author for advice. She told me that case studies from her students demonstrated time and again that their normal reflexology sequence reduced both the severity and frequency of migraine headaches and back pain, so I decided to go with a standard reflexology sequence that incorporated all reflex zones. We do after all, treat from a holistic perspective.

The next step was to try and establish some sort of funding for my research. Most, if not all research requires a lot of funding and I was tasked by Sheelagh to find out if there was any funding that might be available for my own research. This perplexed me somewhat, as I had assumed the university were funding me. I was wrong, what the university were doing was paying for my university bench fees, there was no stipend for my research, so no spare money for equipment, or testing packs, or for me personally. I was, at the time, running a busy clinic from home and working part-time as a secretary for the School Improvement Service, so thought it would be okay. Funding for CAM research was, and still is sparse. I had no idea where to look and as I was working, I naively didn't see the importance of it. I also didn't realise the impact not having funding would have on my research. This would prove to be particularly important when working on the chronic pain study because chronic pain involves sensory, cognitive, and psychological dimensions, and although pain is very much a subjective experience there are a few biochemical markers that may have proved useful for demonstrating the efficacy of reflexology.[10][11] In fact biochemical markers are extremely useful because they provide clinically relevant measurements to help us evaluate normal biological processes and thus support the subjective evaluation of our therapy.[12] Without funding support, I would need to rely on other objective and subjective formulations.

Where you carry out your research can also have implications on the outcome of your study and the room that I was currently using at the end of Sheelagh's lab was not the right place for me to carry out experiments. Rooms were, I was told, at a premium, so it wasn't likely that I would be able to occupy a space of my own. As luck would have it, there was a room opposite Sheelagh's laboratory, but it was barely big enough for a desk and chair let alone a couch or Lafuma chair. Nonetheless, I moved over to the new room, where I sat alone, not yet carrying out any experiments but rather, still focussing on my protocols and what I might need. I had a list of actions to take from both Ivor and Sheelagh and before I could even begin the experiments, I had to:

- decide what I wanted to do for the whole programme,
- decide on the 'control' method I was going to use and how I was going to approach it
and,
- define the number of participants I would need for the acute pain study

Control methods

To scientifically evaluate the efficacy of something you need to compare your treatment with something else, such as a positive control – something you know has worked before because it shows that your method is correct and that it works. At the time of my research, there was a dearth of reflexology literature that I could call upon for insight. I knew that Lynne Booth of Vertical Reflex Therapy (VRT) fame had carried out some research, so I wrote to her to find out what control methods she had used. Lynne explained that she hadn't used a control method for her research because it had been a small study on those for whom she had provided treatments, and so she was unable to help. Fortunately, Ivor had carried out some research on the use of acupuncture for pain[13] in which they had used a sham Transcutaneous Electrical Nerve Stimulation (T.E.N.S.). He suggested that I might use two different modes of T.E.N.S to strengthen my research evidence, so the protocol would include: -

- T.E.N.S that is not switched on – acting as the placebo
- T.E.N.S switched on – acting as the control
- Reflexology – acting as the active treatment

This would mean using the same participant on three separate occasions under each of these conditions whilst at the same time carrying out the ice pain test (cold pressor test). But first I needed to find out what Transcutaneous Electrical Nerve Stimulation (T.E.N.S) was and what it did. I discovered that T.E.N.S is a non-invasive stimulation technique used on peripheral nerves to relieve pain. Small rubber pads are placed over the skin close to the site of pain and pulsed electrical currents are delivered to the underlying nerves. It is used in pain medicine because it works by interrupting the pain signal in the spinal cord, so that the message doesn't reach the brain and this is known as the 'pain gating mechanism'.[14][15] The pain-relieving effect occurs from a non-painful impulse which creates an electrical paraesthesia directly underneath the electrodes. It doesn't have any known side-effects and produces a form of pain relief that can be used for short periods throughout the day, alongside medication, exercise, or on its own. It sounded like it would be a good option for my research, so we went with it.

In February 2003 I met with Ivor again and this time he was talking about somatosensory evoked potentials (SSEPs). Oh my god, what the heck is that all about? I was to learn that evoke potentials could demonstrate whether reflexology was gating the pain signal to the brain at the level of the spinal cord, which might also help to prove the mechanism of action of reflexology for pain management.

An ex-pharmacy graduate from Portsmouth was now a Porton Down big wig in chemical warfare and they were testing some equipment called the CBS5010 or customized biotelemetry solution. It was used for remote physiological testing and negated the need for cumbersome wiring attachments. Ivor thought it would be useful to measure the electrophysiology of brain wave patterns and so he suggested it might be worth meeting with this lady to see if she would loan me the equipment for my experiments. Electroencephalography (EEG) is what measures different brain wave patterns and Ivor explained that during drug use this form of testing can establish how long the drug works and whether it causes drowsiness or stimulates a person. For my research it would provide a more reliable measurement of central nervous system arousal which tells me if reflexology involves activation of the part of the brain that controls your levels of wakefulness, together with its effects on the autonomic and endocrine systems.[16] We arranged to meet this important lady on

28th March, and I was tasked with preparing a short presentation on my planned research to present at the meeting to try and engage their support.

The meeting went well and initially they were keen for me to use the equipment, but I needed to rework the project description, gain ethical approval, and produce a timeline. Once I had all this in place, I would be able to start the tests. After obtaining results I would then need to return to Porton Down where they would analyse the results for me. I can't actually recall why, but unfortunately this never happened, and the equipment stayed at Porton Down. Another disappointment, to say the least. In the meantime, Sheelagh had asked me to contact one of the professors of pain management at the Queen Alexandra Hospital (QAH) in Portsmouth and also my own rheumatology consultant to see if either of them would be interested in collaborating with me for the chronic pain study. I'd proposed that we measure the effectiveness of reflexology on arthritic pain, partly because I was getting some good results with my own client base and partly because I had suffered arthritic pain since I was a teenager. Sadly, neither was interested but that isn't unusual when carrying out research. You may hear of different leads from a variety of people only to find after investigating them that they don't go anywhere.

Part of my research was to establish if there was a link between the nervous system and reflexology and whether I could evaluate it in a measurable way. My knowledge of the nervous system was limited to what I had learned from my basic anatomy and physiology training and didn't even come close to what I now needed to know at a research level. In October 2002 I started attending lectures alongside undergraduates on the subject of neurophysiology. It incorporated forty-two hours of lectures with a further six hours of laboratory work, specifically geared towards pharmacy/pharmacology students. It was nothing like the A&P stuff I had done at college, in fact the terminology was so complex I thought the lecturer was talking a completely different language. Apart from the divisions of the nervous system I was lost, especially when he started talking about glial cells, astrocytes, and action potentials. Looking back on it now, it was an extremely valuable learning curve and one which I hope the reflexology community will adopt a version of in future courses. At the time of writing, we do not know for sure how reflexology works, there are of course many theories, but without a deeper understanding of the physiological processes involved, we may never fully achieve the true mechanism of action for reflexology.

THE TENACIOUS STUDENT | Dr CAROL A. SAMUEL

My meeting with Sheelagh in February 2003 gave me a whole new list of action points but one of the main priorities was that I had to produce two papers in the first year. The first paper was a write up providing an overview of reflexology across the world, basically a form of literature review, and the second was to formulate a project description. Two of the research papers I had found were in German, but it seemed they were valuable to my literature review, so I was tasked with trying to translate them. My level of German understanding was miniscule, having only done a little during my first two years at secondary school, but Sheelagh challenged me to use a translation programme on the computer which she said would help. It didn't! At the time I hadn't met Simone, a German national who was to become a close friend and colleague, so I called on a work colleague who was also German and paid her to translate them for me. She did a cracking job but struggled with the scientific and medical terminology, which did not translate well.

On the recommendation of the QAH professor we had met previously, we got in touch with the Portsmouth Institute of Medicine, Health and Social Care (PIMHS). Sheelagh and I arranged to meet with the research and development manager from this team in early March of 2003 with a view to discussing the possibility of some collaborative research for reflexology and chronic pain. We were however referred to the director of research for PIMHS within the university as she was responsible for the health services design aspect of research. At about the same time I met Ivor again, who this time suggested that he would be keen to work on neuropathic pain, as in diabetic neuropathy, so when I met with the director of research, that was the core of our discussion. She was extremely helpful and suggested that I attend some seminars with Professor George Lewith, who was then the professor of health research in the department of primary care at the University of Southampton. She thought that it would be beneficial to be part of another research group and he was about to give a lecture on chronic mechanical neck pain using CAM which may help my learning. Professor Lewith and I met on several occasions after this seminar and he proved to be an influential advocate of my research, but more on that later.

On the 10th April 2003 I carried out the first tests with Ivor as the participant. I gave him a 45-minute session of standard reflexology, following which he plunged his non-dominant hand into a bucket of crushed ice. I took measurements at 15-minute intervals for both pain threshold (the first sensation of pain) and pain tolerance (the time at which pain becomes intolerable) following his treatment. The results showed there was an increase of 24 seconds in his pain threshold at 30 minutes post treatment and of 186 seconds in his pain tolerance levels at 45 minutes post treatment when compared to the results achieved prior to reflexology. This small experiment told us that tolerance to pain increased over time, but pain threshold decreased over time. After the experiment Ivor experienced some painful pins and needles in both hands for about a week. He said it was a histamine-like itch in both hands but more so in the dominant right hand (the one he had plunged into the ice) but that putting his hands into warm water alleviated his pain. As he experienced the pins and needles in both hands, I wasn't sure if it was related to the ice immersion or something intrinsic to Ivor and so Sheelagh suggested that I try it out on some of the other PhD students for practice. As I didn't yet have a real protocol or format in place and no ethical approval, that wasn't possible.

In May 2003 Ivor suggested that I start more experiments by reviewing the physiological impact of reflexology and once again I wasn't sure what he meant by that. In my experience, each of my clients responded in their own way, depending on the presenting condition. He went on to explain that physiological measurements were useful because they influence pain as well as other physiological processes, so it was important to quantify any such changes using well defined experimental testing procedures. For example, when someone is stressed there is an increase in heart rate, blood pressure and muscle tension, because the sympathetic nervous system is on high alert.[17] I needed to establish if there were any acute changes in the autonomic function of participants directly following a reflexology treatment and then for two hours post treatment.

Some of the suggestions put forward were to:

- Measure blood pressure and changes in heartbeat and flow rate to review the effect on the parasympathetic nervous system.
- Use the CBS5010 - customized biotelemetry solution and affix it to the trapezius muscle to measure muscle tension before, during and after treatment.
- Look at alpha waves using traditional electrodes to obtain a measure of the normal state of wakefulness when the participants were resting.
- Use somatosensory evoke potentials to measure pain and establish whether reflexology was gating the pain.
- Use galvanic skin resistance measurements to show alterations in sympathetic nervous system activity and changes in autonomic function.

It was now July 2003 and I had yet to start any real experiments but once again Ivor was making recommendations. If I were to look at acute physiological changes then

I may as well look at acute mental pain as it would give a clear picture of the short-term effects of treatment. To do this I could do some psychometric performance tests such as those used in computer games where reaction times are measured, or perhaps look at memory games. The idea was proposed because if reflexology were releasing endogenous chemicals, it could affect how one performs these tasks. Off on a tangent again, I needed to find out what psychometric tests were available, where I could get hold of them, and how I would use them. In addition to this he also spoke about personality traits and how this might affect the outcomes of the study. There was just so much to think about, and you can see from the back 'n' forth nature of my conversations that we were in many ways, all over the place, and it really did take quite some time to settle down to the experiments. Amongst all of this Ivor was suggesting that I needed to become a neurophysiologist to fully understand what I was doing and that perhaps I could teach neuroscience with a pastoral role for first year students. He felt I had the right personality for such a role and that I could maybe even teach basic physiology. Whilst I understood that he wanted me to become part of the university, I was not looking for an academic role at that time.

The hypothesis

By now a whole year had elapsed since I started my research, I still did not have ethical approval and we were still discussing the experimental procedures before finally settling on three to start off.

- Physiological experiments to review heart rate, blood pressure and muscle tension
- An ice pain experiment to look at pain threshold and tolerance levels
- Psychological performance – reaction times, working memory, recognition memory and visual acuity.

Each of these had their own merits and I was still on a massive learning curve, but it was time to produce my hypothesis. After many hours of discussion, I finally settled on:

> *Reflexology has a clear cut, statistically valid effect on acute and/or chronic pain.*

Now all I had to do was prove it.

By November 2003 Sheelagh had asked me to produce a poster about reflexology for display at the 'Royal College of Nursing' in London. The only results I had so far, were those I had from the single experiment I had carried out on Ivor, but apparently this was good enough. In addition to the research, Sheelagh had set up a group to discuss the ongoing development or rather modification of the new BSc course in Natural and Complementary Medicine for which I had previously been interviewed. In its original format it hadn't been validated so she asked that I be involved in its further development. She handed me the paperwork and asked me to put forward some suggestions. There was a lot to read and even more to do to get it to a point where it could be revalidated.

In the meantime, Ivor once again volunteered himself for testing using ice pain. This time I was doing the experiment twice. I was to repeat the earlier tests I had carried out on him but this time I would also be measuring his heart rate during the ice pain test and recording his blood pressure but not pain threshold or tolerance levels. This was because there is some evidence that changes in heart rate, blood pressure and core temperature are affected by psychological and physical stress and so they might add to someone's perception of pain.[18][19][20] Plunging your hand into a bucket of crushed ice, when there is no other reason than to inflict pain, is an extremely stressful thing to do but I needed to look at the effect of using reflexology in this case and to compare it with something else known as a control treatment.

The importance of a control arm in research

I mentioned earlier that I used sham T.E.N.S equipment for the control arm of my research, but why is a control arm important in clinical trials? The idea of a control arm in any clinical trial is to control for any non-specific factors that might produce benefits, but are not a direct result of the intervention itself. In an ideal world a three-armed protocol, where you use an active drug, a placebo and an active control are preferable in order to eliminate bias. Those in the control arm might not receive any intervention at all, or they may receive an old treament method, drugs, or some kind of device, whereas in the placebo arm the treatment on offer may act in a similar way to the active treatment but is non-specific. An example might be using foot massage vs a specific reflexology sequence. The purpose is to reduce any bias and to compare each with the other for effectiveness.

Sheelagh's lab technician produced a machine that had a digitised running meter display on its facing surface, along with a whole load of dials which I used as a sham T.E.N.S machine. The narrative I gave the participants was that T.E.N.S releases mediators in the central nervous system to alleviate pain and that it had recently been established that T.E.N.S at a very low frequency works on the d-delta 2 fibres to block pain. This is of course a false statement as there is no such thing as a d-delta 2 nerve fibre. It worked really well across my experimental procedures, so well in fact, that when I tweaked with the dials on the machine some of the participants told me the stimulus was too high for them. This is what you call an active placebo or control.

I used real T.E.N.S pads to attach to the arm not being immersed in the ice (the dominant arm) and these were connected to a crocodile clip, which was attached to the back of the machine. The machine itself was simply showing a running digitised meter-reading without any electrical output. The results from the testing on Ivor looked interesting and I learned a few lessons from it. As a result I changed the procedure for the ice plunge study and finally created my protocol for the experiments in February 2004, almost eighteen months after I had commenced my research.

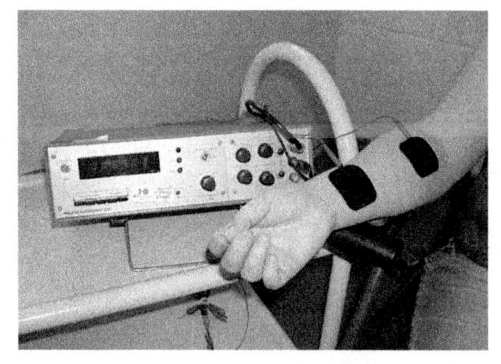

Plunging your hand into a bucket of crushed ice affects A-delta nerve fibres initially, the type that produce a short, sharp, pricking sensation. This means they detect the first pain sensation of pain, known as the pain threshold. When you leave the hand immersed in the ice you start to affect the c-fibres which have a much slower transmission rate and produce a diffuse, dull aching type of pain. This can help inform us about our tolerance levels for pain. The ice pain test was therefore perfect for looking at the effects of reflexology on the combination of both pain threshold and tolerance.

There were a couple of questions I was trying to answer from my experiments to prove my hypothesis:

1. Does reflexology gate the pain signal to the brain?
2. Is the effect of reflexology localised and creating the release of prostaglandins and/or central, creating an analgesic effect?

A-delta fibres are not very responsive to morphine, but c-fibres are which means that if participants had a high tolerance to pain following reflexology, there was a likelihood that it was acting more on c-fibres, thereby interrupting the slow transmission signal to the brain. If the effect were greater on the A-delta fibres, it would impact the pain threshold levels more. If I could prove this, maybe I could demonstrate that reflexology gates the pain signal to the brain.

The question was, how was I going to prove it?

Looking Back

My first 18 months as a research student proved to be a huge learning curve. I realised very quickly that regular meetings with my supervisors were vital to my progression and that I needed to be proactive and not wait for someone to show me the way. Research really is a self-directed learning programme, and you are expected to develop your own ideas, theories, and methods.

A person (especially if they are working as a practitioner) must be really motivated and driven to get a higher degree as there are many pitfalls along the way to achieving your goal. For me personally, it was most definitely a time when I felt quite alone and largely out of my depth. Ivor was full of ideas which was great, but the difficulties arose because for a large percentage of time I really didn't have a clue what he was talking about. I might have asked questions, if I had been able to understand, but for me, it only highlighted my lack of knowledge.

The only true wisdom is in knowing you know nothing
Socrates

It did however make me want to look deeper into the subject of neurophysiology, so that was a good thing. After all, if I didn't understand what he was asking me to do, how on earth was I going to be able to carry out the research or indeed, write about it? It makes perfect sense now that I can stand back from it, and I absolutely needed to fully understand the function of neurotransmitters and other hormones released by the body and their relevance in pain, but at the time it seemed such a daunting prospect.

I struggled a lot with the whole idea of the research but at the same time was completely fascinated by the discoveries I had made already, and how I might use that knowledge to further my learning and development. I was certainly looking forward to carrying out the experiments now that I had a protocol and ethical approvals in place. The next challenge presented itself when I started to recruit people to the first experiments.

THE TENACIOUS STUDENT | Dr CAROL A. SAMUEL

CHAPTER 3
Losing my way

Start by doing what's necessary; then do what's possible and suddenly you are doing the impossible
Francis of Assissi

On the move again, and this time I was moved into a room with the lecturer who had eventually been recruited for the BSc in Natural and Complementary Medicine course. Although we got on well initially, over a period of time we started to clash, and she constantly challenged my thinking, my ideas, and my relationship with Sheelagh. I didn't have her knowledge around universities, nor her intelligence and I didn't have an undergraduate degree. In fact, in the end, I found her rather off-hand and snobbish with me.

The lab itself was a walk-through section within the pharmacy department which meant that technicians needed to enter the room from time to time to collect various bits and pieces. It was a set up that didn't last long, since it wouldn't work for my experimental procedures. There was one more room change before I could finally settle. This time I was in a space which had served as a cloakroom/storeroom, sandwiched between two labs, used for biomedical sciences students. There was a door at either end, which meant that students could access from either lab which proved challenging in terms of privacy, so I asked that one of the doors remain permanently locked to prevent entry. Here is where I stayed for the remainder of my tenure and where I was to carry out my experimental procedures. In the narrow room of just five x twelve feet, there was space for a treatment table and a small desk. I was lucky to have a room at all, so I wasn't about to complain over the lack of space, so I simply adorned the room with some plants and put up some posters and paintings to make it my own.

It was time to start the first 'real' experiments and invite some participants to the study. I created an advert and posted it on the notice boards across the faculty. I also stepped out of my comfort zone to introduce myself to some of the other PhD students and staff so that I could see if I could canvass their support for my research.

Inclusions and Exclusions

To ensure you are treating the right group of participants, you must make sure that your research has both an inclusion and an exclusion criterion.[1] This means you are only using those who fit within that criteria and are creating a very distinct group of participants for your research model. I was told that without this my research would not be as strong as it needed to be. It was important therefore to design my study to include only those participants that would fit the criteria I had set, to prove my hypothesis. Furthermore, I needed a clear scientific or clinical rationale before deciding who I would include and who I would exclude from my research design; some of the things I have needed to consider were:

- *Is my hypothesis gender specific?*
  If my research had been looking at the effects of reflexology on prostate cancer for example, I might only include male clients, since prostate cancer is a male condition. However, as my research was about pain, it was fine to include both males and females.

- *Does my hypothesis exclude a specific age range?*
  Again, if I was looking at the benefits of reflexology on constipation in children, I may well have needed to specify an age range for those children, since in nursing practice, you are considered a child up to the age of 18. In my own research I found that there was some evidence that as we age our pain threshold and tolerance levels reduce, I therefore only included participants between 18 – 60 years old.[2]

- *Do my participants need to be experiencing a specific set of symptoms?*
  Initially I was looking at clients with acute pain, and I was inflicting that pain, so all I needed to include were healthy subjects with no underlying pain condition.

- *Medications*
  I needed to ensure that none of my participants were taking medication for their pain as this would cause confusion in any results. You can do it, but you would need to be able to account for this in your statistical analyses by using specific equations, so I made it so that anyone taking medications for pain were excluded from my study.

- *Would a smoker change the outcome?*
  Smoking can affect the way certain drugs impact physiological processes within the body and may also have an impact on the pain response[3][4] so for my research it was important to consider it.

- *Are there any cultural, cognitive or language barriers to consenting my clients?*
  If you feel that participants of a different culture would be unable to comprehend your instructions for the study, or perhaps be unable to understand a study survey due to language or cognitive issues, you might need to exclude them and give the correct rationale for doing so.

After consideration of these factors, the general criteria for inclusion into my study were: -

- free from any ongoing pain condition
- no previous experience of either reflexology or Transcutaneous Electrical Nerve Stimulation (T.E.N.S)
- aged between 18 – 60 years

Participants were excluded if they: -

- had an ongoing pain problem, and/or were being treated for this condition by their own GP/consultant,
- taking prescribed or over-the-counter medication for ongoing pain,
- had previous experience of either reflexology or T.E.N.S,
- had an interest in the outcomes of the experiments,

- had severe psychiatric or somatic illness,
- had established pregnancy at project start,
- had or currently have a thrombosis,
- had Raynauds Syndrome or other neurological disorders, or
- suffered from clinical hypertension for which they received regular medication.

It was of course possible and quite feasible that a participant who had volunteered to take part in the experiments wasn't aware that they might be suffering from clinical hypertension, but this would become apparent during the experimental procedure. The criterion for exclusion was that the subject's blood pressure (diastolic/systolic) did not normally exceed 20% of those published for the participants' age.

It was now April 2004 and participants for the first of my ice pain experiments had been recruited to the pilot study. With an increasing workload my time was split between my part-time work at the surgery, where I was now employed, my home clinic and university.

My home clinic consisted a separate building at the end of the garden, purpose built for me so that I could run my clinic at home, but not actually in the house. There was plenty of space for a treatment room and office area and with the surrounding garden it had an energy that provided both me and my clients with a sense of inner peace, a place for quietude and reflection.

This inner peace didn't last and the more time I spent in there writing for my research, the more I felt trapped in it. The energy of the place changed, and I started to use the room as a place to hide from the realities of everything going on around me.

My marriage had from time to time been changeable, to say the least. It was one of those situations where I felt that whatever I did it wasn't going to be enough, and that I wasn't enough! Sam and I had met when I was a purchasing special projects manager and a woman with confidence and strength, who could and would be able to speak with anyone at any level and not feel intimidated. I went through a tough period and became quite cold and analytical in my work but retraining in holistic therapies changed me and I grew softer and more approachable. I became more empathetic to the difficulties others were facing and subsequently more vulnerable, although I was always the last to admit it.

I remember attending the Association of Reflexologists conference in Warwick in July that year. Dr Christine Page had given a wonderful talk on spirituality and was promoting her new book 'Spiritual Alchemy', so I queued to have her sign my copy of the book, and as I stood in front of her, she said to me *"no regrets"*. It was a strange thing to say I thought, but for some reason it seemed to resonate with me. I recall a passage in the book that read, *'nobody can make us happy or unhappy; when we fail to believe this, we quickly give our power away'*.[5] I hadn't been happy for a while and with the added pressures of the PhD in my mind I realised that I had lost control of my life. Part of it was that I felt my marriage was falling apart, part was that I felt under pressure because I had made, what appeared to be little progress in my research. Things weren't great when I arrived home, Sam and I had a huge fight, and I came to the realisation that maybe we would be better off apart. What I didn't know at the time was that relationship problems were not an unusual occurrence for doctoral students.[6]

I was now in a position to analyse the results of my first experiment. To say that I knew nothing about statistics, would not be the complete truth, but certainly it wasn't my favourite subject. Despite having gained a qualification in business maths and statistics for my foundation degree in 'Purchasing and Supply Management', I considered maths as one of my weakest subject areas and tried to avoid it wherever I could. Getting my head around statistics and using statistical programmes was probably one of the most stressful parts of my journey throughout the whole PhD. Nonetheless in August Ivor attempted to explain things I had never heard of before, like confidence intervals, analysis of variance, Fisher exact scores, parametric and non-parametric statistics. My head was just so full of angst about my marriage and my ability to take in this new information was almost non-existent. I really didn't feel I could take much more, but I couldn't stop. It was like a drug that I couldn't and wouldn't give up. Ivor's patience was an absolute godsend and he invited and encouraged me bit by bit to learn a little more.

The results we had obtained from the first participants in the ice-pain tests already showed a significant effect from reflexology on both pain threshold and tolerance levels compared to the sham T.E.N.S control. The results also demonstrated that reflexology was having a beneficial impact on heart rate; for example, heart rate was lower in the group receiving reflexology than it was in the control group. This was important because heart rate is thought to increase as pain increases.[7] My results were demonstrating that the effect on pain threshold and tolerance was independent of any autonomic changes in the heart rate and therefore an important validation for reflexology. Of course, it was early days and there was a lot more testing to carry out before I could say for sure that reflexology was indeed having a beneficial effect for pain.

The Transfer Report

Alongside all this excitement I was also trying to write up my transfer report. My first attempt needed a lot of rejigging and Ivor's initial advice had been to write it as a paper, which I had attempted to do. I submitted what I had written and was asked to change it...something that was to happen time and again with my writing.

I mentioned the transfer report in chapter 2 as one of the first things I was told about when I joined the faculty. As a researcher you generally start out on a Master of Philosophy degree (MPhil) and then transfer across to a Doctor of Philosophy (PhD). The report is usually written:

- after you have had time to carry out an in-depth literature review, and
- when you have had an opportunity to carry out the first part of your research

The timescale is roughly 12-18 months after your initial registration, and I was already well past that. The document itself is usually composed of between 5 – 10,000 words and is meant to demonstrate your ability to carry out independent research to a PhD level. So, within the document you have to provide: -

- A short review and discussion of the work you have already completed (literature review).
- An outline of the research and the progress you have made.
- A statement of any formal training you have completed.
- The timetable for the remaining work moving forward.
- A statement of the next stage(s) of the research.

You also have to demonstrate that you are providing an 'original' contribution to the field under investigation...in my case, this was pain management with reflexology, but you also have to show that you are able to complete the work in a timely manner.

Once the report is submitted, it is then sent to a couple of assessors. Portsmouth didn't have a complementary therapy department and there were no immediate or obvious choices for assessors to review my transfer report. Eventually however Sheelagh and Ivor did decide on the two assessors, one was a principal lecturer in biomedical sciences who had some interest in acupuncture, whilst the other was a senior lecturer in psychology. As part of the transfer from MPhil to PhD you may also need to undergo a formal interview with those assessors as well as your supervisors. It is supposed to prepare you for your *'viva vocé'* exam which takes place once you have finally submitted your PhD thesis. It is an oral defence of your work, sometimes referred to simply as the viva. Although I submitted my transfer report in October 2004, I never did have any kind of formal interview with my assessors.

In early 2004 I signed up to the nerve reflexology diploma with Nico Pauly, with the idea that I would be able to enhance my neuroanatomy and physiology knowledge and be able to apply it to pain physiology from a practical perspective. In addition to that I was asked to sign up for the post graduate course in scientific research methods that was being offered for lab scientists. I was pleased that I was finally going to get some formal training in research but didn't realise until February 2005 that the course I had been signed up for was not the right one for me as a practitioner. I discovered too late that the training I should have undertaken was a one-year Masters' degree in Scientific Research Methods aimed at clinicians and which was being run by the School of Health Sciences and Social Work within the university. Needless to say, there was no funding available for me to do this either. In hindsight I feel that I've missed out on a lot of research training that could have made my life a whole lot easier, and that still concerns me to this day.

Tsunami

To say that the past few months had been stressful, would be to play it down. My husband and I struggled to communicate, and my work and business was suffering badly, but I could not walk away and decided to give our marriage another shot. We had already booked ourselves a holiday to Sri Lanka for Christmas and agreed we would take the holiday together to try and rebuild our relationship. We had been having a wonderful holiday, where we were able to connect with one another again and I think, we found a new respect for one another too. Boxing day 2004 started just like any other day. I recall one of the couples we had befriended was talking at breakfast about a tremor that had occurred in the early hours of the morning. They mentioned that some of the things on their dressing table had fallen to the floor. We joked as you do, about the earth moving for them, wink, wink, but otherwise nothing else was said and everything went on as usual. After breakfast we set our things down on a sun lounger and along with another friend went for our usual stroll/swim in the sea. We made light mention of the fact that the tide seemed to be a little strong that day because it was dragging us along the coast away from the entrance to our hotel. After a short while and without saying anything to each other we tried to get out of the sea but each time we moved to get out, the sea seemed to be pulling us back in. I lost my bikini bottoms a couple of times and one of our friends was losing his trunks, we laughed at each other as we struggled to pull them back up. A local man was shouting at us, but of course he was doing so in Sinhalese, so we didn't know what he was shouting about.

Like most hotels along the waterfront our hotel had a perimeter fence to prevent local people accessing the hotel grounds and selling their wares. As we were getting out of the water, we realised we were some distance from the entrance to the hotel and attempted to get closer by walking along the shore. On the beach, just on the other side of our hotel perimeter fence was a huge steel pipe which someone said had been placed there a few days previously by workers with elephants.

The sea seemed to be coming closer to us and we couldn't reach the entrance, so we decided to walk behind the pipe. Sam was walking in front of me, and our friend was behind me; when Sam reached the far end of the pipe, I was about halfway along it. Suddenly there was a huge surge and the sea hit land knocking me sideways and forcing the pipe to roll onto my legs. I remember screaming that I was trapped and felt the water rising but then I felt abnormally calm. It really was the strangest experience, almost like I was out of my body watching it all happen, but not really feeling it. I certainly don't recall how I got out or who got me out. I do remember the local man who had been shouting earlier, was pulling at me at one point. I also remember being lifted by my husband and our friend who then created a chair with their arms to carry me up to the reception area which was on the first floor of the hotel. The water was chasing us as we moved amongst the debris that was caught up in the wave, it seemed to rise up the steps with us and I started then to feel the panic around me.

My injuries looked much worse than they were, so they were keen to get me to hospital. There was a huge dent in my right leg across the tibia and cuts and bruising all around it, so I was a little concerned that it may be broken. My left leg, which would have been the leg on top as I fell, and closer to the pipe, rather strangely, only had cuts and bruises. As the panic rose around us people were running all over the place shouting and screaming.

We had been staying in a cabana; these were separate buildings away from the main part of the hotel with a ground floor and an upper floor. We had an upper floor room and Sam was keen to get me some dry clothes for the journey to hospital. He was gone quite some time, and people seemed to be talking about a second wave. I was terrified that he would be caught up in it and when he eventually arrived back at reception he was covered in cuts and bruises. He had been chest high in water and had been hit several times by drifting debris underneath the water that had torn away from its moorings but otherwise, he said, he was okay. He told me later that he thought he wasn't going to make it when the second wave came through, and that it was only because he hung onto a bar attached to a wall, that he managed not to go under the water. I am not sure how he managed it, but the clothes he went to fetch were dry, but more importantly he was back by my side.

The hotel customer liaison lady had managed to locate a doctor in the hotel who was on holiday. She attended me and had wanted to use some iodine before dressing my leg but had nothing with her to clean my wounds. By now I had already concluded that I hadn't broken anything despite the massive dent, and as part of my own holiday travel first aid kit I always carry essential oils. The doctor gave me the dressing and I cleaned up my own wounds with warm water and tea tree oil. I declined an offer of being taken to hospital since by now, the telephone lines had been affected and we were hearing of more and more devastation across the island, so I didn't think my dent justified a trip. All holiday residents who had been in the cabanas had to be moved into the main hotel that night. Those who had been in the ground floor rooms had nothing left other than what they had stood up in and we were unable to return to our own room until the next day.

On the evening of the tsunami, we couldn't reach our family by phone but knew they would hear about it on the news, so we just kept trying throughout the night. I eventually managed to get hold of one of my sisters who then passed the details across the rest of the family. Our daughters cleverly worked out between them from a previous phone call we had made, that we were on the West coast of Sri Lanka in a place called Kalutara. Although there was much desolation here, it had been Galle in the South, where we were originally going to stay, that had been hit the worst; they were nonetheless relieved to hear that we were safe. We spent a fretful night looking out of the window waiting for the next wave to come but thankfully, it never did. Many of the hotel guests helped in the clean-up process, but as I was unable to stand for any length of time I could only watch and listen to the shocking news that was unfolding around us. We returned to the UK on the 28th December as originally planned, but neither of us were prepared for hearing the full extent of the devastation caused by the damage from the tsunami.

Post-Traumatic Stress Disorder

Over the coming months my physical injuries healed but we were both out of sorts for some time, neither of us realising why we should feel like this. At some point across our lifetime, we will all experience stress in one form or another and most short-term stresses are a positive acknowledgement that helps us to focus our energy on what we need to do at that particular time. It would be fair to say that some people feel excited by stress and in that situation, it can help improve their performance. In contrast however, long term stress is often seen as a state of anxiety and concern; it's then that it may start to affect our general pathology and turn chronic. It is most definitely unpleasant, and it can decrease our levels of performance leading to longer term mental and physical ill health. That said, stress isn't an illness as such, but a state that threatens the body's ability to maintain a normal internal environment, which is controlled by the neuro, immune, and endocrine functions.[8] From a physiological perspective, stressful conditions put our body into a constant state of arousal that triggers the 'fight or flight' response. In this situation it is more difficult for us to achieve stability and maintain homeostasis to within a normal range.[9]

In stressful situations the HPA axis plays a role in balancing the activity of the autonomic nervous system through a series of hormonal signals. For example, when the brain perceives something as dangerous the sympathetic nervous system goes on high alert, then as the danger or stressful event subsides, the parasympathetic nervous system takes control, and our body returns to normal. But when you're experiencing chronic stress this repeated activity in the HPA axis turns off the negative feedback loop so that circulation of cortisol, released from the adrenal glands, continues to circulate. This causes an ongoing neurochemical exchange which creates imbalance and initiates a long list of negative responses in the body. But why am I telling you this?

During my nerve reflexology training I learned that when the sympathetic nervous system is in overdrive for long periods of time, the parasympathetic nervous system struggles to recover it. Something in this statement struck a chord with me and I never forgot it, because that was how I felt in the early part of 2005…in overdrive, confused both mentally and emotionally! In a state of chronic stress running like crazy on a treadmill that I couldn't get off. The steroid hormone cortisol circulates through our blood and it has many functions, but when you are exposed to high levels of it, it can have a detrimental effect on the body. Its role is to assist in the metabolism of fats, proteins, and carbohydrates, but unfortunately when we are in a state of high stress there is a tendency to crave more carbohydrates, which results in increased fat deposits, weight gain and inflammation.

My stress levels were high, and I had by now started to consume large amounts of carbs, sugars and what I call stodge for comfort which resulted in huge increases in my weight. My GP was so alarmed by my cholesterol and triglyceride levels that he advised me to take statins, which I refused. I knew for me there was a stress connection and that I may be experiencing periods of prolonged cortisol and adrenaline release which was also triggering an increased triglyceride reading, which in turn can boost 'bad' cholesterol.[10] Of course, none of us likes to think we are unhealthy, but I did keep eating rubbish and as part of the consequences of doing so my body became more and more inflamed. Rather interestingly I also learned that when the negative feedback loop is unstable, there is a significant decrease in the release of peripheral thyroid hormones which can depress metabolic function thereby increasing weight gain; now it made sense.

We know that within the immune system, cortisol works as a protective mechanism to prevent any kind of turbulence of the inflammatory response, and that this happens through the release of *anti*-inflammatory cytokines. However, an increase in cortisol circulation can suppress this activity and instead of releasing *anti*-inflammatory cytokines it generates the release of *pro*-inflammatory cytokines which increase inflammation. You may have heard about pro-inflammatory cytokines more recently when listening to discussions on the epidemiology of COVID-19. Importantly an increase in the level of inflammation can have a damaging effect on the cardiovascular system creating atherosclerosis,[11] on collagen fibres through the reduction of collagen synthesis and in decreased bone development.[12] Hence the plethora of symptoms in those who may now be experiencing Long Covid. For me, having had a long history of osteoarthritis my bone health wasn't great, and the prolonged stress that I was now under was seriously increasing my inflammatory markers.

I was also having an issue with my memory, and this is another stress-related concern that is indicative of too much cortisol circulation. This can impact the retrieval of stored information, and subsequently can also impair our learning ability.[13][14] Hindsight is a wonderful thing and of course I didn't know any of this back in 2005 but I was nonetheless right there in that highly stressed state. To me it seemed that as quickly as I learned something, it would simply go straight back out again. I couldn't hold onto any information for long, which in turn increased my stress levels, further increasing circulation of pro-inflammatory cytokines in my body. I was caught up in a vicious cycle that I couldn't stop.

> *Every change in the physiological state is accompanied by an appropriate change in the mental emotional state, conscious or unconscious, and conversely, every change in the mental emotional state, conscious or unconscious, is accompanied by an appropriate change in the physiological state.*
>
> **Elmer Green, Mayo Clinic¡**

I knew that my arthritis was getting worse, that I found it difficult to concentrate and store information but at the time I didn't realise exactly what was occurring in my own body. I didn't consciously bury my head in the sand, I was just so focussed on getting the work done for my PhD that I didn't know what was happening or where I was going anymore, so in February 2005, two months after the tsunami I met with Ivor to discuss the progress of my PhD.

I had been so shocked at what I had seen in Sri Lanka and felt so helpless to support the local community there after the event, that I sensed that what I had been doing in my research was completely pointless. What was the point of learning about how to support someone in pain when I couldn't physically nurse someone in pain? I couldn't attend to their injuries, I couldn't even attend properly to my own, in fact, the whole experience of the tsunami literally knocked me sideways in more ways than one, and I totally lost my way. I felt guilty, guilty that I had survived and that so many others had lost their lives. Children and adults alike, some like me had already had a life experience, others hadn't even begun theirs yet. Why did I survive, and they didn't? What, or who was it that was protecting me, keeping me safe, and why? There were so many things going on in my head, so much that I couldn't evaluate, that I couldn't process, but still I didn't realise that what I was experiencing was all perfectly natural. No one told me, no one talked to me or offered any help or advice, or support. I just had to get on with it, we, just had to get on with it.

Any kind of chronic activity in the stress system can lead to a whole host of disorders because almost all our immune responses are controlled by steroid hormones. This means that both our immune and inflammatory responses are greatly impeded as a result and as such can increase our levels of pain. In fact, pro-inflammatory cytokines released into our cells can trigger lots of unpleasant symptoms which, as I mentioned earlier can alter our neurochemistry and neuroendocrine communication systems. We are taught that inflammation is implied through redness, heat, swelling and pain, but the unseen effects of inflammation can often cause more damage than is outwardly visible. Chronic inflammation is known to impact conditions such as asthma, arthritis, diabetes, atherosclerosis, and some cancers too, and in April 2005 I discovered what felt like a lump in my left breast.

I went to see my GP who agreed that indeed there was a lump in my left breast, and I was referred to the local breast clinic for a mammogram. A couple of weeks later I was invited to attend the clinic again to undergo a fine needle aspiration along with an ultrasound scan. When the procedure was carried out the consultant didn't use the scans to guide him, instead he simply felt for the lump and stuck the needle in to remove some fluid. I didn't know it at the time, but this is not on its own a particularly reliable method of determining breast cancer.[15] Two weeks passed and I had not heard anything from the hospital so I rang the breast clinic, and they couldn't find my notes. Two days later I received a call to say that the fluid was clear, and everything was fine, I just had a lumpy breast. Well, that's okay then, isn't it!

As I mentioned previously when the sympathetic nervous system is under duress the HPA axis prepares our body for the 'fight or flight' response. When this system is overloaded it's unable to function effectively so whilst stress has both good and bad attributes, it is, unfortunately, a major factor in the perpetuation of chronic pain conditions.[16] Luckily for us the endogenous opioid system, our own in-built pain mechanism, can in fact help alleviate pain that is triggered by fear, anxiety, and stress. It does this through a phenomenon referred to as stress-induced analgesia and both fear and anxiety are considered imminent threats to the body, which motivate our defence mechanisms to induce a state of hypervigilance. Unfortunately paying more attention to pain increases our perception of it and subsequently also our sensitivity to it, which has an overall effect on our emotions and the neural processes that shape our experiences of pain.[17] In short, stress can either suppress pain (stress-induced analgesia) or exacerbate it (stress-induced hyperalgesia) and this really depends on the type of stress, the length of time experiencing that stress and the intensity, both emotionally and physically. I seemed to hurt more and more every single day and was extremely anxious; so unbeknownst to me I was already in a state of sympathetic overdrive.

PhD to MPhil

During my discussions with Ivor, I had agreed to change my programme from that of PhD back to an MPhil with the focus placed more on pain than the current physiological/psychometric testing I was planning to do. Ivor explained that I would need at least another year to complete the MPhil and that it would still be a good outcome for me. At the same time, I had attended an open day at Portsmouth hospital where they were recruiting for new nursing undergraduates to study at Southampton University. I applied for a place in children's nursing and eventually received a notification of acceptance to start in October of that year.

In the meantime, I had work to progress with my research, and set about preparing for my next round of experiments.

CHAPTER 3 | LOSING MY WAY

Looking Back

In these past two years I lost my way completely. Throughout 2004/5 my relationships with everyone suffered and I became too damned tired, to even give a shit. In fact, I seemed to have lost total control of my life altogether. I hurt inside and out, and I couldn't figure out why. I was a good person, I worked hard to get to where I thought I was going, and yet I was so unhappy.

Looking back now I can see that there was no single event that tipped me over the edge, nor one single thing that I had any real control over. My relationship with Sam was a shared responsibility, but I was so focussed on my research that I lost sight of us. I didn't invest in our marriage the way that I should have done and in return he stopped investing in it too.

I know that I am not alone with this and have shared similar experiences with colleagues who were also doing a PhD. It took the event of the tsunami to make me stop and realise just how much I had to lose in my relationship with Sam and that despite what might be termed the usual marriage-related concerns, we were in fact good together.

I was carrying out research on something I knew very little about, I was being told to learn and absorb a huge amount of information, to direct my own learning and to become an authority on my subject matter. I was also trying to hold onto a difficult relationship, run a clinic, be a parent, grandparent, and wife, continue to work and to succeed in all these things.

I struggled to hit the reset button on my life, to stop and think about what I was doing and why. Instead of focussing on what I could do, I was focussing on what I couldn't do.

THE TENACIOUS STUDENT | Dr CAROL A. SAMUEL

I felt that I was weak, that I was no longer the strong, confident, self-assured woman I had once been, that I couldn't ask questions and get answers that made any sense to me. Through all of this though, I learned resilience, I learned that things are never as bad as they seem on the surface, that when you are faced with adversity you have two choices, you can run away and hide, or you can put on your big girl pants and fight.

CHAPTER 4
Not good enough?

Focus on what you can do, not on what you can't.
Stephen Hawkins

As we continued through 2005 the tsunami was still leaving its mark on us both. Sam was experiencing violent headaches and the most awful cough; so, following a visit to the GP he was referred to hospital for further investigations where they carried out, amongst other things, a computer tomography (CT) scan on his head. Whilst we were waiting to speak with the consultant, I took a glance at his notes which revealed they were looking for a tumour. I kept quiet at the time as I didn't feel it was appropriate right there and then to tell him, but at the same time I felt absolutely terrified of what the results might reveal. Fortunately, for us both the test revealed no apparent lesions or tumour, and the headaches were put down to stress. It would be some time later before we would discover that he had also had pneumonia, but it was not picked up at that time.

I struggled to move forward and felt as though I was walking through treacle, it was such a strange feeling, like I was here, but I wasn't. There is something called the freeze response which is a reaction to a fight or flight situation in which you feel powerless to do anything. It can completely overwhelm you and leave you in an almost self-paralyzing condition where the body tends to lock-down inside and go numb...was this me? I can't know for sure, but certainly I blocked the events out of my mind and instead focussed on where I was going. The tsunami had hit me hard, and I was behind in my research methods coursework, so I had to apply for an extension of time. In a supporting letter our practice nurse had simply written that I was in the tsunami and was being treated for a leg injury I had sustained, and that my husband had suffered a malaise that concerned me. Talk about an understatement!

It was time to focus my attention on the next round of experiments and in this round of tests I was going to expand on the results of the first experimental results and compare my standard reflexology with a light touch reflexology and a no treatment control. The reason for this is that pharmacological studies show that drugs, such as morphine, codeine, and pethidine display dose-related analgesic effects.[1][2][3][4] So the stronger the drug or the combination of drugs, the greater the effect. In a similar scenario, altering the intensity or frequency of stimulation in CAM therapies, such as T.E.N.S or electro-acupuncture, can also influence the analgesic effect.[5][6][7][8][9] It's possible therefore that reflexology has a dose-related response too, so it was of interest to me to determine whether there was a difference in the effects of light and standard reflexology for my pain threshold and tolerance experiment.

It was difficult to recruit participants to this experiment as they were going to have to attend on three separate occasions and each visit would require three hours of their valuable time. I wasn't offering any payment for their attendance, as there was none available to me, hence I think, the difficulties I encountered when trying to engage for it. The question of how I was going to measure the difference between my light and standard reflexology pressure came to light. What might be deemed a light pressure to me may well be someone else's standard. How do you define the difference? Everything in science needs to be measured and if you are saying that you are applying a different pressure, you must be able to measure that difference, so I needed to find a way that I could do that in a very constructive way. I trawled the internet for help and managed to locate a company in the USA who were looking at foot pressure in walking and weight bearing. It was a bit tenuous, but I felt it was a good starting point. After many emails back and forth I was able to explain what I was looking for, and we talked about the equipment they were using to capture and record pressure between two contacting surfaces. This was going to be a very innovative piece of work and they hadn't come across anything quite like this before but assured me they would be able to adapt what they had to meet my needs.

I was still writing my literature review and writing scientifically was proving difficult for me. No 'touchy feely' sentences Sheelagh said, no colloquial terms, short sentences, and lots of referencing. Third person, past participle is the way to write, and it truly was a whole new ball game and one that I needed to get my head around super quick. It was also around about this time that Sheelagh suddenly suggested she and Ivor might change roles, so that he would become my director of studies and she would become my second supervisor. It seemed to me to be a bit out of the blue, but she said it was in fact Ivor who was directing the research.

My appraisal was set for 21st July 2005 and in preparation for that meeting I continued to think about how I would measure the pressure differences of the two reflexology techniques I planned to use in the next experiment. I knew from my own purchasing days that Sheelagh would want me to obtain at least two or three quotes for the equipment, so despite the fact that I had already started negotiating with the USA, I had to locate more companies who might be able to offer us the right kit. No one had done this before, and there wasn't much around, so I only managed to find one other company that might offer something similar. In the end we agreed to go with the American team who were prepared to loan us the sensor equipment for just two weeks, at a cost of $1160, the equivalent UK cost at that time was around £590. Our plan was to hire the equipment at the beginning of September and see how it worked for what I had in mind. Sheelagh was excited to be working with pressure and thought that the measurements we could obtain would form a valuable chapter in my thesis. She was certainly much more adept in this subject matter than she had been on pain and reflexology. I don't know what happened or how it came about but based, I think, mainly on this chapter and the involvement she would have in it, she then decided that she would stay as my director of studies and that Ivor would retain the role of supervisor.

I met with Ivor a few days later to discuss the equipment we were going to hire, and he thought we would need to hire it for much longer than the two weeks we had scheduled. For a start, once we received the equipment, I would need to calibrate it, learn how to use it, test it on subjects and before that, I would need to practice on something that could provide me with a tactile feedback. Ivor wasn't confident that I would get all that done in two weeks. On top of that, I would also need to recruit participants to the study, which, as I had already discovered, was no mean feat. As he had a wont to do, he then suggested that perhaps we use the equipment to look at whether a normal walking pressure could stimulate analgesia. Based on the fact that walking stimulates mechanosensitive receptors in the feet,[10] he explained that as nerves release neurotransmitters it might be that the effect of reflexology on the body is bought about by spatial or temporal summation.

What that meant in terms of neurophysiology, I had no idea. So, I looked it up and learned that it is what determines an action potential, which is the movement of an electrical signal along a neuron. It tells you whether the potential to fire that signal is generated by a combination of excitatory and inhibitory signals from multiple simultaneous inputs (spatial summation), or from repeated inputs (temporal summation). Basically, if I used the sensor product to test normal walking pressure and then compared it with the pressures applied in reflexology using the body at rest with the feet up as the control, I would be able to test his theory. After all, what we needed was an estimation of pressure. I could see his point, especially as the sensor equipment currently on offer was a film that could be used between two contacting surfaces, so participants would be able to place the film between their foot and a sock. Certainly, it was food for thought.

In August 2005 Sheelagh had decided that we would not have any more 'formal' meetings but that I would send regular emails to them both to keep them up to date with my progress. At Sheelagh's bequest I wrote to the team in America and suggested that we would probably need the pressure testing equipment for one month and that if we found it valuable, we would purchase it to give us time to complete the research at our own pace. Initially we borrowed it for two-weeks and set a delivery date for 10th October because neither Sheelagh nor Ivor were available for support prior to that date. Before then, or rather alongside that, Ivor asked me to prepare a poster presentation for the National Health Service (NHS) Biennial Conference so that I could showcase the results of my first experiment. He also said that I would need to be prepared to present those results in front of a group of NHS medics. It was a very scary thought, but you need to step out of your comfort zone sometimes and I was certainly beginning to step out of mine.

---

*If you can see your path laid out in front of you
step by step, you know it's not your path.
Your own path, you make with every step
you take. That's why it's your path.*
Joseph Campbell

CHAPTER 4 | NOT GOOD ENOUGH

I don't really remember how it came about, maybe it was talking to my friend who had been a nurse almost her entire life, or perhaps it was when I was in meditation. My friend had told me that children's nursing is not just about small children but includes adolescents up to the age of 18. She said there was a lot of lifting involved which could put a tremendous strain on my already arthritic joints. Whatever the reason, I concluded that I didn't really want to go into nursing, it was simply a knee-jerk reaction to the tsunami and my feelings of inadequacy at that time. Something had bought me to this path; I didn't seek out a PhD nor did I ever feel I had the wherewithal to do one, but here I was and something inside me knew it was my right path. I told Ivor about my decision first and he told me that I would need to do an awful lot of research to complete the PhD, that even if I spent a further three years from that point getting people to participate in the study, it would be impossible. He said he thought that I should continue with the MPhil and then go for an educational project grant with the Arthritis Research Council the following year. Prior to that, I would need to write and get something published, so for now at least, I was persuaded to continue the path of an MPhil despite the fact that after the submission of my transfer report, I had already been approved for progression to a full PhD. It riled me and I couldn't let it go because I knew that the PhD was what I was meant to achieve, I knew it was my destiny and the feeling was so strong that I simply could not ignore it, but at that time, neither Sheelagh nor Ivor were supportive of that pathway. We met again in December 2005 and all I seemed to hear were problems as to why I couldn't achieve my goals. I had so far only completed two experiments, the first ice pain experiment showed that reflexology had a significant effect on both pain threshold and tolerance, it also showed there were changes in heart rate, but it was nowhere near enough evidence. I needed to expand the theory as I only had basic results and would need a lot more for a PhD.

A chapter on physics and the compliance of pressure would be needed to discuss the pressure sensor testing we were carrying out, and I had already started recruiting for my next round of tests. The results so far were all over the place and were not replicating those of the first experiment. It was also proving extremely difficult to recruit for the third round of tests and our statistician had calculated that I needed a particular number of participants to show an effect, this is known as the 'power calculation' and is similar to the 'number needed to treat' in a clinical trial for medications.

It was explained to me that a power calculation helps to confirm a hypothesis and determine the true effect of the treatment.[11] It forms a crucial part of the planning for data collection to ensure you get an effect that is real and not false. The idea is that you are creating the correct sample size for your study that you haven't yet carried out, so your subject knowledge forms an important part of the calculation. You have to decide what you think will happen, it's a bit like gazing through a crystal ball to seek the meaning of life. You are ostensibly guessing whether your prediction correctly infers that an effect exists in your study design. If your study has a 95% power, then it has a 95% chance of demonstrating an effect and the result is presented as $p=<0.05$ or $p=<0.01$ with p being the probability of demonstrating that less than 5% or 1% of the result is due to chance. Hence you have a real effect from your treatment in the population you are treating.

The number needed to treat (NNT) is a calculation used in clinical trials of the average number of people that need to be treated to prevent one poor response.[12] At least one person has to benefit from the treatment compared to those in the control arm of the research which means that the ideal NNT would be 1. This would indicate that everyone in the trial would benefit from the treatment and no one would benefit from the control. It is usually calculated for trials where medications are involved and is a risk ratio of the medication causing harm but as I wasn't using any medications, this wasn't an appropriate calculation for me.

For my second ice pain experiment, the power calculations used to determine the number of participants that should be recruited for the experiments were based on the tolerance data obtained in my previous ice pain experiment. Because this was where we saw the greatest effect on the first tests, the statistician estimated that the maximum difference between groups would occur at 120 minutes post treatment. It was calculated that for 90% confidence in the result, the power sample size needed to be 19, but to detect a difference with a power greater than, or equal to 95% required at least 30 participants. My aim therefore was to recruit a minimum of thirty in this experiment. This meant that I needed thirty people who were willing to attend for three sessions one week apart, for three hours each time. A total of nine hours' worth of commitment without being paid.

But there was a further issue I needed to address in this experiment that I had not previously considered. Most of those who participated in my initial ice pain experiment were female and there is some evidence that for experimentally induced pain, females when compared to men, respond with reduced pain threshold and tolerance levels.[13][14] This would mean the results may be more clinically relevant to females than for males.[15][16] Whilst this infers that females are the best human model for pain studies, to demonstrate efficacy across a wider population I needed to recruit not only more male subjects, but also people from the ethnic minority groups to see if I was getting the same effect. All of these factors need to be taken into consideration when carrying out research trials and sometimes it's only when you are in the thick of it and have had a chance to read the literature, that you can fully appreciate the real-life implications to what you are doing.

Having initially hired the sensor equipment in October 2005 for the pressure testing experiment we soon discovered that the sensors were creating a lot of 'noise' in the feedback system. What I mean by that is that the signal responses were creating a lot of additional data and obscuring the true picture of the feedback from the sensors. The sensors themselves had to be worn under a gloved thumb and broke easily when I applied pressure to the foot, so modifications were required, and it was three months later before I actually got to carry out the testing again; all of which was eating into my research time. As part of this particular experiment, I was asked to create a project on pressure and reflexology for the pharmacy undergraduate students so that they might consider it as a research choice for their dissertation. The idea being that I would guide their study and use the material they obtained for supporting my PhD. I now needed to get to grips with the new sensor heads, the updated software programme and devise the project for the undergraduate who would eventually adopt my project idea for their dissertation.

Compliance of pressure

Physics is the area of science that tells us all about the compliance of pressure, and I needed to have a clear understanding of it so that I could write the chapter I needed to put into my thesis. This was another steep learning curve but a necessary part of my overall research plan.

There are many questions for which we don't know the answers in reflexology, for example:

- What physiological changes occur when reflexology pressure is applied to the feet?
- How does the skin adapt when pressure is applied and what neuronal changes take place?

- Does it matter how deep we work for reflexology to be effective?
- Are other cell changes taking place?
- Is the pressure itself sensed in the plasma or the cell?
- What happens in the circulatory system...blood and lymph?
- Are there autonomic changes occurring from the pressure applied?
- How can we tell if endorphins are released?

Many of these questions would require a lot more work, a lot more money and many different types of testing. I was concerned, for now at least, with the difference between my light, standard and static pressure applications. It was an incredibly exciting and certainly innovative piece of research to carry out.

We know that collagen is the structural protein responsible for tissues such as bone, cartilage, tendons and ligaments[17][18] and that it changes its geometric shape under pressure to accommodate deformation.[19] We also know that it is the elastin within the Extra Cellular Matrix (ECM) that provides stretch and ensures that the shape of the tissue is recovered afterwards. In fact, all body movement involves the transfer of forces between different segments of the kinetic chain, and an increased tension in one area must be balanced by an increased tension in another in order to maintain shape and support the various structures. One of the pieces of research I read during this particular experiment indicated there were 104 cutaneous mechanoreceptors in the foot sole which are responsive to a variety of environmental and sensory stimuli. They are composed mostly (70%) of rapidly adapting type I Meissner corpuscles, with large randomly distributed receptive fields around the metatarsal-tarsal regions,[20] but I wasn't really sure what that meant in terms of pressure. I found out that this type of receptor is termed a phasic touch receptor because it detects change in texture and responds to light touch and slow vibration. It adapts to constant or static stimuli at a fast rate and its ability to deform and change position generates an action potential or nerve impulse in the nervous system. Now we're getting somewhere.

Although functional magnetic resonance imaging (fMRI) studies have demonstrated a degree of correlation between the reflex points in the feet and somatotopical regions of the brain,[21] in reflexology the relationship between mechanosensitisation on the foot sole and adaptive responses is not fully understood, so anything that can help shed light on this process is of value in terms of the mechanism of action.

What is it about pressure?

As reflexologists we use our skill to utilise an applied pressure that initiates a reflex response from mechanosensitive receptors in the skin. We are taught that the effectiveness of reflexology to affect an organ or physiological response is reliant on the intensity of the stimulus, but is this true?

According to Tiran and Chummum[22] pressure sensitive receptors in the feet are triggered when pressure is applied to them during a reflexology stimulus, inducing physiological change through peripheral vasodilation, but of course we don't know this for sure. Whilst there have been a few studies over the years looking at reflexology on circulation the research is still inconclusive.[23]

In Morrell reflexology a light pressure is used, and it suggests that *"the stimulus should be light and have the ability to reach the patient on a subtle level in order to evoke relaxation and restore homeostasis"*. Poole[24] and Evans[25] both used light touch reflexology for their research protocols and were able to demonstrate an effect on pain levels, together with stress and anxiety, which gave me more reasons to test it again.

Standard reflexology is of course attributed to the method defined by Ingham[26] in which the pressure is described as being firm. In the Rwo Shur Method[27] proffered by Father Josef it is said that the most beneficial use of reflexology is found with a much deeper pressure, utilising a knuckling technique or a rolling dowel. This is of course similar to that proposed by Anthony Porter in Advanced Reflexology Techniques (ART). Hanne Marquardt on the other hand proffers there are no fixed rules for determining the intensity of the stimulus and recommends the treatment should fall within the pain thresholds of the patient being treated.[28] On the other hand, in nerve reflexology Veldhuizen and Pauly used the thumb in a static hold over the foot bones to elicit relief of tension in thoracic paraspinal muscles.[29] As you can see there are many ways to evoke a beneficial response in reflexology. Many of the research results have been attributed to the Ingham method of reflexology[30][31] but no one had actually measured the force of applied pressures in their experiments.

In our general clinical practice, the amount of pressure we use during any given reflexology session varies according to the general health, age, and size of the client. We might also take into consideration the skin surface type and only apply the level of pressure needed to effectively gain a physiological response. For example, a foot that is calloused requires a much greater pressure than a softer foot[32] but regardless of these scenarios, the most commonly utilised reflexology technique is that of Ingham. The pressure used exerts an intermittent on/off caterpillar-like dynamic motion, generally applied using the medial aspect of the thumb. This caterpillar-like stimulus appears to mimic the phasic activity of rapidly adapting mechanoreceptors with their small receptive fields, producing transient responses to the onset and offset of the stimulus.

At the time of this experiment there was no available data recommending the level of force that should be applied and most practitioners, as I have already mentioned, work within the bounds of the feet presented before them *i.e.,* they adapt the treatment according to the physiology, sex, age, and general demeanour of their patient. Meissner corpuscles, one of three types of mechanoreceptor, are free nerve endings that transmit information from mechanical deformation such as touch, pressure, vibration, and sound from the external and internal environment and then translate them into electrical signals. As we age there is a considerable reduction in the number of Meissner corpuscles,[33] which also begs the question, do older people become more sensitive to treatment? They are sensitive to light touch, so does firmer pressure undo the effect of reflexology and if so, is it the Pacinian corpuscle that is creating an effect via a vibratory response, and does it really actually make any difference? After all, they are all mechanoreceptors. What I needed to do was use different foot types with a wide age range of people to test the sensors out. It would be impossible to answer all these questions without an extended knowledge of the tissue tensegrity, and some very specialized equipment.

The original sensors were tested on a 15-month-old baby, a middle-aged man and a 75-year-old woman, each of them with a different foot type. As I mentioned earlier the sensors supplied were self-adhesive and were meant to stay in place, but as I moved my thumb a sensor either snapped or slipped off. I tried using a latex glove to keep them in place, but they were difficult and extremely awkward to use. There was no flexibility in the leads supplied with them and they were tightly packed into the sensor device which meant I could not manipulate them as I worked the feet.

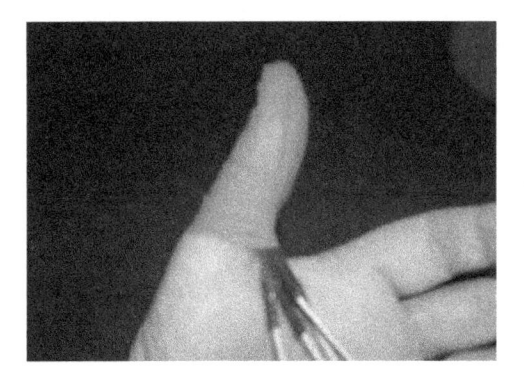

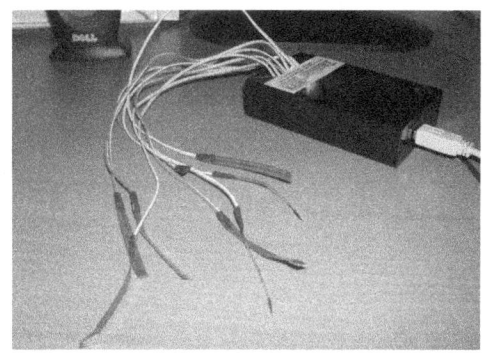

The team in the USA changed the shape of the sensor, provided both a large and a small size to accommodate the change in surface area and updated the software programme. I still had to use a latex glove to keep them in place, but they were far more flexible than the first set had been.

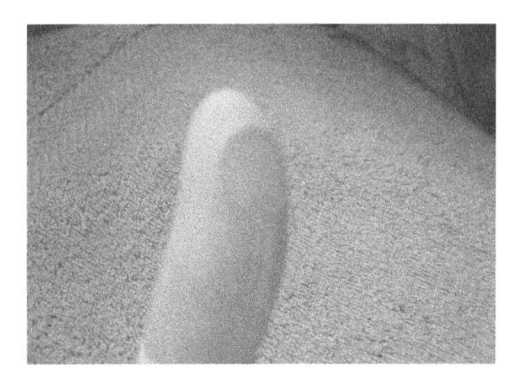

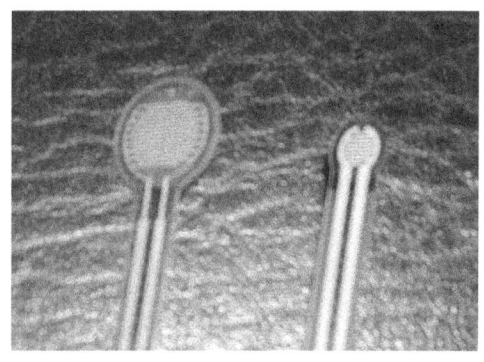

Having set my protocol for the work to be carried out I met with Emily who was, in April 2006, to become my project student. It seemed strange to be taking on a young student for my research but there was a lot to do, and a young inquisitive mind was exactly what I needed. Emily didn't know anything about reflexology, so she wasn't biased in her approach to the testing either. We started testing the sensors on balloons that we had blown up to different sizes in the hope that we would be able to get some measurements of pressure and familiarise ourselves with the equipment and software. We initially measured in millimetres of haemoglobin (mmHG) as one would for blood pressure, but soon discovered this was not an acceptable measurement for pressure between two contacting surface areas. Sheelagh recommended we convert these figures to pounds per square inch (psi) and then into kilopascals (kPa) as this was the standard international unit requirement. It was a lot of messing about, but it had to be right.

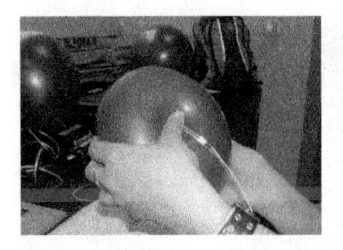

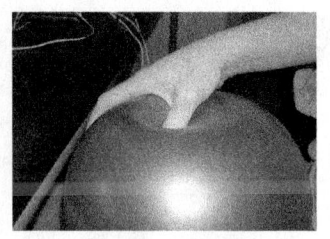

With a view to evaluating whether the pressure differed every time I did it or whether it remained consistent, regardless of the age, gender, type of foot, I selected a group of people to participate in the study. I used the medial border (spine reflexes), the medial malleoli, the heel and foot arch on which to experiment as this would accommodate all different tissue changes of the foot and allow me to apply standard, light, and static pressures.

Financial setback

When I originally signed up for an MPhil/PhD in September 2002 my application finance form clearly stated that my fees were being paid by the Dean for a six-year period. However, in November 2005 I received an invoice from the faculty for my tuition fees. I was at a loss to understand why I was suddenly receiving invoices for something I was not meant to be paying. It was more stress and took several emails and phone calls to resolve. The university had stopped paying my tuition fees after three years, thinking that I was a full- time student and not part-time. I argued that the agreement was for six years and held my ground until they changed their mind. They finally agreed to pay half the fee for a further 12 months, after which time, I was expected to fund myself.

In March 2006 Sheelagh decided we were going to have weekly meetings again, I needed to find out how the effects of electro pressure and acupressure were measured on the skin, review the theory behind the sensor device, find out how it worked and write a full report on everything I had done to date. I was told to be calm, cold, and analytical when discussing my data and that I should aim to submit it within four weeks. Although much of this would be done in conjunction with my project student, she was also under pressure to complete her dissertation. In May Sheelagh set me another test, to draw a schematic of an action potential, to look up the cell membrane potentials, find out what the cell membrane is made of and what ions move in and out in exact numbers. It seems we were back to chemistry again. Furthermore, I needed to understand the Nernst potential and the Nernst equation and look at the relationship between the concentration of ions and potential. Basically, I needed to be sure of the in-depth physiology of what happens when pressure is applied to the skin. Once again, this was a huge chapter and a massive learning curve. At the time of writing my thesis I could have explained what the Nernst potential and equation were, but like most things that you learn, unless you are using it on a regular basis, you soon post it to the back of your memory. It's the 'use it or lose it' scenario of brain plasticity.

Alongside the work on the pressure measurements, I was still trying to recruit for the next experiment and the progress was slow. I was becoming increasingly frustrated and dissatisfied with the support I was getting from Sheelagh and Ivor and was giving some serious thought about moving my entire programme of research to Southampton University. In November 2006 I arranged a meeting with Professor George Lewith at the University of Southampton. I hoped that he would give me a more balanced view of my research and help me to decide what I might be able to do with it. It was a good meeting, not only did he help me make more sense of what I was doing but he also provoked and helped change the way I planned for future experiments. I began to see more clearly what it was I was trying to find out; that's not to say that I didn't have any idea in the first place, but now it just seemed to make more sense. Everything that I had so far done at Portsmouth was heavily science orientated so talking with George was an absolute breath of fresh air. He took a role on both sides of the fence, as a medic and as a CAM practitioner, which seemed to give much more meaning to what he was suggesting. Yes, there was the science of course, but it seemed George understood on more levels than either Sheelagh or Ivor from a holistic perspective, and I came away from that meeting feeling completely recharged and now with more excitement about any further research too.

I had already mentioned to Sheelagh and Ivor that I was going to be meeting with George and that I was considering a transfer to Southampton, so George suggested that I keep a record of our meeting and everything we had discussed, making sure that I copied Sheelagh and Ivor in with notes. Rather interestingly George had been part of the education board who had validated the course written by Sheelagh for the BSc in Natural and Complementary Therapies, so they already knew one another. George was a director of the International Society for Complementary Medicine Research so he suggested, indeed recommended, that I write an abstract about my results so far and aim to present them at a congress on CAM in Munich set for May 2007, but I wasn't sure Sheelagh would pay for me to go even if the abstract were accepted.

Confusing results

In December 2006 Ivor and I met again because the results of my experiment, the second ice pain experiment, were all over the place. I had so far treated 27 of the 30 participants I needed, but some of them were responding early with increased threshold and tolerance levels, whilst others were responding later in the timeline. When you analyse data like this, you find that they level out and there is no apparent effect of treatment. As I was doing the work on pressure, he suggested that I make a subjective judgement about the foot, for example is the foot very calloused, is it soft, spongy etc. If someone's foot is more calloused, could it be that thicker skin means they are reaching their maximum response times sooner?

There was another suggestion from one of the other lecturers. She was a biomedical scientist and thought that I might be able to measure resting cortisol levels; she said that if the participants had high cortisol levels, they may also have a higher pain threshold which might be skewing my results. I didn't know how to do cortisol testing or how to analyse any results I might get from that type of testing, but as there were no additional funding options open to me to find the money to have the biomedical team carry out the tests, I couldn't do it anyway.

The results of the second ice pain experiment really threw a huge curve ball at me, what was happening here? Was reflexology having an effect on pain threshold and/or tolerance, or was my first experiment a fluke?

CHAPTER 4 | NOT GOOD ENOUGH

Looking Back

There were parts of 2005/6 that were so very satisfying. Knowing that I was doing something so innovative with pressure testing was huge, but learning physics, chemistry and everything that went alongside that, was incredibly difficult for me.

I had never started out to be a scientist, I was finding it increasingly difficult to absorb any more information and still make sense of it.

Although I have written about it in a previous chapter, I didn't consider from a practitioner or personal perspective, the effects of stress on my body, nor did I realise the pain I would place on those around me. My battles with Sheelagh and Ivor to be accepted for a full PhD were still not resolved and I found myself seeking support elsewhere. I didn't know where I was with things, one time we would have no meetings, then we would have meetings every week. I would start out with one experiment, which would suddenly become two, three or more experiments. I was doing my utmost to keep up with everything, but it was like trying to hold onto water and I felt it was all slipping away from me.

The meeting with George was a turning point because I could see more clearly what I needed to achieve and how to go about it, but I needed Sheelagh and Ivor to have confidence in my ability to achieve that, and they did not.

I had thought I had achieved a lot in this period and was more determined than ever not to throw it away on a qualification I was not comfortable with. What I needed now was to establish how I could persuade them both that I was good enough!

THE TENACIOUS STUDENT | Dr CAROL A. SAMUEL

CHAPTER 5
Fighting back – the battle is not yet over.

First, they ignore you, then they laugh at you, then they fight you, then you win.

Mahatma Ghandi

On 1st February 2007 during a meeting with Sheelagh I was told that as things stood, she didn't think I could get a PhD. She told me I needed to learn a whole lot more to get to grips with the compliance of pressure, neurophysiology, and pain science, and she thought I would be unable to defend my work in a *'Viva Voce'* examination because I couldn't remember things and I was too defensive. In addition, she told me she had spoken to Ivor whilst I was away, and he agreed with her.

I find it extremely difficult to articulate my feelings from that time within this text and to say that I was furious, frustrated, defensive, outraged and incensed would all do those emotions an injustice.

My reply to Sheelagh was: *"I will get my PhD, I know I have a lot to learn but I will do it, with or without your support. You cannot make the decision without my input".*

But I didn't know for a fact whether I needed them or not, whether I needed their support or not, so I had to speak with someone who could provide me with some clear advice. I went to see Roz, one of the other lecturers, and one of the two people who had approved my transfer report from MPhil to PhD. She advised me to go to registry and/or the student research tutor who would be able to advise me on the most appropriate path.

In March 2007 following the recommendation given by Roz, I met the Research Degrees officer at university. Up until this point I was still expected to submit for my MPhil by the end of September with a viva exam 6 – 8 weeks later. I was informed that I had a couple of choices, I could prepare for a PhD and allow the examiners to make the decision, or I could ask either my head of school or the Faculty of Research Design Chair (FRDC) to intervene, but in the meantime, I needed to discuss things with Sheelagh and Ivor. It's not really a conversation I wanted to have, but I arranged to meet them both on the 13th March and told them I had been to the academic registry for advice because I wasn't happy about their decision not to support my progression to a PhD. Ivor told me that their decision was made because there were still many unanswered questions to my research, my work was still inconclusive and I needed more participants, which clearly, I was having difficulty with. They concluded that right now, neither of them believed I could achieve a PhD and again, both recommended I stop at an MPhil. They said that it was still a good academic qualification for someone with my background.

I came away from that meeting feeling hurt, feeling angry and rejected, but above all, determined that they were not going to take this away from me after I had given so much of my life to it already! They knew what I had been through to get this far, they knew that my home life was again going through a difficult period and that I had passed that point of no return. I cannot put into words how it felt to know that those who were supposed to be guiding me, thought me so useless and fragile. It's true I was fragile, but at the time I had to push those feelings to the back of my mind and the knock-on effect of that, was that I found an inner strength, a stubborn refusal to give up and an ability to hang on even though, if I had given in, it would probably have made my life much easier.

CHAPTER 5 | FIGHTING BACK – THE BATTLE IS NOT YET OVER

You may encounter many defeats, but you must not be defeated, in fact, it may be necessary to encounter the defeats, so you can know who you are, what you can rise from, how you can still come out of it.

Maya Angelou

The research degrees officer had told me that I would be able to submit a PhD thesis without their support, and that if they were unwilling to appoint examiners, the FRDC could bypass them on my behalf. She explained that the important thing was how to get around this and of course what was best for me in the long term. She recommended that I send formal written notification to Sheelagh and Ivor telling them the full extent of our discussions. Sheelagh's response was that I would need to think carefully about this whole scenario, especially since they were not in agreement with me. I was asked to put together a project plan for the next two years and to incorporate six months for writing up. Basically, she said it was time for me to lead the research properly, and in hindsight that is not an unusual request. I now needed to say what experimental procedures I would undertake, produce a Gantt chart, which is basically a project management tool for showing the timeline of the experiments, and show exactly what I was going to do next and why. She gave me a month to complete this task and told me she would not pay for any further conferences or courses; she did however agree to put aside £1000 out of her own budget which was to be used for payment to encourage participants into the trials.

We were to go back to having weekly meetings again and I would need to provide a set of minutes summarising the discussions and actions. She said that in mid-October I would have to go through a review process to see whether I had made sufficient progress for a PhD, or if I would submit for an MPhil. On top of that, I would also need to attend an internal viva exam probably with my neurophysiology lecturer as the examiner. This was to serve two purposes following which a decision would be made involving all parties regarding the progression route.

The two purposes were: -

- to evaluate the research progress in terms of the data I had collected, and
- to review my ability to stand up to a viva voce examination

In all of this I still had to continue with my research and my ability to remember what I had heard, what I had read and what I had done was dreadful, and I struggled to recall a time in the past 12-18 months when it was different. I had to get my act together, to get my head in the right place or this would end here and now, and I was not going to let that happen, so I continued with the next experimental procedure which was all about habituation and adaptation.

I needed to carry out this experiment because there is a type of tolerance to drugs known as tachyphylaxis, which is a rapid decrease in your response to repeated doses of a drug over a short period of time. What it means is that larger doses are needed to achieve the same effect previously encountered. In day to day life you often see this with smokers because of the effects of nicotine[1] or with those in pain using opioid medications,[2] and in physiological terms it is a type of tolerance called adaptation.[3] You might remember me telling you that in my previous experiment's reflexology had improved both pain threshold and tolerance when the participants were subjected to repeated exposure to ice. Because there was some evidence that repeated exposure to cold pain could create a similar form of adaptive response[4][5] I needed to establish whether this was the case in my ice pain experiments.

I recruited just four participants to this study who repeatedly exposed their hand to ice every fifteen minutes for an hour, every day for four consecutive days. It was a useful experiment and supported my earlier findings that participants hadn't adapted to daily ice plunges either during the session, or in the days between attending the sessions. Basically, adaptation to cold pain didn't happen and this gave added value to my results because it confirmed that I was achieving real results which were not based on an adaptive or habitual response to the ice plunge.

Review of Direction of Study

The review of my status as a PhD student was now official and on the 16th April 2007 I received a formal confirmation letter of the action I had taken and Sheelagh and Ivor's response to it. They declared two important reasons for not supporting my path to a PhD in this letter, and they were:

a) It was their considered academic opinion that I would have considerable difficulties in defending a PhD thesis in a Viva Voce examination, whereas the MPhil pathway would be a more accessible option for me.
b) They were very concerned not only about my ability to recruit sufficient participants for my studies within the allowed timescale for the project, but also with the breadth and depth of my experimental work and the lack of data I had collected.

In the past 12-18 months their academic opinion was that I had made inadequate progress and they had grave concerns about my ability to complete my studies to the level required of a PhD. Their academic judgement was that considering the progress I had made over the four and half years I had been there, I was unlikely to be able to complete my project to the level and standard commensurate with a PhD degree; so in their opinion the MPhil was the best and most appropriate course of action for me. Despite the fact that it went against their academic judgement, I was given six months in which to demonstrate that I was capable of gaining substantial progress with my research and so I set about preparing my six-month plan for submission to them on 14th May. There was still no guarantee that I would be successful, and the tasks they had set me were challenging me on every level, but I was determined not to give up.

If I were to achieve my goals and get the PhD, something had to give. I couldn't continue to work part-time at the surgery, run a clinic, a home, and maintain healthy relationships with people, so I made the decision to relinquish my role at the surgery and reduce my clinic time. It was a good decision for my research and provided flexibility in the times that I could now be available for participants, but it was a disaster for my relationship with Sam. When I had taken on this programme of study, he was my greatest supporter, so proud of me, but the more time I spent away from him, the bigger the wedge between us. I couldn't put into words what this meant to me, and in an argument one day, I told him that I was prepared to sacrifice our marriage to get my PhD.

I prepared my report for the next 12-month period, stating the experiments I had thus far carried out, and those I planned to undertake. I needed to up my game and ensure that I had everything in place by the end of my trial period. It was time to fight back, to manage my supervisors effectively and show them what I could really do.

THE TENACIOUS STUDENT | Dr CAROL A. SAMUEL

Without data, you are just another person with an opinion
Andreas Schleicher

I still needed a further three participants to complete the second round of ice pain tests and the plan was to do some testing on Somatosensory Evoke Potentials (SSEPs). You might be wondering why I needed to do this type of testing. Evoke potentials are the electrical signals generated by the nervous system in response to touch, and evoke potential waves occur in the first 30 milliseconds of an EEG recording, which means they can be used to measure pain. So, this test was going to help me show whether reflexology was 'gating' the pain signal to the brain (i.e., stopping it reaching the brain) and hopefully, also provide me with an indication of what reflexology does to central nervous system arousal which, I had proposed, might provide a reliable measurement to view the mode of action of reflexology. The outcome measures are recorded using a standard electroencephalogram (EEG), but the downside was that you couldn't see the results with the naked eye, so it required specialised averaging equipment. Signal averaging is a specialised analysis of the data, and we didn't have that resource at Portsmouth and when I discussed it with Ivor, he said that I would either have to work with Porton Down and/or representatives from Newcastle University where Ivor had contacts who held the correct equipment. It was yet another blow to my experimental pathway.

My next proposal was based on chronic neuropathic pain and I had hoped to carry out this work with our local hospital, but of course ethics would be required, and this can sometimes take forever. I then also had to put together the resource requirements and costs. The total costs for the experimental procedures were somewhere in the region of around £61k, which seems ridiculous I know, but it was in fact a realistic calculation.

Of course, all of this was a test of my ability to prepare for a PhD, they wanted to see that I could in fact put together my own study programme, that I understood the financial implications, the ethical considerations and the time course involved. There was no way that I was going to be able to find the resources for funding this project, after all I had already tried my hand at gaining appropriate funding for my research, without success. What I did however was demonstrate my determination, my commitment, and my resilience to pressure. In some ways it was as though they had formally accepted my stubbornness and it was that which spurred me on, but at the same time absolutely terrified me. I did at least so far, have the result I needed together with their assurances that they would continue to provide me with all necessary help for my success.

At our first weekly meeting following the formal letter of notification, Sheelagh suggested that I review the pressure element of my research and decide which of the experiments would provide the best data for my thesis. As there was such a huge learning curve in terms of physics, she suggested it may be prudent to work out how much the pressure work melds with my overall plan for the thesis. As pain itself is such a vast and complicated subject, I first had to demonstrate that there was an effect from the reflexology treatment. She now felt that the pressure testing would detract from the main study on pain. I was both confused and concerned. I didn't understand the point of carrying out the experiments if they weren't going to form part of the thesis.

Sheelagh had been keen to see me produce a paper from my research, but as there was insufficient data to be able to do that, the idea was set aside. She did however say that when the time comes, she would give her support and guidance in helping me to write. This seemed like a small turning point for me, but she also made it clear that she would want to see it in a proper scientifically validated journal rather than something like Complementary Therapies in Medicine. Her emphasis was always, that my work should be reviewed from a scientific perspective particularly as I would be judged via a scientific degree.

On top of everything else my hearing was becoming decidedly worse, and I struggled to hear what people were saying to me. As a child I had a hearing aid in my right ear up until the age of 11, but when puberty kicked in, I decided that it wasn't a cool look. They weren't as discreet as they are these days, and I didn't want to have to cope with the bullying that had gone with wearing the one I had, so I stopped wearing it. However, my hearing now seemed to be slipping away quickly. I wasn't altogether sure if I were having a problem hearing what was being said, or whether I simply stopped listening because my brain was overloaded with information that I couldn't compute. The problem seemed to start whenever I went into a meeting with Ivor, which ostensibly should have taken around 30 minutes, but more often than not, I would still be there three hours later. Ivor has such a kangaroo brain, he is a real scientist, and his thoughts jump from one subject to another, which eventually do come together, but the process of getting there for me was incredibly painful to listen to. I already had so much new information in my head that everything seemed to merge together, and I simply couldn't decipher what I needed to keep and what was just Ivor filling in the gaps. My colleagues often used to joke when I said I was meeting Ivor that they would see me next week. I would tell Sam I was going into a meeting and hoped to be home by a certain time, which never seemed to happen, which of course didn't bode well for our relationship. What made the whole thing worse was that I would come out of the meeting not actually knowing if my original question had been answered, and so I was even more confused than when I went in. Anyway, the more I struggled the more frustrated I became and subsequently the more I seemed to switch off from the world around me, so I made an appointment with my GP who referred me for an MRI scan. He was a little concerned that I may have developed a tumour in my ear but thankfully it wasn't, they did however discover that I had irreparable damage to my inner ear. How that happened, I do not know.

The upshot of this was that I sought permission to record my meetings with Sheelagh and Ivor so that I could play them back in my own time and pull out the salient points for action. Whilst they were a little perturbed by my request, they did at least agree with it. So, from this point forward I recorded our conversations, wrote them up as minutes and made a clear note of the actions I needed to take. If I was going to achieve my goals for this research, I knew that I needed to take control of the meetings we were holding. Sheelagh and Ivor were both very generous with their time, but it was difficult sometimes to pin them down so that I had a reasonable timeline for producing what was required of me. In addition to providing them both with minutes of our meetings, my business head told me that I needed to ensure we also had dates in place for the action points. It was no good me getting things done for them to review, if they then took 3-4 weeks to get back to me with their responses. I was learning that my supervisors needed me to present them with good quality written work, written in a scientific manner and that the grammar and layout needed to be very professional, so I set about requesting formal feedback and introduced 'track changes' for any written work I presented. This provided me with a history of all the changes requested and allowed each of us to either accept or reject those changes. There would be no more of, *"I asked you to write this"* or *"you need to do this in your text"* to remember, as it would all be documented. This was great for Sheelagh, but not so great for Ivor who was not as conversant with using Microsoft Word.

CHAPTER 5 | FIGHTING BACK – THE BATTLE IS NOT YET OVER

One of the major dissatisfactions with the lifestyle of a research worker is that nobody else either understands or cares about what it is that the researcher is doing.[6]

The life of a researcher can be extremely isolating and there are times throughout your journey that you question whether it is a worthwhile thing to do. What are you expecting to get at the end of it and what, if any kudos there may be as a result of completing it? I didn't know the answer to any of those questions, I wasn't sure I had even asked myself why I was doing it in the first place, I just happened to be in the right place at the right time, I think.

Making friends when you are working alone is extremely difficult, particularly when you are the only person in the entire university who is carrying out research work in complementary medicine and not only that but doing it in a science faculty. I just seemed so out of place and I was so very lonely, so intimidated by boffins; I mean, these were serious academics, and I didn't understand what half of them were talking about most of the time, and constantly asked myself what on earth I was doing here.

As time moved on, I started to make some real friends, not many, but a handful of people with whom I could discuss the difficulties associated with doing a PhD. All of them younger than me and who had come through the usual undergraduate route to get to where they were. Sam was the same age as my daughter, her PhD was about 'proteomic and transcriptomic analysis of prostate cancer progression' and she had previously done a BSc in genetics. Simone, who was only a couple of years older than Sam was originally from Germany, she was looking at 'the effects of lycopene at cellular and molecular level'. She was applying lycopene to prostate cancer cells and normal prostate cells to look at growth (inhibition) and gene expression. I was in awe of them both. Here they were, these young women making huge strides in their research and I couldn't even repeat their subject headings, let alone understand them. Claire was Sam's supervisor and one of the biomedical sciences lecturer's, but not much older than her, then there was Roz who was also a lecturer in biomedical sciences. Each of them had been participants in my research and remain friends to this day. In fact, Roz is now a Traditional Chinese Medicine (TCM) practitioner and lectures on acupuncture and

Claire is now a medical writer who also worked alongside me when I became a Research Fellow at the University of Surrey.

BBC documentary

Sometime between March and April I was approached by BBC television to participate in a documentary they were running about alternative therapies. The programme was to be a short series about three therapies - meditation, hypnotherapy, and reflexology. The programme was to be presented by Professor Kathy Sykes from the University of Bristol. She had asked if she would be able to participate in my research and then do a short piece about it for the programme, I was both excited and cautious at the same time. I mentioned it to Sheelagh, because as my director of studies I needed to gain her approval, but she wasn't keen and said that she felt uncomfortable about it, and anyway I was busy preparing for my first overseas conference in Munich, so the answer was no. I remember watching the series when it finally arrived on television and in each one Professor Sykes tried the therapies herself and then shared her reactions, making note of the claims made by those she had interviewed and how their opinions compared to the clinical and scientific evidence.

It seems I would have been in good company had I agreed to participate as one of those she interviewed was Dwight Byers. Dwight had said that *"he thought the mechanism of reflexology could be via a relay to the brain, then to the area or region, and believed it may work via the neurological system"*. He also talked about mineral deposits that short-circuit the reflexes, which could be uric acid, but in all honesty, he said that he didn't really know.

It was at this point that I was glad I didn't participate because there is still no solid evidence to suggest that mineral/crystal deposits exist in the feet. Indeed, when she then went on to speak with the Emeritus Professor Paul Dieppe who is one of the world's most pre-eminent researchers on osteoarthritis, he said that *"he had never seen uric acid crystals in the soles of the feet and that you certainly can't dissolve them just by rubbing"*. He went on to explain that they only appear in certain circumstances in the body and are usually found in the ends of the toes and fingers in those experiencing gout.

In my thesis I wrote that there is no evidence in any of the medical literature to support the theory of crystal deposits in the foot, nor that any such crystals can be eliminated by pressure or rubbing. Gout, stones and calcium pyrophosphate dehydrate crystal deposition disease, a form of rheumatoid arthritis,[7] are the only known forms of crystal deposits in the tissues of the human body. The presence of these is managed through conservative pharmacological means[8] and not by any form of pressure management. Ingham's idea that pressure on the feet can grind down crystal deposits found in the ends of nerves[9] is still without any form of scientific basis. Rather interestingly Dr Alice Roberts who was an anatomist, teaching medical students at the University of Bristol said *"I can't see how nerves from the feet can affect any of the internal organs. The nerves from the feet enter the spinal cord at the fourth lumbar and first sacral segment and there are no nerves in this area that go to the viscera"*. Whilst anatomically this is correct, in terms of reflexology we have discovered that some of the nerve reflex points in the feet do in fact serve the viscera. Many of these are used by qualified nerve reflexologists across the world with great effect by using anatomical areas of reflection.

Professor Tallis from the University of Manchester said that he thought reflexology could work via the placebo response and that it is hope, attention and care that is producing the effect. However, Ted Kaptchuk, Associate Professor at Harvard University and a world authority on placebo said, *"when I monitored a reflexology session, in a particular situation, the lavender aroma, the subdued lighting, the positive affirmations given during treatment, all built up trust through the session and that amplified the sensation of touch"*. He went on to explain that the whole thing could be a mix of ritual and belief, which would be enough to make it work. I am however delighted to acknowledge that my own research proved without doubt that reflexology is not simply a placebo response.

There were more interviews and discussions, this time with the Emeritus Professor of Cancer Rehabilitation at the University of Hull, Leslie Walker. He spoke about research he had carried out to look at alternative methods to relax cancer patients' and had compared Indian head massage with reflexology. Patients also had access to a drop-in centre and of course, their normal medication. The outcome of his study was that both treatments provided benefits in terms of relaxation and improvement in quality of life (QoL) scores. Both were statistically and clinically significant, even though the significance was only small. So, the question asked was whether the response to treatment could simply be a response to touch alone? To add further enquiry to this question Professor Sykes met with Jim Coan a psychology professor from the University of Virginia. He had carried out studies using electric shocks and MRI scans. The participants of his study were warned by an 'X' image that they might get an electric shock and an 'O' image if there was to be no shock. He compared no hand holding, hand holding by a stranger and hand holding by a loved one and found that responses to stress (indicated by changes in MRI readings) were much less when the subject's hand was held by a loved one. From this study he concluded that touch from someone close has a really powerful effect and has a profound impact on the brain. Does this mean that if you give reflexology to someone with whom you are close, you will have a better outcome? It is another as yet, unanswered question.

The whole programme was finally summarised by Professor Sykes when she concluded that the best thing to do in looking at research into reflexology was to study physiological changes, so I was pleased that I was already doing this, albeit at a fairly basic level.

In May 2007, Sheelagh permitted my travel to Munich to give a presentation of my results at the International Congress on Complementary Medicine Research in Munich, as recommended by Professor Lewith. I was incredibly nervous and felt a little out of my depth as I listened to some of the other speakers at the conference. Not because I didn't appreciate what they were talking about, simply because it takes me a while to assimilate new information and I didn't feel confident enough to be able to ask the right kind of questions straight away. On the other hand, people were approaching me to ask about my research and I felt very competent in responding to their questions. I was incredibly grateful for the support of my dear friend, Griet Rondel, a Belgian physiotherapist who specialises in the gut/brain axis and emotions with nerve reflexology. Griet had taken time out of her busy practice to drive from Belgium to Munich to hear me speak, she then took me under her wing and back to Belgium so that I might spend a few days with her and her family. We had met only on a few previous occasions, but immediately hit it off, she has an amazing library of knowledge and is my 'go to' person for anything related to the gut/brain issues.

When I returned to the UK, I sat down with Ivor to discuss the next round of testing. It was important that we quantify any physiological changes that may occur following reflexology by using well defined experimental testing procedures, so we agreed that I should carry out some testing in this area.

There are a couple of things you often hear when people are discussing the effects of complementary therapies, both of which may play a major role in the outcome of treatments and they are: -

- the placebo effect, and
- the relationship between the therapist and the patient

The patient-therapist relationship is possibly one of the major limitations in any study where there is close contact between the two people involved[10] and may be interpreted as having a large placebo effect. In fact, being listened to is an extremely important part of the healing process[11] and relevant in any interaction between a patient and therapist. In order to avoid some of the pitfalls associated with the patient-therapist relationship, we discouraged participants from discussing their personal health issues and made no attempt to provide support on health matters during the experimental procedures. As there is quite a growing body of evidence on the therapeutic alliance and how personalities within a therapeutic relationship can impact the outcome of the treatment[12][13][14] Ivor and I discussed carrying out some form of psychological testing as well. The idea being that the data obtained would give an insight into the relationship between the personalities of my participants and myself, as the therapist.

We used an adapted version of the Eysenck personality questionnaire to see if personality traits such as extraversion and introversion correlated with the experimental outcomes. The Eysenck theory stipulates that the terms extraversion/introversion (E) relate to the level of arousal in the reticular formation and cortical areas of the brain. Furthermore, it proposes that introverts are typically more aroused than extraverts. This therefore becomes relevant in pain science because the level of arousal in pain subjects is an important marker for the cognitive/affective processes involved in their pain experience.[15] Using the biopsychosocial model of pain this helps us identify whether they are the type of person who may or may not catastrophize their pain because of their personality traits.[16][17] It is worth knowing that from a psychological perspective one's personality has the ability to moderate the entire pain experience.

Physiological Stress

There is another mechanism that is used to suppress pain and that is something called stress-induced analgesia, which has the ability to change basic physiological functions such as heart rate, blood pressure and core body temperature.[18][19][20][21][22][23] I established from the research literature that reflexology has a beneficial effect on the autonomic nervous system and that it has a favourable effect on stress[24] and anxiety related ailments too.[25][26] What many may not be aware of though, is that a person's perception of pain can change as a result of physical and psychological stress, and of course this can also induce changes in heart rate, blood pressure and core body temperature.[27][28][29]

I was about to carry out an experiment on the physiological impact of reflexology. One of the purposes of this experiment was to establish whether changes in basal physiological function were affected by a standard reflexology protocol without the addition of ice. I also needed to establish whether or not, standard reflexology alone, induced stress. I am sure it would seem quite inconceivable to some people that reflexology should induce stress, but I knew from trying to treat my husband with reflexology that not everyone found it a comfortable experience, so it was important to rule this out.

When I first looked at what to measure for this experiment, I was going to look at muscle tension because I thought it would tell me if the subject was relaxing during reflexology, but of course for this I also needed muscle testing equipment, which I didn't have. One of the lecturers within the department did however have this equipment so I asked if I could use it. When we trialled it, we discovered the equipment had not been looked after properly within the lab and didn't work, so like many others, this idea was also shelved. Ivor suggested that perhaps we could use EEG (electroencephalography) equipment to see if reflexology had any effect without any external stimuli. For example, by not talking to the participants during reflexology we could observe their levels of arousal within the brain and see whether they fully relaxed during treatment. Anecdotally of course, we have all had those clients who simply drift off to sleep during a session[30] but unfortunately anecdotes don't stand up to scientific evaluation. EEG lets us look at the alpha waves and these waves provide information about wakeful relaxation. We were aiming to establish whether alpha based neuromodulation would produce an analgesic response through the relaxation effect of reflexology. We knew that the ideal equipment for measuring this was at Porton Down and that I would need to see if I could get hold of it, but guess what, I couldn't. In terms of finding the right equipment I just kept on hitting the same brick wall, over and over again.

Physiological measurements

The relationship between pain and blood pressure is not well understood[31] but by measuring blood pressure before, during and after reflexology I had hoped to gain an insight into what was happening in the autonomic nervous system. We know of course that when the body is in a state of fight or flight, the release of adrenaline encourages smaller blood vessels to contract and ensures there is sufficient blood supply in major muscle groups for action. But the heart is a muscle too so I also needed to measure heart rate as this would help demonstrate whether reflexology was affecting the parasympathetic nervous system and lowering heart rate as it had done in my previous experiments.

Ivor started talking about ionotropic and chronotropic changes in the heart and had asked me to look at what adrenaline does to the heart. I needed to answer the question whether the heart rate (chronotropic effect) or the force of the contraction (ionotropic effect) was more important, and then decide which of the two to measure. I summarised that I needed to look at the chronotropic effect of the heart because that would tell me about the heart rate and rhythm, which is innervated by our electrical conduction system, the nerves, and therefore it would tell me what the autonomic nervous system was up to. Adrenaline which is present during any fight or flight situation is released by the medulla of the adrenal glands in times of stress, so it is a powerful cardiac stimulant that increases heart rate. It is also released by the autonomic nervous system in times of pain and there was some evidence that an increase in heart rate could influence the analgesic effect.[32] I needed to establish whether reflexology impacted analgesia through a surge in adrenaline, which in turn might mask the body's ability to feel pain.

Temperature is another basal physiological function, and the normal human range varies depending on an individual's metabolic rate, the time of day and the area of the body from which it is taken. It is generally standardised to 37°C, fluctuating by approximately 1°C in ±24 hours, usually in the early hours of the morning and late afternoon.[33] You might also see fluctuations in women during the luteal phase following ovulation, when temperature may increase by approximately 0.5°C until the beginning of the next menstrual cycle.[34] Importantly for me temperature also provides an insight into the effects of stress on our body systems, including stress associated with pain and inflammation.[35][36][37] Indeed, psychological stress is known to increase both body temperature and blood pressure.[38][39][40] As reflexologists we often suggest that treatment has a calming effect on the stress response which, in turn, suggests a lowering of body temperature; however, as no one had measured body temperature as part of the physiological responses to treatment, I felt this too might be helpful for my experiment.

Another point for consideration is that when someone is consciously tense or apprehensive they go through what is termed a transitory emotional state which increases the activity within the sympathetic nervous system.[41] So, in addition to the physical measurements (quantitative) I also needed to take some subjective measurements (qualitative). I had already done this during the first two experiments and had designed a 'subjective rating questionnaire' which basically asked subjects about their level of arousal, anxiety, and discomfort at various periods across the experimental procedures.

All in all, the results concluded that reflexology produced significant decreases in heart rate during treatment compared with the sham T.E.N.S (control). Heart rate was also significantly lower than in the control group for up to 40 minutes following treatment, however the effect on blood pressure and core body temperature was small and insignificant. My results for the subjective responses showed high scores, which indicated that the participants were not anxious, so there was no relationship between subjective anxiety and any of the physiological outcome measures. This led to the conclusion that reflexology as a treatment does not in itself, act as a stressor.

My goal across all these experiments was to prove beyond a shadow of a doubt the validity of my statement that *'reflexology attenuates pain'*.

Moving forward my next steps were to:

- Review chronic exposure to reflexology to establish whether reflexology was going to work on someone already in pain?

- Establish whether they become tolerant to the treatment and if so, do you have to do more treatments to reach the same result as you do with medications (cumulative effect) and,
- Establish if reflexology, when used as an adjunct to clinical treatments, will have a long-term effect?

I was back in control, at least in part. Now all I needed to do was figure out what experiments to prepare for next, and recruit for them. I had more time on my hands to dedicate to the research, but that didn't necessarily mean that I would be able to get the right number of participants to the study.

Looking Back

My naivety as a researcher did not help me in accepting that I was on a lone journey. That it was of course my responsibility to lead the research because that's what is required of a PhD.

In hindsight I can see that Sheelagh and Ivor were generous in their response to my assault on their support, that they were doing everything they possibly could to direct someone like me, with my background, to get the best possible result, but I didn't see it that way at the time.

I found my fight, my strength, and my determination and yet despite this I was still struggling both at home and at university.

When I think about what I said to Sam about choosing my PhD over him, I am absolutely repulsed by my behaviour, but so powerful was my desire to succeed in reaching my goal, nothing else mattered. What he went through during my PhD and what he must have felt at the time has haunted me for many years. It does however help me to understand why only the strongest relationships seem to survive a PhD, and I am glad of that.

I was tired of the battles, being on full alert all the time and wondering who was going to try and trip me up next. It felt like a war and I wasn't sure I was winning. I hid myself away in my clinic at the bottom of the garden and tried desperately to find some semblance of order.

I cried a lot, but I also argued a lot. I questioned my ability to complete the work on more than one occasion. I questioned my knowledge; my interpretation skills and my confidence at the time was at rock bottom. I kidded myself I was in control, but I knew that I wasn't. There was still so much to do, so much to learn and not much time to prove that I had what it took to complete a PhD.

CHAPTER 6
Throwing everything at it

She was unstoppable, not because she did not have failures or doubts, but because she continued on despite them.

Beau Taplin

By September I was having to spend a lot of time writing up the results of what I had so far learned from my experiments. It was meant to form the start of my thesis and writing it would help explain why I had done each experiment, discuss the results and prompt any follow-up experiments that may still be needed. Of course, every piece of research prompts further research, so there will always be more to do, but I had hoped I would not have too many more experiments to complete for my PhD. October came and went, and Sheelagh and Ivor had still made no decision on whether I was to continue to submit for an MPhil as they had suggested, or whether they now supported my progression to a PhD.

I mentioned in previous chapters that statistics is one of my weakest subjects, so I struggled a lot to understand the meaning of my results and needed a lot of support in this area. Most researchers would have a separate statistician as part of their project team, in a paid role, but I didn't have that luxury. I was however able to discuss my results with the principal lecturer for statistics who tried to guide me on the methods to use and the reasons for those methods, but quite honestly it was like he was speaking a different language. I joined various classes and workshops and had a great deal of help from Ivor, who was very well versed in statistical analysis. With a huge amount of guidance, I gradually came to understand and appreciate the full extent of my experimental results, but I was warned that I might need to add various caveats when discussing them, mainly because when you carry out research you have a certain criterion within which you are working, so you cannot easily extrapolate results to the wider population.

Because I am a visual learner, I like pictures and I have found that when I create a graph of the results, I am better able to understand what is happening in the experiment. Fortunately, I am also quite adept at creating graphs so that made a big difference to me when it came to interpreting what I had actually gained from my outcome measures. Nonetheless statistical analysis was an absolute nightmare and was to come back time and time again to challenge my entire thesis as you will see.

A novel idea

I did in fact have further experiments to complete and the next round of experiments was something entirely different. As a researcher you have to be objective and think on your feet. We were beginning to question whether the effect of treatment was based just on touch alone, for example:

- is touch providing some added form of psychological effect that helps create the response, or does reflexology have its own separate and specific effect?

We know from the research evidence that tactile therapies produce a number of physiological responses, some of which include changes in heart rate[1] and blood pressure.[2] There is also some evidence that they can alter the perception of pain, stress, anxiety and depression,[3] so I needed to establish if my results were due to the stimulus or simply human touch. Reflexology is known as a manually applied therapy i.e., a tactile therapy, but there is an increasingly profitable market in the commercial industries for mechanically applied reflexology treatments. The use of mechanical stimulators is largely associated with experiments in the elderly, those who are bedridden but also in astronauts who experience atrophy of skeletal muscles due to gravitational changes.[4] You need only to look on google for reflexology machines and you will see that there are a number of advertisements for commercially available machines on the market today. Each one of these claims to be reflexology, and there is of course some scientific evidence for their use in the improvement of circulatory disorders.[5]

In patients who may be at risk of falls it is important to observe control of the human erect posture, and in one study[6] they used viscoelastic gels with vibrating elements embedded under the foot so that they could assess the effectiveness of these gels in enhancing proprioceptive feedback. Proprioception is important for reducing postural sway as it feeds information back to your brain about the position of your limbs and joints in space.[7] In another study, nine healthy subjects underwent a mechanical stimulation to the sole of the foot to assess the specific benefits of improving neuromuscular activity in human erect proprioceptive feedback responses,[8] so there was already some evidence in the literature for mechanical stimulators on the foot. One of the other areas in which mechanical foot stimulators is used is in exercise programmes for astronauts and there was a study carried out by Layne et al.[9] where they used a dynamic foot stimulus device to apply a certain pressure value (172 kPa) to the medial, lateral and heel regions of the foot sole for 250 milliseconds. What they found was, that when there is a limited or loss of weight-bearing activity, mechanical stimulation of the feet can attenuate muscle atrophy and functionality. That's an important result and for them it made a valuable contribution for astronauts whose muscles atrophy because they are unable to bear weight in space. Usually when we are weight-bearing our muscles contract, but when we are unable to bear weight, the muscles don't contract and eventually weaken and lose strength. The outcome of this study was helpful, and the mechanical stimulators were used alongside existing passive exercise programmes for astronauts.

At the time, the only sources of literature for the use of a mechanical stimulation to monitor the effects of reflexology, were those that had been carried out to evaluate heart rate changes in normal healthy subjects.[10] In one particular study researchers applied mechanical stimulation with a device known as a 'massager scroller', which was applied to the soles of both feet just below the toes for 20 minutes. They measured heart rate variability using an electro-cardiogram and recorded the results for the variation in time between each heartbeat which indicated that the heart became more random, with a trend toward chaos. Chaos in heart rate variability is a positive aspect of cardiac dynamics because the fluctuations show a better state of health.

In my previous experiments using manually applied reflexology I was able to demonstrate significant increases in pain tolerance levels following an ice plunge, but of course I didn't know how much of that was down to human touch, therapist interaction or reflexology stimulation.

As I mentioned earlier tactile stimulation and talking to a patient is known to impact on physiological functions such as heart rate, blood pressure and temperature[11][12][13][14][15][16][17] so I now needed to check out whether applying reflexology by mechanical means gave me the same results.

The principal aims were to identify whether: -

a) the therapist was necessary for the effect of treatment and whether,
b) mechanical reflexology-like stimulation affected pain threshold and tolerance levels in an ice pain experiment.

The questions I was trying to answer here were:

- *Does manual reflexology produce a better outcome than mechanical reflexology?*
  If my results proved manual reflexology had a better outcome, it might indicate that human touch *is* an essential element of the treatment, but it might also be down to the interaction with the therapist.

- *Is the response to mechanical reflexology equal to that of manual reflexology?*
  If the responses were equal for both manually applied and mechanically applied reflexology, I would be able to say that one might expect a bigger response from using the whole foot because larger contact surfaces yield the greatest amount of spatial summation. You might recall that temporal summation is about successive stimuli on one nerve but that simultaneous stimuli from many nerve fibres is called spatial summation.

- *Does mechanical reflexology produce a better effect than manual reflexology?*
  In this case I would be able to say that the therapist interaction in the treatment doesn't seem to be all that important.

The initial recruitment of subjects drew interest from 59 first year pharmacy students. However, when e-mails were sent explaining the ice pain procedure and the time commitment involved, 41 of these withdrew. Of the remaining 18 subjects only 12 participated, so as you can see, recruitment issues ensued despite my best efforts and despite the fact that in this particular experiment they were paid to participate and coerced with the suggestion that *'it would look good on their CV when they do their pharmacy registration year'*. We invested in a 'Scholl Ionic Rejuvenator Foot Massager' to provide reflexology-like stimulation to healthy participants who were subjected to ice pain. The equipment was composed of a curved bed of raised nodules with an additional circle of vibrating acupressure pads located on either side. It had two massage modes, high and low, and the low mode was used for the experiments with a running time of 20 minutes.

The reason we only gave 20 minutes on the machine was because of the manufacturer's guidelines for use, but of course in manually applied treatments the session is generally around 45 minutes. There is always something else to consider, and the time difference between the two treatments could have introduced another variable into the experimental procedure. However, because the results of my previous experiments had shown that 30 and 45 min (respectively) of standard and light reflexology applied manually significantly increased pain tolerance, I didn't really see this as too much of a problem.

Anyway, as it turned out it demonstrated that the method of administration for reflexology might be a factor in its efficacy. The reason for this may be because manually applied reflexology is more discriminative, and it might therefore elicit its responses through phasic stimulation of Meissner corpuscles in the foot sole. In contrast the mechanical reflexology stimulus is much less discriminative and therefore less likely to elicit such a response.[18]

It was nonetheless a remarkably interesting study and the results showed that mechanical reflexology significantly increased the perception of pain, which was in direct contrast to the results I had obtained from the manual reflexology experiments I had carried out. In trying to figure out why I should get such an opposite effect I considered whether it might be due to the set-up of the equipment. Most of the commercially available stimulators consisted of a flat platform usually in the shape of the feet and had raised rubberised nodules that covered the entire foot surface, whilst the equipment I used had large central floating heads which were vibrating under the arch of the foot. It is possible therefore that this central platform might have caused some form of irritation to participants in this study especially since there are a limited number of receptor units in the arch of the foot[19] and it can often be an extremely sensitive area too.[20]

The summary outcome of this experiment was that it is likely that the relaxation response we attribute to manually applied reflexology, in addition to the normal responses achieved by touch, together contribute to the overall effect.[21] There is a caveat however and that is, that if we assume that mechanically stimulated reflexology impacts the mechanoreceptors of the feet in a similar way to manually applied treatments, we may be able to speculate that treatment given by a therapist is of greater therapeutic value. Do bear in mind that I did not directly compare manual reflexology with mechanical reflexology in this experiment, but against a sham T.E.N.S control as I had done in previous experiments. It would be good therefore to compare manually applied reflexology to mechanical reflexology and a control arm in the future. Anyone up for it?

Pharmacy students

One of the things PhD and Masters' students may be asked to do during their research journey, is teach. The reason for this is because a large majority of PhD students plan for a career in academia when they have successfully achieved their PhD, and if you have already done some teaching it looks good on your CV. In fact, as part of a PhD research stipend, which is a grant that you do not have to repay, you are sometimes expected to carry out some teaching of undergraduate classes. If you are lucky enough to get a stipend it can come with conditions but in my case, there was no stipend, so there weren't any such expectations. That said, Sheelagh had already tried to recruit me to lecture on the BSc Natural and Complementary Medicine course at the start of my PhD, but without success. It was just as well really because the course didn't get validated, was then rewritten to include biomedical sciences, and ultimately didn't run because no one signed up for it. Nonetheless, Sheelagh felt it was important that I take a class of first year pharmacy students and tell them about complementary therapies, and in particular, reflexology. Putting the lecture together didn't faze me, I had been a college lecturer for six years and was quite comfortable teaching what I knew. The issue for me was the response I got from the students, honestly, I sometimes question whether youngsters go to university to learn, or simply for the camaraderie and social aspect. I had one student who kept falling asleep and I stopped short of chucking him out of the class, which was just as well really, as I was told later that I couldn't do that, they were paying students and if they chose to sleep during a lecture, that was their issue not mine. I never took another class after this experience and decided that academia here at Portsmouth was not my future, although at that point in time, I really didn't know what was.

At the start of 2008 Sheelagh suggested that I might consider an exchange visit to China, so that I could learn more about how the Chinese approach reflexology, after all, historically this is where it was all supposed to have started.[22][23] I wasn't sure where I was going to find the time to do that when I was already struggling to get everything else together, writing my thesis, carrying out further experiments, analysing the stats and planning future work. Besides which, I didn't think it would go down too well at home either. It's not that Sam would ever have prevented me from doing what I wanted to do, but I was already spending far more time at university than I was at home, so taking what might have appeared to be a bit of a 'jolly' I felt would not sit well. It was a lovely idea and had things been different I may well have taken up the offer but in the end I declined. I can sit and think about missed opportunities as much as I like, but I believe everything happens for a reason and although we may not see it clearly at the time, somewhere along the way, it will become apparent.

Final experiment

By February 2008 I had carried out and completed six separate experiments, but it was time to do more. My acute pain studies had shown a significant benefit for reflexology on pain threshold and tolerance levels, and I needed to consider looking at whether the effect was sustainable over time. In my earlier experiments I had only given reflexology to each participant once across their experimental journey, I now needed to establish whether the same outcome was repeatable and be objective about any conditioned responses that may occur. Because a conditioned response is a learned response to a stimulus, a previous experience of a stimulus will automatically evoke a response all on its own, so the next stage was going to help me decide if reflexology was creating a similar kind of conditioned response in participants.

When reflexologists provide treatments, they generally recommend and indeed, are taught, that a course of treatments is preferable to a single session. Many are led to believe that a single session does little more than provide relaxation to the patient so as to provide the correct healing environment.[24][25][26] The overall number of treatment sessions is often assessed on a weekly basis and of course depends on many other factors, including the responsiveness of the individual client. It has however been noted that single treatment trials of reflexology do not represent standard clinical practice[27] and it was therefore important to evaluate the full benefits of reflexology from continued use.

So, the main questions for this piece of research were:

- whether standard reflexology produces a sustained effect over three weeks of treatment,
- whether there was any tolerance to the treatment, i.e., was there a decrease in effect over time and,
- whether participants become more sensitive to treatment the more sessions you provide.

This experiment was fraught with challenges, not least of which, as previously, was to recruit for it. I was proposing to carry out six sessions in total, three weeks where they would attend for reflexology and three weeks where they would cross-over and have sham T.E.N.S. This meant that I would need to ask participants to attend once a week for six weeks, for three hours each time; taking up a total of eighteen hours of their valuable time. It was a big ask and needless to say there weren't many takers.

It was time to rethink. My approach to that was to examine what had happened in the previous experiments and see how I could still get the data I needed but in less time. My previous results showed that the latency for the minimum and maximum pain threshold and tolerance levels was less than 120 minutes, therefore a two-hour session once a week was probably going to be more achievable than three-hour sessions and would still give me an accurate result. In other words, instead of having to attend for eighteen hours in total, they were now being asked to attend for twelve hours. Still quite an ask, but there was no other way around it if I was going to successfully replicate my previous results. One of the other concerns for me in this experiment was the carry-over effect. A carry-over effect isn't unusual in cross-over studies where participants attend both arms of the experimental procedure, i.e., reflexology and a control treatment and can happen when the effects in one treatment period are carried over to subsequent treatment periods.[28] However, in the reflexology literature I could see that in previous research studies the effects of treatment were transient to within each session[29][30] which meant there were no obvious carry-over effects to subsequent weeks.

You may recall that I had experienced an immense difficulty in recruiting for all of my experimental procedures, and of course it was in some ways quite understandable when you know that I was inflicting normal healthy people with pain. Our own life experience may tell of the horrible cold and numbness you get in your fingers and toes when you are playing in the snow, or the pain from the pins and needles that hits you when you start to warm up again and everything starts to come back to life. It's not a nice experience and despite offering to pay people to participate, the difficulties ensued. In the end many of the participants in this experiment had been recruited previously, and so had prior experience of both reflexology and the control procedures. The downside to this is that it introduces a level of bias in the results but if you can account and justify for that bias in your text, it will help the reader formulate a critical and independent review of those results.[31]

This was the last of the experimental procedures I had to carry out and I was pleased to see that the results demonstrated that repeated reflexology treatments produce increases in both pain threshold and tolerance that are stable over time when compared to sham T.E.N.S (control). The only difference here was that in my previous experiments I had shown an effect on heart rate too, but in this round of tests there were no cumulative effects on either blood pressure or heart rate. Quite comfortingly the overall result was mimicking previous research carried out[32][33] and indicated that reflexology produces an effect of relaxation within each session, but that it does not appear to produce cumulative effects on basal physiological function that may be of any long-term benefit. The take home point here is that the benefits of relaxation alone are sufficient to justify reflexology as an aid to those suffering from chronic unrelenting pain[34] and of course, this makes absolute sense when you think about it. Much of the pain response occurs because of stress, when you are stressed you tense your muscles, so anything that will relax you, will also help release muscle tension and subsequently pain.[35][36] My final experiment was now complete, and I needed to get down to the business of writing up my thesis.

A mind that is stretched by a new idea can never go back to its original dimensions

Oliver Wendell-Holmes

Scientific writing

An important part of any doctoral thesis is your skill in putting across your work so that it reflects your ability to demonstrate original research in the experimental procedures you have carried out, so in May 2008 I met with Sheelagh to discuss writing my thesis. I still didn't know if I was writing for an MPhil. or a PhD. Her suggestion was that it would take a good nine months to write up, but before that I would have another appraisal. Both Sheelagh and Ivor would decide on the sufficiency of my experiments and Ivor would check them for content. She told me that I would now easily get an MPhil. but I should aim for a PhD. Did this mean they were supporting my road to a PhD? Not yet it seemed.

Between them they would decide who my internal and external examiners were going to be, and I would have absolutely no say in it, as they would be based on my personality and my ability in a viva situation. I was a little confused here as I hadn't yet had any form of viva, so on what basis were they determining my abilities? Besides, it was my understanding that your examiners represent your academic peer group, which in my case was reflexology or complementary and alternative medicine (CAM). Usually, the internal examiner is someone in your department, who would understand the work you have been doing but obviously not your supervisor, whilst the external examiner would be someone from another university who was familiar with your field of research. You would normally know who those examiners are going to be before you complete your writing, so that if you have objections to those selected, you can voice your concerns to your supervisors. Sheelagh said that whether I go for an MPhil. or a PhD really depended on how well I write. I needed to give a clear explanation from a scientific point of view because I was investigating a therapy from a scientific perspective and her advice to me was that I write an 'excellent thesis'.

And so, it was, my writing was to start following my appraisal in June. I was expected to complete the first draft for the introductory chapter and the experimental chapters by the beginning of September and the remainder of it by the end of December, with a view to submitting my entire thesis by the revised date of 31st March 2009, several months past my original expected submission date of September 2008.

I had already started writing prior to this meeting with Sheelagh so I was able to submit my first draft to Ivor in July. It was to start a whole new cycle of rewriting vast amounts of information. There were questions coming up that I hadn't even considered might be important to put into my thesis. It wasn't simply a case of giving background information about reflexology and the experiments, but also about including the history, theories, neurological relationships if there were any, of reflexology. It was to include a whole chapter on pain, its history, types of pain, the different methods currently used to treat pain, on what other therapies were beneficial for pain and how that compared to reflexology. Placebo effects in pain management, medications used for pain, hypnosis, relaxation, acupuncture, acupressure, and a whole lot more that I hadn't even thought about.

First things first in that case, I needed to set out what would go in each chapter and then set about writing it.

Looking Back

In 2007 I became very detached from what I called 'everyday living' and instead threw myself heart and soul into proving that I had what it takes to complete a PhD. At the end of the year, I still didn't know whether I had achieved that, but both Sheelagh and Ivor were still supporting me, so I was at least meeting the targets they had set.

From a personal perspective there were more challenges within my family unit which were to form the start of a long period of hardship for my daughter and subsequently for me. As a parent you cannot neglect or hide away from the troubles of your children and as much as you hope that your own experiences will be lessons for them, they are not. I could see what was happening for her and yet I could do nothing about it, my advice and suggestions were viewed as an attack and she simply withdrew into herself, which left me frustrated and anxious for her.

I know I have an incredibly strong mothering instinct, whether with my own or with others, both old and young, and I cannot help but want to help them, which has, across my lifetime often been to my own detriment. I discovered there is a fine line between help and interference, and I remember my colleague Sam, who is the same age as my daughter, saying to me, *"why is it that I can ask my mum a question and completely ignore her response, yet when I get a similar response from you it doesn't seem like an attack"?* It was a bit of a wake-up call for me and made me realise that those closest to you are the hardest to help.

My husband felt, and rightly so, that I was giving my time to everyone and everything but him and us, so once again it was testing our relationship. In my determination to succeed, I had not allowed myself to see that for what it really was.

At university I felt I was making progress and although I had completed the experiments there was a whole new set of challenges ahead of me in preparing my PhD thesis.

CHAPTER 7
Writing the Thesis

Along with a healthy dose of luck, the key attributes needed to produce a worthy PhD thesis are a readiness to accept failure; resilience; persistence; the ability to troubleshoot; dedication; independence; and a willingness to commit to very hard work – together with curiosity and a passion for research.

Irini Topalidou – Nature

https://www.nature.com/articles/d41586-018-06905-0

Having completed my final experiments I now needed to get my head down and write, write for the opportunity of obtaining my PhD and to prove that I could excel where others thought I would fail. Scientific writing is often dry and difficult to read, and I didn't want to produce a thesis that would not be appreciated by my peers, so I set about writing in a way that I understood with the thought that if I understood it, so would my peers. You will know from what you have already read in this book that I came into research as a non-academic and had no skills in writing beyond what I had learned in secondary education. My English teacher always remarked that my grammar, spelling, and comprehension was good, so I drew on that knowledge when I started writing and thought I was doing okay, only to be told that I had taken a completely incorrect approach to the writing of my thesis.

Scientific writing first and foremost means being organised, making sure that what you are writing is accurate, that it is written in the correct context and that you are referencing correctly without plagiarising the work of others. It is a complex form of writing and requires short sentences, written in past participle and without the use of colloquial terms, so for me, that meant taking out all of my personality, all of my understanding and starting from scratch.

The first chapter in any thesis is the background information, the section that explains the bigger picture before drilling down to the subject matter and your reasons for carrying out the research. In this section I needed to discuss what was happening in the field of CAM as a whole, what the government view was and give some worldwide statistics on its prevalence and use within a medical hierarchy. Here in the UK at that time, 28.3% of the adult population had used one of eight therapies, they were acupuncture, chiropractic, homoeopathy, hypnotherapy, medical herbalism, osteopathy, reflexology, and aromatherapy. Most users were female and 46.6% of them were lifetime users, whilst the annual spend on CAM equated to £580 million, of which 90% was from private purchase.[1] Today those figures have increased exponentially both here in the UK and in Europe[2][3] so anything that helps to build up the knowledge base and evidence for complementary therapies is going to prove extremely beneficial in the long term and will help develop our path for integrated health.

When you start to look at your subject matter in more detail you have to put in your literature review, so this bit was all about reflexology, the work that had already been carried out by others with reflexology and pain, and where my research was going to add to the existing knowledge base. Although the research into the benefits of reflexology is now beginning to develop, at the time of writing my thesis there was little to draw on, particularly in the area of pain management. Those of you who are practitioners will know that reflexology treatments generally include a complete 'package of care' that reviews lifestyle, diet, and exercise which addresses the possible cause of a condition and not just the presenting symptoms. However, my research presented more of a challenge for examining the benefits of reflexology in the management of pain because it was carried out in a laboratory environment without the benefit of the care package or the advantage of a holistic approach. I started writing about the history of reflexology, but then also needed to look at it in relation to Eastern medical practices such as acupressure, acupuncture and auriculotherapy. Why? Because the entire Eastern theory of medicine seems to be related to lines or zones that run through the body, and it is this connection that many have suggested ties reflexology with Eastern medical practices.[4][5][6] That wasn't enough though, as this was after all a scientific thesis, so I was told to write about the Eastern theories and how they relate to the neurological practices introduced by Sir Henry Head way back in the 1800's,[7][8] but more on this in my next book perhaps!

I wrote about the theoretical basis of reflexology in pain management and a whole section on the history of pain, through to medications used for pain and what CAM therapies are available to support those in pain. There was a lot to get my head around in this section, but I was feeling much more confident in my knowledge and found writing about it extremely fulfilling. Having completed the first chapter, it was time to move onto the second chapter – the methods section. This shouldn't really have been a difficult chapter but having been told that you need to reference everything, this was how I wrote it, only for Ivor to tell me that putting in a rationale for this section was all wrong. When you write up your methods section you should be writing it more like a recipe book. You don't say that you are baking a cake because of this or that, you just say how you need to do it so that others who may want to replicate or build on your work can follow the exact same procedures with the exact same equipment. Once I had got my head around that, it was easier to put it together in the correct format. What I lacked for this section though was an image or chart for reflexology. There are many and varied charts on the market today and I wanted to provide something that was quite unique. My niece, Tina Signorelli, was at the time starting out as an art undergraduate at the University of Portsmouth, so I asked her if she would consider creating something, and this is what she did for me.

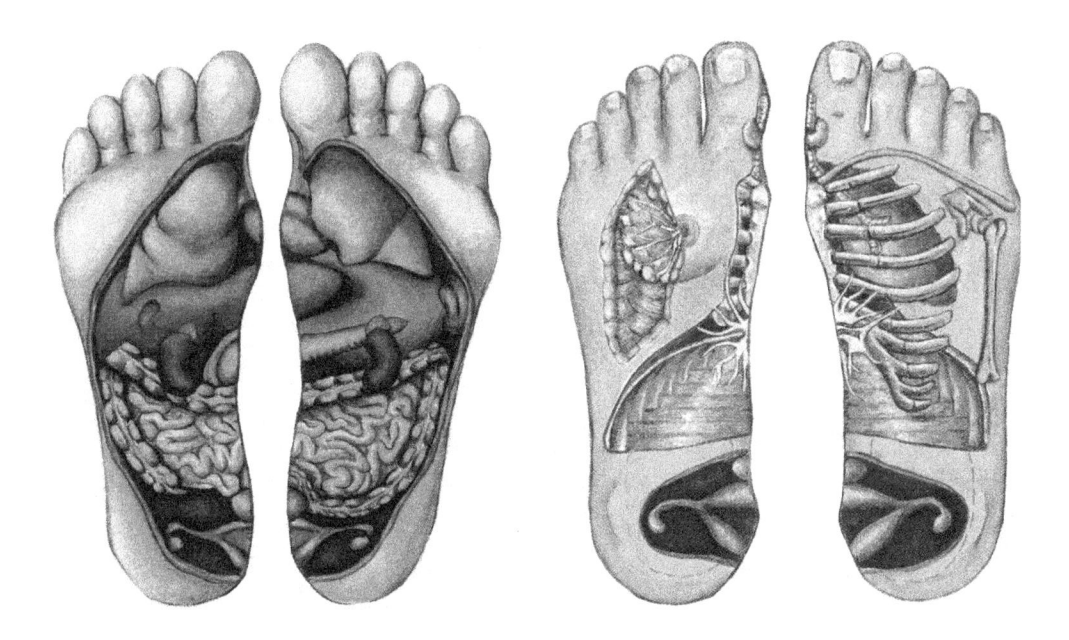

I was so proud of her and what she had produced. She was not a reflexologist and knew absolutely nothing about it, but she certainly understood how to draw and to interpret my needs. She went on to complete her studies with a first-class honours degree and then progressed to a Master of Art. I am delighted that she continues to share her artistic talents teaching children. She has produced two incredible charts of the nervous system on the feet for me, which are not only anatomically correct, but provide an insight into areas of the feet not previously shown on many charts available today. She is also the artist who created the illustration for the front cover of this book.

In July 2008 I met with Ivor to review what I had written so far. You think you are doing really well but then someone comes along to piss on your chips. It seems that there were still a lot of questions I needed to answer before making statements in my thesis, and I needed to give a whole lot more time and effort to the section on pain. It had taken me quite some time to get to where I was, but it wasn't enough. As a science-based thesis I needed to write about the sensory nervous system and skin receptors, to discuss the neurotransmitters that get exchanged at a cellular level and to thoroughly understand it. We know of course that the true mechanism of action of reflexology has yet to be clinically demonstrated, but sensory receptors seem to play an important role.[9][10][11] Indeed, the body responds to a number of chemical exchanges that are instigated by the movement of ions in and out of the cells, so I needed to provide a clear explanation of this within my thesis.

I was proposing that pain sensation is reduced in reflexology *via* the gate control mechanism, it was not a new theory and had been discussed by others before me.[12][13][14] The 'gate control' theory was first postulated by Melzack and Wall[15] when they suggested that the physical perception of pain was not a direct result of stimulating small pain receptors (Aδ and C nerve fibres) in the skin, but was modulated by larger non-pain (Aβ) fibres that closed the transmission signal (gate) to the brain. These modulating receptors are said to interfere with the pain signal at the level of the spinal cord by releasing natural endorphins.[16]

We have still to confirm the mechanism of reflexology, but this was certainly a logical starting point. However, in the experiment I had carried out using light, standard and no reflexology, the results were confusing. What I saw in the results was that some people responded early to reflexology and others responded late, and a few didn't respond at all. When this happens in an experiment, the results are all over the place and it is extremely difficult to make any assumptions from them.

There were a few things to consider: for example, in a normal reflexology practice there is an open environment where our clients can discuss personal and health issues, but in my experimental environment this didn't happen. Participants to the study were not permitted to discuss their health, their personal life or anything else that might influence the outcome of the experiment, and the reason for this was so that I could be clear about the effects of treatment. What I mean by that is that I needed to know if the effect I was achieving was from the reflexology stimulation or the interaction between us. If I didn't allow that interaction, then I could state with greater clarity that the effect was from the treatment.

The pain/pleasure conundrum was another thing to consider because there was some suggestion that when giving reflexology some participants were finding it pleasurable. You may not think it's important but there was a published paper in the journal Nature[17] about pain and pleasure, and Ivor said it would be essential for me to understand it because it would provide me with information about the type of person I was using in the experiments. I was a little confused about what he meant by that, so he explained. If there is an interaction between pain and pleasure, and participants deemed reflexology as a pleasurable experience, some people may get an analgesic response from it because pleasure itself releases endogenous opioid peptides.[18] When people feel good about something the body releases dopamine too which works alongside opioid peptides, and this creates a link between wanting and liking. If you have a lot of dopamine release you get an increase in your locomotor activity (seek your reward) which is what happens to people who take speed, it gives you the incentive to do something, the pleasurable bit. With reflexology we are providing a manual treatment that a client may find enjoyable, we are changing the neurochemistry of their pain, and perhaps inducing the release of opioid peptides, which may therefore attenuate pain. It was therefore another theory to consider.

If for example, my volunteer participants didn't like foot massage, one would anticipate that they wouldn't have volunteered in the first place. Some may have been curious of course, but the normal person has certain pain/pleasure thresholds, and some others are more on the masochistic side, where pain itself can be pleasurable. These things are multifaceted, so in addition to the theory on pain gating, I needed to contribute something to the thesis about this too. It was starting to get a little more complex and I was absolutely fascinated but already mentally exhausted.

The target for submission of my thesis was originally September 2008 and when I started writing Sam and I knew this was the home run. What we didn't allow for was the amount of time it would take me to write, or the number of times I would have to rewrite what I had already done. I would spend hours at a time with Ivor who was challenging everything I had written with a question, this in turn meant that I had to look at more research papers but in areas that I hadn't even envisaged would be relevant to reflexology. Relationships were beginning to suffer again, and I struggled not to use Sam for my frustrations and anger. We seemed to be walking on eggshells with each other and in hindsight I can see that much of that was down to me, but when you are in the thick of it, it is those closest to you that take the brunt of your frustration.

At my next meeting with Ivor, he told me who he was proposing as my examiners. The external examiner was Professor John Golding from Westminster University who had originally trained as a biochemist at Oxford. He also had a degree in psychology and had done research on psychoactive drugs and pain relief, as well as research related to acupuncture and acupressure. My internal examiner was going to be either the head of the science faculty, Dr John Wong, or Dr Roz Gibbs. Dr Wong was a pharmacologist who taught pain science to undergraduates within the faculty, so I could see why he might be appropriate, and Roz was the biomedical sciences lecturer who had already approved my transfer from MPhil to PhD but also had an interest in acupuncture. Roz had participated in my research and was also by now a friend, so Ivor thought her an inappropriate choice and instead made the decision to ask Dr Wong to be my internal examiner.

It was time to look at the results more closely and to try and standardise things. As I mentioned earlier, in one of my experiments the threshold and tolerance scores were all over the place. There seemed to be two categories of people, those who responded to reflexology and those who didn't, so I needed to take another look at the literature for T.E.N.S and acupuncture to see if anything similar had happened in other research trials. This would provide me with some form of justification for dividing the two populations. I was trying to establish whether reflexology produced an analgesic effect, so I took a really close look at the data and sectioned out groups of responders and non-responders. I examined the different ways of analysing the data and at any correlation between heart rate and levels of arousal, but pain tolerance was the important factor in my evaluations. We all have similar pain threshold levels, for example we would all feel heat pain at around 45 - 50°C but pain tolerance can make the difference between taking huge amounts of medication and being able to reduce that intake because it is dependent on many contributory factors.

Alongside my meetings with Ivor with whom I was discussing the pain experiments, I was also meeting with Sheelagh who was trying to guide my writing. Her role was to direct my introductory chapter, the overall formatting of the thesis and the chapter on pressure. There were all sorts of things to consider in my writing aside from what was happening with my experimental results. She quite rightly said that I needed to stand back from it and be critical of the work of others, to think about what I may be asked by a skeptic as well as someone interested, to be careful about terms I did not fully understand and do more research before writing about them. I wasn't permitted to use terms that were unscientific, and whilst all of this was good advice, it was also extremely stressful and made me feel very inept.

I was also meeting with the statistician who was trying to explain yet another set of statistical measurements that might be useful to me for my group of participants who were presenting with varied results. All in all, I felt as though once again I had information overload and my brain just would not take it all in, and I eventually became sick with bronchitis and lost my voice.

I took Sheelagh's advice and did another literature search, rewrote huge sections of text, and hoped I had done enough in the first sections to satisfy the requirements of my thesis, then I had a meeting with Ivor. It was November 2008 and I had already missed the deadline for my thesis submission. The writing of my experimental work, aside from the pressure chapter was being directed by Ivor and there were still many unanswered questions.

Each year in January Ivor would travel to Thailand to teach for around 3 – 4 weeks, but this year he told me that one of his other PhD students was due to submit his thesis and was not playing ball. He explained that he still had to do the appraisals for his post-doctoral students and mark two sets of papers for 160 students when he returned, and he also had to prepare four posters for a conference. It was his way of saying that my work was going on a bit of a back burner for a while. Between now and Christmas I was to see him just once and before then I needed to rewrite my materials and methods section, write my individual chapters with the discussion sections, and give him what I had completed in readiness for his trip. This basically meant that Christmas 2008 was going to be all about writing for me. In addition to that Sheelagh had been reviewing my introductory chapter and the chapter on pressure and suggested we meet again just before the Christmas break with a view to 'getting my teeth into the changes required' over the holiday period.

It wasn't going to be the Christmas break Sam and I had envisaged and now I had to go home and tell him, and I was seriously not looking forward to it. I did however take a slight glimmer of hope from Sheelagh when she said *"I want you to finish because it has been a difficult PhD, it is a difficult subject and you have had a lot of learning and growing up to do. Your qualifications made you look as though you had the right experience, my only worry is, what I have always said, that you may have difficulty with the viva, but you are much better now, you are not as defensive as you used to be"*. She had not told me outright that she thought I could do it, but at least she was giving me her full support now, and I took hope from that statement and prayed that I could put that across to Sam when I got home. As far as he was concerned it was the same old stuff, I was still putting more time into my PhD than our marriage and I got that, but what he didn't see was how demoralising this was for me, how my confidence was failing and how exhausted I was with it all.

New Year, new hope

I met with Ivor on 6th January 2009 as planned and we started to break down the experimental chapters and the things I needed to give more attention to. For example, in the physiological responses to reflexology I was trying to fully understand and present my work for what I thought was happening. I could see that there was a correlation between heart rate and pain threshold and tolerance levels, so Ivor had suggested that the kind of questions I needed to address from this were: -

- Could this be related to circulating catecholamines (adrenaline/noradrenaline) which increase heart rate, blood pressure, breathing rate, muscle strength, and mental alertness?
- Could it be reflex bradycardia - a reduced heart rate that responds to the baroreceptor reflex, to prevent abnormal increases in blood pressure? or,
- Local prostaglandin release which has many different functions within the cell, but which also act as inflammatory mediators?

My understanding of physiology was better than when I had first started my research, but Ivor's questions were throwing me all over the place and it seemed

I still needed to learn more and more. Once again, I was questioning myself and my knowledge and whether I would ever get this PhD completed. I was to ignore the editorial changes to my text and instead look more closely at the data. The responders and non-responders were throwing my results and I needed to get a handle on what was really happening here, so I had to look at their results on an individual basis. This meant charting every single participant result in a graph for their responses to light and standard reflexology and then comparing that to the no treatment (control).

> *The study of philosophy is not that we may know what men have thought, but what the truth of things is*
> **Thomas Aquinas**

When I looked at the data for the individual participants in this way it showed that although there was a difference in the latency of response, there was also a difference in who did and did not respond to treatment. It wasn't the first time this effect had been demonstrated in complementary therapies and in Western populations around 20-30% of people don't respond to CAM treatments.[19] In fact, there is a wide magnitude of responses in acupuncture, T.E.N.S and also hypnosis experiments[20][21][22][23][24][25] but it is not unique to CAM therapies. When I looked at the effects of responders and non-responders to medications I saw that up to 33% of people don't respond to the pain relieving effects of 10mg of morphine, and that there also exists a group of responders and non-responders with non-steroidal anti-inflammatory medications too.[26]

We don't know what predisposes an individual to respond to a certain treatment, but there is some suggestion that genetics may play a role. Around 50% of patients with neuropathic pain don't achieve any sort of satisfactory pain relief from a single therapy alone and codeine has no effect if an individual is unable to metabolise it to morphine.[27][28] The problem with this is that the effect of responders and non-responders make it extremely difficult for CAM research to establish the true effects of treatment. Certainly, if there are any future studies around pain, researchers should take this point into consideration when doing power calculations and evaluating results. On a positive note, my results did in fact indicate that they reflect normal differences in populations of pain sufferers who more often than not have a diverse and multi-dimensional variation in their pain. This tells us that *'one size does not fit all'* and that treatment for pain must take a more multi-dimensional approach based on the biopsychosocial model.[29][30][31][32] My results were also consistent with those achieved by others for reflexology, acupuncture, and T.E.N.S.[33] It was good to get to the bottom of this chapter and to see how my results compared to those seen in other CAM therapies across the world, and it did give me the confidence to discuss pain as a very individualistic and personal experience.

When I started presenting my results, I was graphing them as histograms, but here I was now, writing up my results and putting my thesis together, when Ivor decides that histograms won't do. So, to show my results in a more acceptable format I needed to create a different type of graph and he recommended a programme called GraphPad Prism...as if there wasn't enough to do already, I now needed to create my graphs using a completely new piece of software.

In addition to this he had also asked that I look at the personalities of the participants who had taken part in the trials to see if there was any correlation between pain responses and personality types. These things may seem small to the reader but when you already feel as though you have done everything, it takes very little to push you over the edge again.

Subjective responses to pain are considered the single most reliable index of the magnitude of pain[34][35] but there are inconsistencies in the reflexology literature in which the subjective level of anxiety has been evaluated. Some researchers have demonstrated that reflexology produces a significant reduction in anxiety,[36][37][38][39] whilst others have shown only transient effects.[40][41] Participants in my experiments didn't show increased levels of anxiety or arousal when conducting ice pain immersions across the range of my experiments. This could have been due to the level of control they had over the ice plunge, i.e., they took their hand out when they had reached their tolerance level, or perhaps it was due to their general personality. In order to look more closely at this Ivor created a modified version of the Eysenck personality questionnaire which I used to assess whether the effects of extraversion and introversion (E-score) were correlated with pain responses. Each of the study participants had completed 41 questions of which 20 were related to the E-score. High E-scores suggest an extravert, whilst low E-scores represent an introvert, but why was it important? As you will have read earlier, my results were not stable across all of my experiments, so I needed to investigate this from every possible angle. Pain is a hugely personal experience and there is some suggestion that your personality will dictate how you respond to it.[42][43] My investigations revealed that although in one of my ice-pain experiments the majority of participants were indeed from an extravert population, there was actually no correlation between personality and their ice-pain responses.

The other part of the subjective experience came from the feedback questionnaires which indicated that a large majority of participants had expressed improved energy levels and improved sleep. Whilst the effect was seen in both the control and reflexology treatments, the greater effect was seen following reflexology. I don't doubt that you may have had similar feedback from your clients over the years and in one randomised-controlled trial of reflexology there were significant improvements in the quality of sleep in postpartum females.[44] I'm sure that the parents amongst you will know that the transition to motherhood often encounters quite a bit of sleep deprivation and poor-quality sleep, so reflexology may certainly seem like a viable option to many new mums. More importantly and relevant to my research was that sleep deprivation is a major concern for sufferers of chronic pain, so it can be extremely distressing.[45] The percentage of patients who visit pain clinics reporting insomnia, or some other form of sleep disorder is as much as 53%, and this may have a detrimental effect on the immune system.[46][47][48]

It would of course be worth carrying out further research to evaluate the effects of reflexology on sleep deprived pain sufferers, particularly as it may be beneficial to the general well-being of patients in pain.

Applying for an extension

By March 2009 I still had a lot of work to do and had run out of time. I had already eaten into the extension I had in place because of the tsunami but Ivor felt that I would not be able to complete on time, so without my knowledge Sheelagh had spoken with academic registry to confirm whether it might be possible to extend again. Clearly, they were still backing me, or they wouldn't have made the request, but at the same time they were telling me that if I wanted it, I would now need to pay for it myself, it was a no-brainer for me. Ivor was still questioning everything I had written; he was really making me think about pain and the role of the various neurotransmitters. I needed to be more specific, more detailed, more focussed. I needed to look at the pain pathways, how the different nerve fibres transmitted their signals to the brain. There were more charts and comparisons to make, more research papers to understand, more to write and rewrite. He was picking holes in everything and of course it was in my own best interests, but you don't see that when you are in the middle of it all. I was exhausted, not just mentally but emotionally and physically too and my health was suffering more and more. I was experiencing huge flare-ups in inflammation, I couldn't sleep, I was tired, tense, and irritable and played that out on anyone who was within my vicinity. I wasn't a nice person, neither was I happy or confident or fun, but I was determined and nothing and no one was going to stop me now.

When you reach the end of your rope, tie a knot in it and hang on
Franklin D Roosevelt

Between Ivor and Sheelagh, they tore my work apart so that I could produce the best of it. They did not tread lightly on my feelings nor did they release their pressure and I know that what they did, was in my best interest, but it was nonetheless, relentless and demoralising. This continued throughout the spring and early summer of 2009, then in August Ivor asked Sheelagh to pay for an extra month's study as he thought I would need to run into September with my thesis. Ivor asked me to get all my chapters in order before he went on leave at the end of August, he was then going to hand it to Sheelagh to read but didn't want me to rush putting it together in terms of the formatting and references.

The plan was to submit by the middle of September at the latest, so this is what I went home and told Sam. I was already over-running, and he was not best pleased when I said there was to be another extension. I had already gone to him in spring and said it would be a couple of months, now a further five months had elapsed, and I was seeking yet another extension. He was disappointed to say the least and I tried to explain, I wanted to be able to talk to him about what I was doing but it just didn't work out that way and although he was still supportive of my journey, the really good days that we used to have were seriously struggling to see the light of day. I felt he was blaming me for everything and in hindsight he may well have been right, but I was struggling too and that's not unusual for any PhD student. When you read the literature on the number of relationship failures for PhD students, it makes for frightening reading, and whilst I was among them it was very threatening and was having a really negative effect on us both. He had always been a fan of Fleetwood Mac and they were playing Wembley arena, so I had tried to get tickets earlier in the year, but they had sold out, then I saw, purely by chance that they had added an additional date. Maybe it was the guilt of not being around at home, or when I was physically home, not being there emotionally, I don't know, but I felt the need to give something back to him, to try and patch up our differences and let him know how hard I was trying to maintain our relationship amongst all the chaos at university. I am pretty certain there was an angel sitting on my shoulder helping me that day because I managed to get front row tickets for the event, he was absolutely ecstatic, and we had an amazing time together. There is no doubt about it though, doing a PhD is a huge psychological investment and trying to balance study at this level whilst maintaining a healthy relationship is an incredibly difficult process.

The middle of September came and went, and I had still not submitted my thesis, I was still moving things around, still trying hard to absorb more detail so that I could be more specific in my discussion sections. Ivor told me that in the viva they want to see at what level you know things, so you need to know things that are not directly related to your thesis. That was a really scary thought, and I didn't know what I was supposed to do with it. He said they want you to have both a specific and a rounded knowledge of your work and my work was complicated by the statistics.

My final discussion chapter wasn't strong enough and it was the most important part of the entire thesis, so I had to get it right. When you are writing your final discussion you have to look at everything you are doing and then ask yourself, how can I prove this, and if I am saying this or that, is it generally true, is there evidence for it? You need to ask yourself questions such as how, why, and what? You have to know how to measure things and demonstrate that you have thought about something beforehand, because your examiners want to see if you can think on your feet. Ivor told me that the worst thing that can happen is that they think your thesis is ok, but that your viva vocé wasn't, so they will call you back for another viva. He explained that in science you have to build on something you have already done so they will ask what you would do next and how you could do it; he didn't think I had the background knowledge for that, but he did say that he had confidence in me. Was this a breakthrough?

Professor Golding, as my external examiner had suggested that I have my viva vocé exam on the 10th December, but Dr Wong couldn't make that date as the university had external auditors arriving and he was going to be heavily involved in that process, so I needed to wait for a new date. In the meantime, there was still more to consider with my writing. When you are making statements in your thesis you have to use a different kind of language to say something speculative, such as, it is likely, or possible or probable. It was these little things that kept coming back to bite me on the bum and meant that I was still changing text, but by now I had just three weeks remaining before I *had* to submit my final thesis. Sheelagh was big on language too and she had a huge influence on what I wrote for my chapter on pressure because of her expertise in this area of science. This particular chapter was a bit of a sticking point as far as my research went. Sheelagh thought it would form a good part of my thesis, but Ivor thought differently. I was having ongoing meetings with Sheelagh about the content of this chapter between April and the end of August and she had made a number of recommendations on how I should write it. The difficulty for me was that it was all about physics and the compliance of pressure and I really was a novice as far as this was concerned. That said, it was an interesting learning curve and helped me relate the compliance of pressure with what goes on in the cell and understand the importance of pressure on skin from a physiological perspective.

When Dr Wong reviewed my thesis prior to my viva there was a whole backlash of comments coming my way. He wasn't impressed with my glossary of terms and said it was too basic, the introduction was too long and added nothing to the quality of the thesis, he didn't believe that I fully understood the concept of my work and he certainly didn't think that the chapter on pressure fitted in with the rest of the thesis. He had picked each chapter apart and suggested that I review, revise, and update them before my final submission, or I may fall foul of his comments during my viva, which would not bode well for me.

My final meeting was with Sheelagh on 21st December 2009, and we spoke at length about the pressure chapter, why I carried out the research, the difficulties we had with the equipment, the differences between force and pressure and whether when I used the mechanical reflexology in my experiments, it was the machine or the participant applying that pressure. She again reiterated what Ivor had said previously, that I could be asked about absolutely anything on my thesis during my viva. I needed to be sure of everything, but she said that I would be able to draw something if I found it difficult to explain, and that if I remained calm when I defend it, I will get it. Wow, 'Merry Christmas Carol', oh and by the way, your viva will be on 12th January 2010. It was the date of my granddaughter's birthday, so I hoped it would be a good omen.

CHAPTER 7 | WRITING THE THESIS

Looking Back

Looking back to the Autumn of 2008 when I started to get ill with an upper respiratory tract infection and lost my voice, I can see how much sense it makes now. From a metaphysical point of view the throat is all about expression of will and the balance between our mental and emotional intention. I felt challenged in writing my thesis and all the additional things I had to research in order to make sense of everything. It wasn't that I didn't have the will to carry it through, far from it, that was my intention right from the start. No, the issue was that every choice I made was about power, who would have it, Sheelagh and Ivor or me?

I wasn't able to fully express my concerns about writing scientifically, so I bottled them up and instead let those thoughts and feelings go inwards. I didn't have control about the way I wrote so I had lost my self-expression and I felt it by losing my voice.

My friend Simone had already graduated so I had really wanted to graduate in 2009 with my other friend Sam, but I remember meeting with Sheelagh in April that year and she told me then that she thought I wouldn't be able to submit my thesis in time to graduate that year. She did however think that I had done really well with writing and told me that if I got a PhD out of it, it would be a tremendous achievement, and if I got an MPhil, it would also be a tremendous achievement.

She said that it would be a shame to rush it when I had come so far, and she was right, but I was still disappointed that I wouldn't be graduating with my friend. She also told me that they had my best interests at heart, and from time to time, tough love was necessary if I was to accomplish my task and achieve my goal of a PhD.

Reflection is an important part of writing and I know now that every step, every phase of this PhD journey has been about developing me into the person I am today.

CHAPTER 8
The final hurdles

> *I was not delivered into this world in defeat, nor does failure course in my veins. I am not a sheep waiting to be prodded by my shepherd. I am a lion and I refuse to talk, to walk, to sleep with the sheep. The slaughterhouse of failure is not my destiny. I will persist until I succeed.*
>
> **Og Mandino**

The term 'Viva Voce' is Latin for 'living voice' and provides you with an opportunity to discuss, or rather defend your research face to face with your examiners. To ease you into the viva, examiners may give you the opportunity to provide a 10-minute overview of your thesis, perhaps by asking you to tell them what the main value of your thesis is, or what you would like to do if you had more time?

More time…for heaven's sake, I would have thought that eight years was plenty long enough for anyone doing a PhD. No, it wasn't about more time as far as I was concerned, it was about having the right financial support so that I could carry out the right kind of testing, with the right support group in an environment where I was not the only person in the entire university carrying out research where others didn't believe in me because it wasn't 'scientific' enough. Who was this person doing airy fairy research on a load of mumbo jumbo? Me, that's who, it was me who was able to show that this load of 'mumbo jumbo' had some credential, that it was scientific and finally with the help of Sheelagh and Ivor, I was able to prove that.

As I mentioned in my previous chapters, you have two examiners, the internal and external. The role of the internal examiner is to uphold the interests of the university and to ensure a fair process. The external examiner on the other hand is responsible for providing impartial advice that is independent of your own university, as well as commenting on the quality of the thesis before a degree can be awarded at the appropriate standard. Both examiners are supposedly selected because they have an interest or have written extensively about your field of research and you should have at least mentioned them in your thesis references. Neither of the two examiners that had been selected for me knew anything about reflexology, but Professor Golding knew a little about complementary and alternative medical practices. Neither had written extensively about it and I had not quoted either of them in my thesis, so this didn't apply to my work.

When you go into your viva exam you quite often attend with your PhD supervisor, however in my case Ivor wasn't available so Sheelagh took his place which, in some ways made me a little more anxious. Whilst she knew an awful lot about the chapter on pressure, she didn't know much about the science of pain, and I was faced with two examiners that did, hence the reason they were both selected.

Sheelagh told me that they weren't there to trip me up, they simply wanted to ensure that I had done the work and that it was a valid piece of research. It was my final stage exam and an opportunity for me to gain a doctorate, a degree that indicates a high, if not *the* highest, level of academic achievement. I needed to have total belief in what I had done, give a balanced view of the outcomes and I would be fine. I wasn't exactly feeling that fine, in fact I made more trips to the toilet that morning than I had ever done, my stomach was doing all sorts of flips and my brain didn't seem to want to function at all.

Once you are in the room with your examiners you may give an introduction of your work and then there is a focussed discussion, it is not, Sheelagh said, an interrogation, though it may feel that way. They will ask you some warm-up questions and it can last anywhere between one and four hours, so just try to enjoy it. I did have some reservations about my examiners and whether or not the viva was really fair given that neither of them had any interest in reflexology, but I knew their combined intelligence on pain was very much based on science and medicine and they were therefore likely to question all that I had learnt about it during my eight years at university. They were both 'real' scientists with a mass of knowledge that absolutely terrified me, especially as my internal examiner taught pain science to pharmacology and pharmacy students here at Portsmouth and I had been one of his students for a while. Ivor had told me to read a few papers written by Professor Golding, my external examiner, so I selected three papers.[1][2][3] Two were related to motion sickness whilst the third was more about the psychological impact of an acute pain stimulus. Ivor then reminded me that Professor Golding had also been a co-author for a paper on using acupuncture and T.E.N.S to measure pain threshold and tolerance;[4] and had carried out research on the effects of acupuncture on somatosensory evoked potentials, hence the link to my research. Professor Golding held a first degree in psychology and there is of course much discussion in the research about the psychology of complementary and alternative medicine.

As part of the preparation for the viva I took a workshop where we were told about all the different issues and concerns post-graduates may experience with a viva voce exam. One of the important points that I took from the workshop was that once you had submitted your thesis you must ensure you read it thoroughly. Now I know that sounds a bit daft, after all you're the one who wrote it, but actually by the time you reach the end of the writing process you really don't want to look at it again and so you become rather immune to its content. You do however need to make sure that you are up to date with the latest knowledge on your topic, and that you are able to identify any gaps in your thesis that may come about because of new information, all of which helps you fully prepare for what may come your way in the viva exam. I was told that 90% of the questions would be based on the thesis so I would need to remember what, where, when, how and why I did things. I also needed to have a plan of action for any future publications I may have been proposing and if I already had any publications under my belt, I would need to append them to the thesis.

I had done my research for the examination. I had put together a set of questions that I thought they would ask me and prepared appropriate answers. Once again it was suggested that I carry out some background research on my examiners to see if I could gain insight into their own research approach. Although by now I knew how to read a research paper and what to look out for, the papers I had read by Professor Golding went a little over my head and to be perfectly honest, I didn't read any of Dr Wong's papers because they were more about pharmacological studies on nociception and fluid intake, so didn't seem relevant to me at the time.[5][6] Why would I complicate an already complicated situation by reading up on something I knew nothing about and in this situation was unlikely to need, too?

THE TENACIOUS STUDENT | Dr CAROL A. SAMUEL

Worrying gets you nowhere, if you turn up worrying about how you're going to perform, you've already lost.

Usain Bolt

My viva socé examination was set for 2.15p.m on 12th January 2010 in Dr Wong's office in the School of Pharmacy and Biomedical Sciences. It was difficult to keep myself occupied during the morning and so I spent as much time as I could re-reading my own questions and hoping that I had guessed they would be the questions I was going to be asked. As always, one of my biggest concerns was whether or not I would hear the question and hear it correctly. Listening is a skill and if you don't hear well like me, you already feel inhibited. It seems to take more energy for me to listen to a question, hear it correctly and interpret it in the right way, and I get particularly stressed if the speaker has a strong accent, so I am not the quickest responder. I tried to meditate, to do some deep breathing and to ground myself fully before walking into the room. Sheelagh went in first, had a chat with the examiners and then invited me to sit.

The very first question they asked me after introducing themselves was asked by Dr Wong and it was meant to put me at my ease, but instead, I completely froze, the words would not leave my mouth and my brain went into scrabble mode. The question he asked was *'tell me about the divisions of the nervous system'?* I stared into space in the hope that I could pluck something out of the ether and then I saw Sheelagh out of the corner of my eye, and I recalled her past words when she said their concerns for me were that I would not be able to cope in the viva exam. I wasn't going to fail them or myself. Dr Wong could clearly see how terrified I was and graciously reworded the question so that it encouraged the correct response. It broke the ice because as soon as he reworded it, I was able to reel off everything the examiners were looking for. The rest of the examination was about defining my work and defending it through my thesis.

There is a certain type of language use in a viva examination, and you are encouraged to use certain phrases as openers in your responses. It was about being confident but not arrogant, being assertive but not aggressive and being open to constructive criticism. I remember one of the viva workshop lecturers clearly stating, 'don't bullshit' and that was at the forefront of my mind throughout. I had the evidence in front of me, they had both read my thesis and had already made some comments prior to recommending the viva, so it should not have been difficult.

CHAPTER 8 | THE FINAL HURDLES

It was of course, mostly due to my nervous state, but as time progressed, we were able to get into a discussion about my work and I relaxed enough to be able to defend it. Where it was appropriate, I said that I wasn't able to answer a particular question, or that whilst I wasn't aware of a particular procedure, I would certainly take their advice and review it for any future research and at the time, I meant it. It was about diplomacy and tact, about not being too defensive of their comments and suggestions, and about finding the right words to use when responding to them. The questioning was all done and dusted within a couple of hours and I was asked to leave the room whilst they deliberated on their recommendation.

The examiners recommendations I was told, are not a verdict but a report on the possibilities and they are: -

- Pass
- Pass with minor corrections, usually typos - you have 3 months to resubmit.
- Submit a revised thesis with or without a further viva exam – you have 12 months to do the revisions.
- MPhil
- Fail

You cannot appeal their decision once it has been made unless it is for procedural reasons.

When I was called back into the room, I was informed that I had passed my viva exam with minor corrections. They would write up an official report and I would receive formal notification from the academic registry in due course. I was elated and yet numb, I didn't know whether to laugh or cry. Was this real, had I finally reached my goal?

Sheelagh asked me to join her in her office so that she could explain things to me. We sat down and she congratulated me. She said, *"I have been an educator for very many years, I have never in all of those years met a student with such tenacity and I am immensely proud of you"*. Those words were the most precious words I had ever heard but a couple of days later she sent me an email to remind me that the PhD wasn't guaranteed until the corrections had been done, which bought me back down to earth and told me that I could not yet celebrate my success.

Corrections

I needed a break before tackling the corrections and so I booked a trip to Scotland to spend time with an elderly friend of mine who was in failing health. It gave me a lot of time to think, too much time perhaps, because I felt a little lost. Life had been full on for the past eight years and it just seemed to suddenly stop, I didn't know what to do. Being with my friend helped fill some of the space and I was pleased to have her company, then on 23rd January Sam and I took a very much needed holiday where we were able to really concentrate only on each other for the first time in, what seemed like, an exceptionally long time. It was such a relief not to have to look at my thesis and I can honestly say that whilst we were away, I didn't even think about what would come next. The years of stressful eating though had taken their toll and I was the heaviest I had ever been in my entire life. I worked out that I had gained almost four stone over the course of my PhD and was feeling every ounce of it. My self-confidence had hit rock bottom, but I was determined that once I got back on an even keel, I would set about tackling my weight and do something to improve my overall health, but in the meantime, I was going to enjoy my time with Sam.

Amongst the post we had accumulated whilst we were away, was the formal notification letter from the academic registry with a sentence telling me of their decision, which read: -

The examiners recommend that you may submit a revised thesis for the degree of Doctor of Philosophy (PhD) and then if acceptable will be exempt from further examination.

I was so thankful that I didn't have to go through another viva and of course I already knew there were corrections to do, but I wasn't yet aware of the extent of those corrections. Included with the letter was the list and a notification that I had a year to re-submit them, which was more than generous for what they had initially termed 'minor' corrections. There was however another fee to pay for re-registration and re-submission of the corrected thesis.

I set about reviewing them; those from Dr Wong were mostly rather picky, he still didn't like my glossary, there were too many typos of which he had provided a full list, my introductory chapter was too lengthy, and he still didn't think that my chapter on pressure fit where it was in the thesis.

CHAPTER 8 | THE FINAL HURDLES

From Professor Golding the corrections were far more detailed and seemed to be picking up on the psychology around my experiments. In an email to Ivor, he was suggesting I carry out further statistical analysis, but we needed to wait to receive further guidance on the type of analysis I was to perform. He recommended I add lots of caveats in the various chapters and change the way I had written some of the conclusions so that the results appeared a little more circumspect than I had originally proposed. I was bloody furious that he would suggest that I hadn't carried out every possible means of statistical analysis to meet the standards required for my conclusions. The thought of having to redo the statistics all over again just gave me such a gut wrenching feeling that I wanted to throw up and throw it all away.

There was a lot to do, and I needed to meet with Sheelagh and Ivor to discuss how I should proceed. When I went to Sheelagh's office in late February 2010, I was told by her lab technician, that she was currently on sick leave with the flu. In the meantime, I went along to see Ivor and we talked through the changes one by one. Most he said, were fairly straight-forward but the statistical testing recommended by Professor Golding was not something either of us were familiar with. The notes Sheelagh had taken during the viva were not particularly clear to Ivor, and the paper Professor Golding had sent across did not refer specifically to the test that he wanted me to do. He had told us the test was called the Pitman Permutation Test and was ostensibly a superior method of analysing the results than those I had used for my experiments.[7] The problem for me was that if it changed my results, which was a possibility, there would be huge amounts of rewriting to do. It threw me into a whole new panic, and I now had to go home and tell Sam that it wasn't over yet.

By late March Sheelagh had still not returned to work and I was struggling to find out where she was and what was going on with her. I spoke with her technician, who was not forthcoming, her other students didn't seem to have any news either, so I went to see the lady with whom I had shared an office in my early days at university. She had become very unfriendly toward me but did tell me that Sheelagh was in hospital. When I asked what hospital and what ward she was in, I was told very clearly that a visit would not be welcomed, she didn't explain herself, she just said I couldn't visit.

I was to discover much later that Sheelagh had been diagnosed with Acute Myeloid Leukaemia, a cancer of the blood which results in the over production of blood cells that don't properly mature.[8] She had a rapidly progressive form of the disease blocking the production of normal healthy cells, and which ultimately reduces the number of red cells, white cells, and platelets. I wasn't aware of her treatment regime and I was given hardly any information, so I had to rely on the snippets I could get as and when I went into university, which wasn't often now. I no longer had a space to call my own and could only attend for meetings with Ivor and to collect mail.

I continued to make the corrections to my thesis, painstakingly going through all the minor issues with typos highlighted by Dr Wong but carrying out the pitman permutation test was proving much more challenging. This was how Ivor described it to me:

This test looks to see if there is a significant difference in variance between the groups at various time points. A t-test asks whether under condition A and condition B, the sample population is from the same or different populations, whilst the Pitman test looks at the variance between them. You will need to do the F (Fisher exact) test, a Pearson moment correlation coefficient and then the rest of the equation.

I look at that again now as I am writing this book and it still invites a certain amount of fear and panic even though I know that if I were to set time aside, I would work my way through it. It quite honestly just looks like a completely different language to me, but this is what I had to work with, and I took every single set of raw data, from every single experiment I had carried out and started the analysis all over again. I spent hour upon hour in my clinic at the bottom of the garden working through the corrections, which meant that I spent less and less time with Sam and that, quite understandably, caused much discontent between us.

In 2005 I found what felt like a pea-sized lump in my left breast which had turned out to be just a lumpy breast, so as I had been invited to a mammogram screening at the local Asda mobile unit in Portsmouth, I thought it best I attend. My appointment was scheduled for 4th June and I duly went along as arranged. The screening was quite unremarkable, and I was told that I would receive a letter from the hospital telling me of the outcome, so I wasn't surprised to receive it. I was however a little perturbed to read that they wanted me to attend for another mammogram, this time at the hospital. The letter explained that sometimes the equipment on the mobile units produces a poor image quality and that 1:14 get called back for the test to be repeated. I told Sam about it and he said he would come along with me. I refused, telling him that it was just another routine test and there was no need for him to take time off work on my account. Truth be told, we were making a fresh start and my head was still in a muddle. I didn't know who I was or what I wanted, my purpose in life or the direction I was going, there was no passion left in me for anything and I didn't want his company.

I had the mammogram late morning of the 21st June, they took four shots on the left breast only, so I was already getting suspicious. They asked me to sit in another waiting area whilst they looked more closely at the scans. After a while I was called in to have an ultrasound scan and needed to keep my arm above my head for 40 minutes, which was extremely uncomfortable. The radiography consultant kept stopping at a point on my left breast, the same place I had found the lump in 2005 and I prayed that if there was something to find, they would find it now. He wanted to do a core biopsy there and then, so they anaesthetised my breast, and he took five tissue samples. When I asked him what he thought, he said *"that on a scale of not being at all concerned, and being genuinely concerned, I am slightly concerned"*. I gave a silent prayer that if it was cancer, that they had found it early enough. I was told that I would get the results of my test in a week's time and I tried to remain positive and upbeat about it all.

I had to tell Sam when I got home not least of all because I had a huge dressing on my breast which was by now very sore and bruised. The appointment for the results was scheduled for the 28th June and I told Sam that I wanted to go on my own because I really thought that it would be alright. When he came home from work the next day, he told me he had booked the day off and that he was coming with me because it was his place to be by my side. I knew he was really worried, but I was trying hard not to be, after all, I couldn't change anything, and I was trying to be positive for both of us.

Life changing news

We met with the consultant and breast care nurse who gave us the news in a really gentle manner. The consultant simply said, *"there is a tumour in your left breast, which is a grade 2 cancer"*. It took a while to take in the news and I looked at Sam to check he was okay. Oh shit, that's not what I had wanted to hear! I gathered myself together and said, okay what's next? My consultant simply replied, *"good, may I examine you"?* The bruises from my biopsy gave a clear indication where the tumour was but I still couldn't feel a lump. He explained that I would need to undergo surgery to remove the lump, they would remove a margin of healthy tissue too which ensures they clear away any stray cells and then they would discuss any additional therapies, such as chemotherapy, radiotherapy and perhaps hormone therapy if necessary. They also needed to check the sentinel node which is the first lymph node to receive the drainage directly from a tumour.[9] I could expect to be called into hospital within the next 2 – 3 weeks but no longer than four weeks. They don't hang about!

I didn't know whether it was the right time to tell anyone else or whether I should wait until after the surgery. Sam and I sat down and discussed it and he thought it might be best to wait, although I felt it important that I tell my daughter Claire. I arranged to meet her at home that afternoon and explained that it was a small lump which they had found early, and my chances of survival were about 85%. She took the news well, in fact much better than I had anticipated. Sam and I agreed later that day that it would be right to tell my mum and dad, who were now both in their 80's. Ever since the tsunami mum had fussed and worried about me so I wasn't looking forward to telling her my news. I drove over that evening and she took it well, in fact she went on to tell me about my aunt in Canada who had previously had surgery for breast cancer and survived, that told me that she was being positive for my sake. I now needed to tell my dad who was already worrying about his younger brother who had been taken into hospital. He was great about it; he was shocked, but he held his feelings in check, and I think that's when I first registered that I get my strength of character from my parents. We decided to tell the rest of the family as the week progressed, together with my closest friends and of course, Ivor. It had been a difficult week and managing my own emotions was hard enough but rather bizarrely I felt that I needed to stay strong for everyone else. It was a mask that came down when I just wanted to get on with things, when I didn't want to have to think too hard about something. That very British, stiff upper lip, I guess.

It was the 1st July, and I had a meeting with Ivor to review the work I had done on the Pitman tests. They looked good but the chapter on the mechanical reflexology testing needed to be rewritten, again. During our meeting, my mobile phone rang so I switched it off without answering so that I could continue my discussions with Ivor. After the meeting I picked up a voice message from my breast care nurse. The message started...*it's nothing to worry about*...which has the completely opposite effect, *but we would like you to have some more tests, would you please give me a call?* When I rang back, it went straight to an answer phone, so I left it until the following day before calling back, and again I got the answer phone. It was mid-morning when the nurse returned my call and I remember I was in my clinic trying to rewrite the mechanical reflexology chapter. She told me that after further examination, the pathologists and radiographers think that I may have lobular tumour rather than a ductal tumour, as they first thought. I didn't know for sure, but my gut told me that this was a worse situation to be in and after hanging up, I completely lost it.

I shouted and screamed at the top of my voice to no one in particular, FUCK OFF, FUCK OFF, FUCK OFF...I won't have it, so you can FUCK OFF! I cried and I mean really cried and I was so angry. It was the first real expression of my feelings since my diagnosis, and I felt better for doing it. Anyway, I gathered myself together and I was determined to learn more so I started looking at all the facts and gathered some data.[10][11][12][13]

The breast care nurse (Julie) had said that I would need to undergo an MRI scan to determine the extent of it and to see if it was in a single point or multiple places. If it was in multiple places I would need to have a full mastectomy. Needless to say, that when I told Sam he was absolutely shattered but incredibly supportive at the same time.

I received a letter to say that I was to undergo my pre-op on 6th July and when Sam and I met with Julie, she told us that on the day of my surgery, he would have to drop me off in the early morning and then leave. He was not a happy bunny. I still had no date for the MRI scan, so Julie chased it up for me and it was scheduled for the 14th July. Apparently, they needed the results before the surgery could commence so I would get the results on the 15th July when she had scheduled a 2.15 appointment slot for me with the consultant. My pre-op took over four hours to complete and I was exhausted. I went to see a friend of mine who gave me some Reiki, the first of many sessions for which I was extremely grateful.

The MRI procedure itself sent me into a panic. I was face down with my arms down by my sides, my breasts lying in two cup holders and a canula pushing a blue dye through my blood vessels which sent great waves of nausea through me. It seemed to take forever, and the radiographer kept telling me when a new cycle was going to start. I hit the alarm button and kept shouting that I was going to be sick, but no one seemed to hear me, then it was over, and they got me out. They said the nausea was an unusual reaction...no shit Sherlock!

I took some time to read through some more research papers when I got home, this time about sentinel node biopsies so that I could prepare myself for what might be ahead of me.[14][15].

The next day Sam and I both had hospital appointments, his was in the fracture clinic at 2.45 and mine was for 2.15. Unfortunately, the breast clinic was running late so I didn't get to see the consultant until 3 o'clock, which meant that Sam was not with me when they gave me the results of my MRI. It was good news, as far as cancer can be good news of course. The cancer showed up only in my left breast so I would need to undergo surgery with a probable wide local excision to remove some lymph nodes and perhaps some radiotherapy. We discussed the sentinel node biopsy procedure and why it was necessary and then talked about the adjuvant therapy. He thought I would probably only need radiotherapy followed by a course of tamoxifen as my cancer was oestrogen receptor positive. I would need to wait until two weeks post-surgery before I would know the real outcome, and we would then discuss whether I needed or indeed wanted any form of reconstruction or reductive procedures.

Day of the surgery

Surgery for the removal of my breast lump was scheduled for 20th July and I felt surprisingly calm about it. Sam took me to the theatre suite at 7.55a.m. as planned, and he was told he could go, but he declined and told the staff that he would not leave my side until the last minute. I knew he was terrified of losing me and that he wasn't as strong or as positive about the outcome. I went through the usual system routines, spoke to the consultant and then the anaesthetist who discussed pain medication post-surgery. When I expressed a wish not to be given morphine because of the side-effects, he agreed and said he would write me up for Ibuprofen or Nurofen. I was number four on the list. Sam and I then walked over to the breast services department so that they could carry out another ultrasound scan and mark me up for surgery. There were two areas marked as the MRI had shown that I did in fact have two tumours taking up around 2.5cm overall.

We then went over to the nuclear medicine department where a nice radiographer allowed Sam to stay in the room whilst the procedure took place. They injected a radioactive dye alongside my nipple which tracked to the hottest lymph nodes

CHAPTER 8 | THE FINAL HURDLES

(sentinel) and then they took pictures and marked up the nodes under my arm. When we finally got back to the theatre suite it was almost lunchtime and my morning surgery slot had been and gone. At 12.40 they told Sam he had to leave as it was time for me to change for theatre, but at 1.20p.m. I was still waiting. When I asked how much longer it was likely to be, I was told perhaps another one to two hours, which upset me a bit because I could have been with Sam for longer.

I had not had anything to eat or drink since 6p.m. the previous evening and by now with the warm weather and the heat in the hospital, my lips felt as though they were sticking together so I took a small sip of water, which was a big mistake. I was called to go to theatre but because I had taken some water, they wouldn't now take me down for my surgery and I was subsequently put to the bottom of the list. They suggested I get dressed and go for a walk. I couldn't phone Sam as I had no money and no phone, and it never occurred to me to ask if I could use the phone in the department. I remembered that Sheelagh was still in hospital, so I went to find her. I didn't know if she was in a position to see me or even if she wanted to see me. The last message I had been given was that I would not be welcome. I found her in an isolation ward, so I needed permission from the nurses before I could go in and see her. I was a little nervous, but she was pleased to see me, which made me feel good.

She noticed I had a hospital wrist band on and asked why, so when I gave her my news, she was upset, but her own news was devastating. She had undergone two courses of chemotherapy already and it wasn't working, they told her that she would not survive and had given her just a month to live. I didn't know what to say, there were no words that would safely leave my lips and be appropriate for her predicament, so I just sat with her and chatted about nothing in particular. She tired quickly so I didn't stay long but promised to visit again when I could. I went back to the theatre suite and got changed again. It was 3.55p.m. when the anaesthetist put the canula into my hand and 6.30p.m. when I woke up in the recovery suite. My consultant had said the surgery had gone well but the sentinel node biopsy had shown there were positive cancer cells...I wasn't sure what that meant and was feeling very scared but not conscious enough to ask any questions. I was to learn later that they had performed a wide-local excision with an axillary clearance; in other words, they had removed the lump along with a percentage of healthy tissue together with seventeen of the lymph nodes under my arm.

When Sam had left the hospital in the morning, the nurse told him they would call him as soon as I was back on the ward. What I didn't know was that Sam had been trying to find out what was happening ever since he left me earlier in the day, and no one seemed to be able to tell him. They took me back to the ward at 7.30p.m. and my daughter and husband arrived shortly after. The relief on his face was palpable and I was in no position to explain what the surgeon had said in recovery at the time, but I was very keen to get home. I was allowed home the next day with a fluid drain in place, but before I left the hospital, I went along to see Sheelagh again, not sure if this might be the last time.

I had been given a little bag to carry the sac which held the fluid from my drain and whilst I was out I somehow managed to squeeze the drain causing a backpressure that moved it from its origin in the side of my breast. We phoned the hospital who simply said to push it back and see how it goes, so I asked Sam to do just that, and we thought it was ok. Anyone who has had cancer will be able to tell you that one of their biggest fears is the risk of lymphoedema and so when I got up the next day to find that my entire side was soaked in fluid, I knew that the drain wasn't working. I was sent back to hospital and the doctor I saw simply confirmed it wasn't working and rather than stitch it back in place, he took it out. It was the weekend and there was hardly anyone around who could or would put the drain back in place. I was told about the risks of a seroma, which is a fluid filled sac at the drain site and knew that I needed the drain to remove the fluid, but the doctor simply said I wouldn't get lymphoedema in the next 48 hours, so I shouldn't worry about it. Julie had told me that the key to preventing lymphoedema was to perform the exercises from the handout they had given me, but I wanted to learn more. I guess that's the thing about being a research scientist, you always want to know the latest advice and recommendations, so I set about reading some research papers again.[16]

The issues with the drain continued across the rest of July and I made several trips to the breast clinic to have the fluid released by needle aspiration. My concerns about lymphoedema grew each time the nurse stuck a needle in me to remove more fluid, particularly as it was one of the many pieces of advice you are given to help prevent lymphoedema:

- avoid any needles on the side of surgery,
- avoid carrying heavy bags/weights on the side of surgery
- improve your range of movement through exercise

- avoid having blood pressure taken on the side of surgery
- keep the skin clean and well moisturised and attend to cuts and grazes immediately

---

Some people are going to leave, but that's not the end of your story. That's the end of their part in your story.
Faraaz Kazi

I was getting bored and tried to tackle more of my thesis corrections but found it extremely difficult to concentrate. I was concerned about Sheelagh as I hadn't heard any more news from anyone and hoped that I might be able to make another visit. I wasn't allowed to drive until 28th July so as soon as I could I went to see her. I met her family who were all exceedingly kind to me, and Sheelagh told me rather proudly that her daughter was expecting her second child in December, she knew then that she would never get to meet her new grandchild. By now she was on oxygen and struggling so I didn't stay long. A couple of days later I received an email from a colleague at university to say that Sheelagh had passed away on the 29th July, the day after my visit. It was so unfair and so incredibly sad. She had taken me through my entire PhD, we fought a lot of battles with each other but all for my greater good, and she wasn't going to be around to see me finish or graduate. I shed many tears that day, the start of many and not all related to Sheelagh's passing.

My cancer diagnosis wasn't the best news I had received but to some extent I guess it wasn't totally unexpected either. I had spent eight years studying under extremely stressful conditions, and because I was totally focussed on achieving my goals, my marriage had hit the wall a few times along the way, which was yet another stressor. As I have mentioned in earlier chapters there is strong evidence that long term chronic stress can impact your immune system. It can increase the output of pro-inflammatory cytokines[17][18] and evidence for inflammation leading to tumorigenesis, or the activation of cancer cells is now firmly embedded in the research literature.[19][20] I tend to liken it to a mould that given the right conditions, gets out of hand. I didn't recognise those conditions in myself, nor did I do much to alleviate them because I was too involved in achieving my goals, so the lesson was a hard one for me to learn. I was now on the edge of a life-changing situation and needed to decide whether or not I wanted to continue treatment for my cancer. A meeting with my Oncologist informed me that the tumour had been a mixed invasive ductal and lobular carcinoma which had already spread to the sentinel lymph node. What this meant was that they were recommending further treatments as they had already observed a metastasis, and the prognosis for this situation was not as positive as perhaps it could have been.[21] Like a lot of women who go through this terrible ordeal, I was in a position where I needed to decide whether or not I wanted to undergo the recommended treatment plan for me of chemotherapy, radiotherapy, and hormone therapy, or whether I wanted to do nothing more. My natural instinct was to rebel and say no, I don't want anything else, but my logical brain told me that I needed more information before I could make that decision.

One of the things about being a researcher is that when something new comes to light you automatically want to be on it straight away, so when I heard about the Oncogene DX test, I did all I could to learn more. This test looks at 21 genes that have an effect on how a cancer is likely to behave and respond to treatment so it was likely to provide information that would help me make an informed decision about any additional treatments, particularly chemotherapy.[22][23] At the time, it was very new, and my Oncologist didn't know what to do with the information, but after many discussions with her she agreed to look into it further.

The test is not suitable for everyone and there are certain criteria you need to fit in order to have it. The value to me was that it was not only a predictive test, in as much that it would tell me if I would benefit from chemotherapy, but it was also prognostic, so was likely to tell me whether or not my cancer was going to return. This test is now available here in the UK through the NHS system along with other similar genomic testing techniques. As luck would have it, at the time of my own cancer diagnosis, the test wasn't available through our NHS system and the cost was nigh on £2000, so I needed to know if I was suitable for it before making the investment. My Oncologist promised to follow it up, but it was another 10 days before she finally came back and said that I really did need to decide about chemotherapy as the recommended time for commencement is usually within 30 days following surgery.[24]

She had said that I had an 80% chance of surviving more than 10 years without any treatment at all, so I was really confused when she was being so pushy...those odds looked pretty good to me. She then said that my risk of relapse if I didn't have treatment was 35%, but having chemotherapy was going to reduce that risk to 15%. Apparently, I had a macromestasis in the sentinel lymph node larger than 2mm which increased my risk of the cancer spreading, but then she said the overall benefit of chemotherapy to me was just 5%. My brain just couldn't compute everything she was saying and even having all the statistical evidence in front of me, my gut was seriously telling me not to go ahead with chemotherapy. It wasn't until I met with Julie, my breast cancer nurse again that it struck a chord. She said, *"for all your research and knowledge, you will never have the same insight as the doctors – they have 'experienced' the effects of cancer from those who have lived and those who have not, so they know what they are talking about and your knowledge & research cannot compete with that"*. And there it was, the facts as they truly were and not as I wanted to see them.

Alongside chemotherapy, which was to start on the 9th September, I still had my thesis corrections to do, and time seemed to be moving along way too quickly. The minor issues highlighted had mostly been sorted, but the statistical analysis was a real bugbear. It was a very lengthy test to perform, and I was struggling again. My plan was to try and complete the changes on four of the experimental chapters so that I could send them to Ivor before going to Scotland again. I was part way through this but still a long way off where I wanted to be with it all. Alongside all of this, we had decided to put the house on the market, and I had to ensure everything was looking it's best if we were going to entice the right buyer. I don't know what I was thinking, it was clearly not a good idea at this time to add yet another stressor to my already challenging lifestyle, but hey, you do daft things sometimes don't you?

The new statistical testing I was carrying out was, as I had feared, changing some of the outcomes, but in a positive way. It meant creating new graphs, changing some of the text and then rewriting the discussion and conclusion for the experiments, but at least I was moving forward.

Looking Back

When Sam and I were first together we played a lot, but when I went to university, I lost the child in me and I think I stopped playing. I forgot how and instead everything he did, said or suggested, seemed to annoy the hell out of me. Life was too serious, and it wasn't only about him, but also about me. Where was my fun, the child, the explorer, the flirtatious girl I had once been with him?

I allowed stress to impact my life, not just a little bit, but a lot, and we paid the price for that. Of course, it was never one sided, but those with whom you relate bounce off you, your moods, your voice, your body language, and it isn't easy to maintain a figure of confidence, peace, and gentleness when you feel your whole world is crumbling beneath you.

Only when you take a step back and reflect on your past can you fully appreciate the lessons that come your way. I felt this last two years had bought many lessons, not least was that I had been pushing myself too hard, and that the long-term consequences of doing that, came at a price.

That I had passed my viva voce examination and only had minor corrections, was I thought, an absolute gem, but trying to get those corrections done when so many other things were going on around me, felt like a whole new mountain to climb.

I was however able to pause for a while when Sheelagh passed away to genuinely appreciate how very much, she had given during my PhD. When I was right there in the thick of it, I didn't see that, and it is only when I could take that step back that I was fully able to embrace the care and concern she had bestowed upon me. She held my hand from day one, she didn't just do that though, she pushed me, she challenged me, she frightened me but most of all, she stood by me, and for that, I will be forever grateful.

CHAPTER 9
A hopeful road

> *The ultimate measure of a man is not where he stands in moments of comfort and convenience, but where he stands at times of challenge and controversy.*
>
> **Martin Luther King**

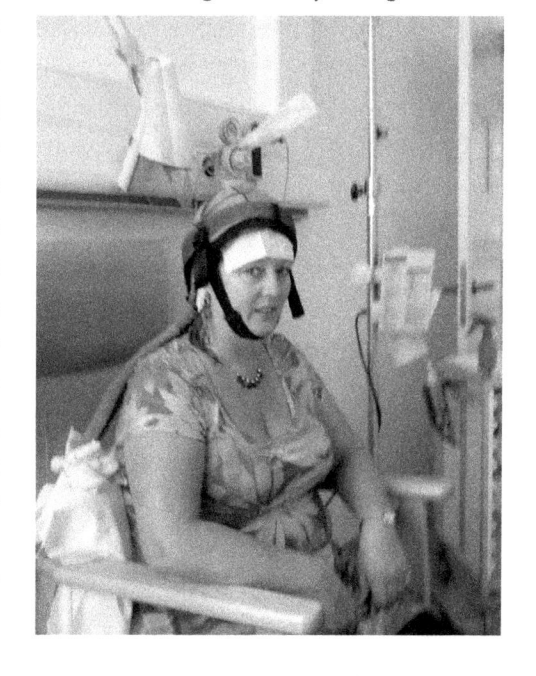

My very first chemotherapy session was on the 9th September as planned. I had received a good reflexology treatment in the morning and my daughter had accompanied me for my 10'clock appointment. My nurse was a pretty young girl who had only been working in chemotherapy for three weeks. She discussed the procedure and asked me whether or not I wanted to wear the cold cap, I was curious, why did I need a cold cap and what did it do? She explained that one of the many downsides to some chemotherapy drugs is that you are likely to lose all your hair, not just your head hair but your entire body hair. The cold cap or scalp cooling as it is sometimes referred, is supposed to offer the opportunity of preventing or reducing head hair loss. I decided that as I had a reasonable head of hair at the time, I would like to at least try and keep it, so I agreed, and she duly wet my hair and put the cap in place. I looked absolutely ridiculous as you can see from the photo, but hey, if it was going to help me keep my hair, it was a small price to pay.

I continued with my corrections as best I could and was grateful to be in a business where I knew so many other practitioners who were willing to offer me their help and support. I received regular reflexology and reiki throughout my course of treatments and an incredibly special friend of mine was providing me with top of the range nutritional supplements. I was however still not happy that the benefits of chemotherapy were worth all the challenges it was likely to present. Sam and I had discussed the idea of me discontinuing the treatment, partly because the advice we received from my Oncologist was a little confusing to us both. She was throwing all sorts of statistics at us and they didn't make any real sense. I met with Ivor just before travelling to Scotland so that I could hand over the corrections I had managed to complete so far. He explained that when they operate, the cells are disturbed and despite them telling me they had got everything, there was a minute chance that one or two cells could have escaped and migrated elsewhere. Then a few days later I heard from my friend in Scotland. She said that her mum had been treated for a melanoma on her arm but that some of the cells had migrated to her bowel and she was now being treated for bowel cancer. Were the angels telling me that I needed to continue treatment? Certainly, everything seemed to be pointing that way, so despite my own reservations I decided I would continue with the chemotherapy. It was, partly out of fear, because I had already been told that I had a macro metastasis in my lymph nodes, and partly for the benefit of my family.

It was the second day of our holiday in Scotland, and I noticed that my hair was full of knots, which was unusual for me. As I started to comb it through, it started to relieve itself from my scalp. I took a shower hoping that the hair conditioner would alleviate the knottiness but the more I massaged my head, the more hair left it, clearly the cold cap wasn't working on me.

Emotionally I was a wreck, crying at the drop of a hat. I lost more and more hair as the week progressed, but Sam hugged me close and reassured me we were in this together. I told myself there was absolutely nothing I could do about it, so I had better just get on with it. Toward the end of the week I hit a catalyst with my hair, I lost as much combing out the knots in one moment than I had done all week. It was time to do something about it, so I made the decision to get it cut short, but that was easier said than done. Peterhead is a small town near Aberdeen in Scotland and there aren't many hair salons, those that were available were fully booked and I ended up in a salon where they didn't speak good English. Despite giving an explanation about chemotherapy hair loss, they really didn't seem to understand my predicament and cut my hair so that I ended up looking like a world war 2 refugee, it wasn't a good look. When I arrived back home, I went to see my local hairdresser who did her best to make me look at least, a little more human.

Facing the future

I was feeling empty. I had spent a lot of years working on my research and despite still having the corrections to do, I needed to find another focus. I wasn't really in a position to continue my clinic work at that point in time and though it may seem odd, given that the research path was such a struggle for me, it somehow felt safe. I was at least part of a bigger community and I had created a circle of friends and colleagues on whom I could rely, even if just for a rant.

Some PhD students are able to secure a position within academia straight after completing their studies, but more often than not such positions are extremely difficult to obtain. There was no natural pathway for me within Portsmouth as I was the only person carrying out research in the field of complementary medicine. I couldn't teach pharmacy students as I didn't have the scientific acumen required, and quite honestly, I really didn't know what I did want to do next. I had found my PhD quite a traumatic experience, but at the same time it had given me a whole new skill set that I wanted to utilise. I certainly didn't want to go back into administrative roles again, so I decided to apply for some post-doctoral research positions with some of the local universities. One such position was for a Research Fellow at the University of Surrey in Guildford. It was a project running in conjunction with Macmillan Cancer Support and the National Cancer Survival Institute to look at the skills and confidence of practitioners working with the late and long-term adverse effects of cancer and its treatments. I had only just been diagnosed with cancer myself and prior to this had no previous in-depth knowledge about it, so I didn't really have the appropriate skills to carry out the research in this particular field, but nothing ventured, nothing gained, and I applied for the post. I was pleasantly surprised when I got invited to interview, but at the same time I was a little reticent about what I was heading into, was I crazy? Surely it was enough that I was going through my own cancer treatments, was I seriously wanting to learn more about it?

As is quite often the case with post-doctoral positions, it was for a fixed-term contract so I thought I would be okay. The interview was set for the afternoon of the 7th October which was the same day as my second chemotherapy session. The chemotherapy department was running late that day, and I wasn't able to use the cold cap for this session; but it's not like it had helped the hair loss after the first session, so I wasn't really too bothered. There were difficulties inserting the canula into my hand and one of the nurses who had tried had pushed the needle too close to the bone. When I arrived at the university for my interview my hand was both swollen and bruised. As is usual for this type of interview there were a team of people present, one of whom was the Professor of Cancer Nursing Practice. The research involved carrying out a mixed method analysis which is useful for research that is both quantitative and qualitative in nature and which is often used within nursing and health sciences.[1][2] I had only a limited experience of carrying out analysis on qualitative data, so I had tried to do some studying prior to the interview. When the job role was explained in more detail, I was a little baffled because it didn't reflect what had been posted in the job description. The professor said they were looking for someone who could hit the ground running and I was, needless to say, a little troubled that my own treatments would inhibit me. It felt to me that the interview didn't go well, and she had noticed the bruising on my hand, so I was duty bound to explain that I had just that morning, had my second chemotherapy session. She was the most supportive interviewer I had ever had the pleasure of meeting and thanked me for my honesty. To my absolute surprise I received an email later that day offering me the job, albeit at a lower salary than had been advertised because I had not yet graduated with a full PhD. It felt that it was a good starting point for me and a golden opportunity to learn more, so I accepted the position.

"Every day presents a new opportunity to grow and press forward to your success. Stay the course believing that where you are right now doesn't matter, as long as you are moving in the right direction."

Germany Kent

Chemo-brain and corrections

It was important to me that I continue to work through the corrections despite the sickness that came in great waves following chemotherapy, so I found myself with my head once again in my thesis trying to make the changes required following the Pitman test revisions. The graphs I was preparing were causing me some anxiety, as they were a little confusing. What made it all the more confusing was that Ivor was suggesting that the charts should be put into the appendix and not in the body of the thesis. It didn't make sense and I wasn't sure whether I was on my head or my arse. The chemotherapy seemed to be having an effect on my thought processes which scared the hell of me. How on earth was I going to continue to make the changes to my thesis and hold down a job in research if I couldn't think clearly?

I spoke with my breast care nurse who explained about the cognitive changes for people going through chemotherapy, often referred to as chemo-brain. She explained that it was quite common amongst cancer patients and might include things like:

- Extreme tiredness, fatigue
- Difficulty remembering things
- An inability to think clearly and being easily distracted

I was certainly beginning to feel that I was affected by it and it threatened my confidence quite markedly. I continued to work on my thesis corrections but felt weak and incompetent.

My diet was absolute shite, and my mouth was getting sore, so I didn't particularly want to eat. It was a rather dramatic way to lose some weight and it just seemed to fall off me. I had found some research about alternatives to anti-emetic drugs[3] and managed to control the sickness with an acupressure band so that at subsequent chemotherapy sessions I was able to refuse all medications other than those that were absolutely essential.

It was two weeks after my interview at Surrey and I still hadn't been given a start date. I had received a telephone call from Occupational Health who were concerned about me starting work whilst I was undergoing treatments. I wasn't sure if they were going to change their mind and it all became very unsettling. Sleep seemed to evade me, and my head was itching all the time, which seemed to trigger even more hair loss, so I made the decision that perhaps I would simply shave it all off, but I still needed to find the courage to do it and resign myself to what was in fact a fait accompli. Then, three weeks after my interview I finally received notification that I could start my new post on 1st November 2010.

In one of my experiments, where I looked at the effects of both standard and light reflexology on pain threshold and tolerance, the results were biphasic, that is, some subjects showed maximum pain tolerance scores in the early time period following treatment, and others showed maximum responses at a later time period following treatment. What this means is that traditional methods of graphically representing and analysing the data showed a distorted interpretation of the treatment effect.

Ivor had told me that in one of the pieces of research he had carried out on T.E.N.S and acupuncture, they had seen a similar response,[4] so he wanted me to separate that experimental chapter and split it into two chapters to offer a clearer rationale of the results. The results had shown that there were large inter-individual (differences between two people) variations between the participants, so I needed to carry out the special permutation test, on top of the other statistical analysis, to retrieve a more accurate result.[5][6][7][8]

You may recall from an earlier chapter, the literature for pain studies using acupuncture and hypnosis indicate that approximately 20 – 30% of participants are considered non-responders.[9][10][11][12][13] This meant that in addition to the other statistical analysis, the data could also be analysed by considering separately those participants who were considered to be "responders" and those who were considered to be "non-responders".

On examining the individual responses of my thirty participants, I was able to identify that twenty-four of them could be classed as responders and that six could be classed as "non-responders" because they showed almost no response. I had already created individual graphs for every single participant to review their pain threshold and tolerance responses, resulting in sixty different graphs, just as a starter. What he was asking me to do now felt like such a daunting task, made all the more difficult because I didn't really understand the permutation test to the level I needed, and right now, my brain just wasn't functioning at full capacity for me to be able to do so. There was however no way around it. If I was to finally get the piece of paper telling me I had achieved a PhD, then I needed to get my finger out of my arse and do all I could to make it happen.

During the August bank holiday weekend, I had been feeling quite good and decided to get up a ladder to cut back my wisteria tree. Don't we all do crazy things sometimes? As I reached the top of the ladder it toppled sideways and I came down with it, directly onto a concrete bench. I fell with my left arm in the air coming down hard onto the bench and turning the whole of the underside of my arm bright pink. I knew it was going to bruise and by the next day it was a very deep shade of purple from my ribs to my elbow...oops! There were in fact no immediate repercussions of that, other than it was extremely sore at the time, but now, two months on, it was beginning to swell all the time and I couldn't feel it underneath at all. In addition to that I was now also having pain under my arm and in the operated breast. My breast care nurse thought it was just the nerves settling down but referred me to my Oncologist so that she could re-examine me. The swelling continued and it appears that in addition to being diagnosed with lymphoedema I had further traumatised my nervous system, hence the numbness on the underside of my arm. I was fitted for a compression sleeve and compression bra, which was definitely not the sexiest looking thing I had ever worn.

As part of the NHS services for cancer patients you are offered a free wig if you want one, but the choices are not the best, so I decided that I would simply shave my head and wear a scarf. Sam had decided that if I were going to be bald, he was going to be bald too, so I invited my daughter over to dinner that evening so that she could record us doing it. It was scary but funny at the same time. I had a glass of wine for a bit of Dutch courage, and we made it a fun evening, but it was surprisingly cold without hair and I can now appreciate why bald-headed men often wear hats.

I had by now completed the changes to the first three experimental chapters and was feeling really good about the progress I had made, but the work I needed to do on the thesis, combined with the work I was doing at Surrey, and my treatments, soon began to take their toll and I started to feel really unwell again. Before each chemotherapy session it is usually necessary to have a complete blood count to check that your body is able to function at its optimal level and that there are enough white blood cells to help fight off any infections. They check: -

- the white cells that help fight infection and prevent the development of leukopenia,
- the red cells that prevent you becoming anaemic, and which help supply the oxygen to your tissues without having to work too hard to do it, and,
- the platelets that prevent your blood from clotting.

At my next chemotherapy session my Oncologist explained that my white cell count was low and that I was neutropenic, which simply means that I had low neutrophil count, a white cell that helps fight infection.

I already had a chest infection which was viral in nature and she explained that if my white cells didn't improve before the next session, I would need to inject myself daily with G-CSF a human growth hormone which increases the white cell count in the bone marrow. By now the veins in my right arm, where they had been injecting chemotherapy drugs, had started to collapse so she also recommended that I have a PICC line inserted. I didn't want either the PICC line or the human growth hormone so I looked to see how else I might be able to boost my immune system. As I wasn't doing well with eating, my friend recommended that I take cruciferous and flavonoid supplements. I established there was evidence that cruciferous vegetables help fight inflammation[14] and flavonoids have antioxidant properties that help prevent oxidative stress.[15] After discussing it with my Oncologist I made the decision to wait another month before starting with the growth hormone treatment to see if my white cell count would improve on its own. I'm all for trying to get your own body working without adding more chemicals. I really thought that my body was going through quite enough without introducing anything else that it had to process in order to function.

In the meantime, I needed to prepare the research I was doing at Surrey and set about how I was going to obtain the evidence I needed for it. I had also been chasing various avenues about lymphatic drainage techniques and hadn't really achieved much. I had however completed another chapter of corrections for my thesis, so felt positive and upbeat. It was time for another chemotherapy session, and even though I arrived early I didn't get seen for another hour. It was an extremely busy unit and during the first drug administration the nurse came over to take my blood pressure.

CHAPTER 9 | A HOPEFUL ROAD

Unfortunately, he had omitted to stop the flow of Epirubicin (a DNA damaging anti-cancer drug) and I had an immediate allergic reaction. On recognising the situation, he immediately stopped the flow and administered Piriton an antihistamine drug. The duty doctor was called, and he seemed to think it was a back flush of the drug whilst taking the blood pressure, but I was to discover later, that the incident wasn't recorded on my file. After 30 minutes they continued with the drug at a much slower pace and also put me on oxygen as I was incredibly light-headed, I couldn't read my book, as I often did, and really felt the need to sleep. As I was leaving the unit, I collapsed and was taken up to a ward for further tests but allowed home later that evening with some additional meds.

I had a meeting planned with Ivor the following day but was feeling really lethargic. Thankfully, the meeting was over in record time for Ivor and there were now only minor changes to make to the two chapters I had recently updated. I had planned to complete all my changes by the end of November, so I really needed to get a spurt on. I went up to the hospital to collect the growth hormone as my white cell count was still worryingly low and the nurse instructed me on how to inject my stomach, which I needed to do on a daily basis, five days post chemotherapy, for a five-day period.

I felt for Sam who was struggling emotionally and having to take care of me. He worked with a girl who had also been diagnosed with breast cancer but wasn't going to make it, so he constantly worried about me and wasn't sleeping. I found myself trying to remain optimistic for him, but I don't think it helped much. It was day five after my chemotherapy session and I needed to start my injections, but I had forgotten what the nurse had told me. Whilst at work, my boss had introduced me to the principal lecturer for chemotherapy training at Surrey and she very kindly showed me how to do it. She recommended that I do them just before bedtime as they can make the bones ache.

They were pleased with my progress so far at Surrey and the development of the study questionnaire I had prepared was almost complete. I needed to validate it with a peer group so we discussed who might be involved in that. However, the travel back and forth to Surrey was beginning to take its toll, the weather was getting worse with snow and ice and it took double the time it should have done due to major road improvements linking Portsmouth to London. Fortunately, my boss had agreed that I could work from home until the end of November because I had so many hospital appointments to attend that month.

I was having more and more difficulty with movement in my left arm and shoulder, so I engaged my friend Gunnel Berry, a very experienced physiotherapist to support me with pain management and exercise regimes. She is also a specialist in whiplash injuries and offers a remarkably successful technique called 'Adapted Reflex Therapy' for working in this and other areas of pain management. My consultant had examined my arm and thought that I had bruised the nerves which were irritated by the excess lymph fluid, so he gave me clearance to go ahead with lymphoedema treatment, which was easier said than done. When I went to see my breast care nurse about lymphatic drainage, she told me that they didn't provide a service for it, which I found truly astonishing. She did however give me details of a local practitioner who provided private treatments, and who came highly recommended. She was great, a gentle woman who really knew what she was doing. I went along for my first session and felt really good for a couple of days, but then the pain and discomfort returned. I was to learn later that in addition to lymphoedema I also had supracalcific tendonitis which seemed to be a progression of my osteoarthritis. Although loss of shoulder movement is not unusual following surgery for breast cancer[16] this further compounded the already restricted movement in my left arm.

Setbacks, disappointments, and frustrations

I had another meeting with Ivor, which didn't go well. He told me that he didn't have time to read through my thesis corrections and that it was unlikely I would be able to submit it before Christmas. I was absolutely devastated and also furious and felt incredibly dejected. He said that if I can get chapter seven and the general discussion done in the next ten days, he would take it with him to Thailand and if I give him a full copy of the whole thesis, he will attempt to read it over Christmas and then give it back to me to amend in the new year. He said I shouldn't worry about my deadline. Whilst I knew he had a heavy workload, the impact it had on my psychological state was too much. I needed it to be over. I hadn't wanted to go past Christmas and into a new year with corrections and still have to work on my PhD thesis. I had to dig down really deep inside in order to pull myself together but right then, I just wanted to throw it away. Sam was almost as furious as me and it took a while for me to gather my own feelings before I could help contain his anger, even though it wasn't directed at me. To help us both calm down he agreed to drive with me to Surrey to find an alternative route to the horrendous road works I was having to encounter on a daily basis, then in the afternoon I set about writing out the full research proposal for my post-doctoral research at Surrey.

The following week was my fourth chemotherapy session, and I was astounded when my Oncologist told me that she knew nothing of the previous incident in relation to backflow of the drug into my arm. When I explained, she wanted to add Piriton and hydrocortisone to my pre-chemo meds just in case I had a further 'allergic' reaction and because by now, the tissue around my wrist was starting to show signs of breaking down. At home, later that day, I received a call from the nurse who had administered the drugs and caused the incident, claiming that I must have been mistaken and that he did not, and would not, have left the drug flowing whilst taking my blood pressure. I couldn't quite believe what I was hearing and knew that I had to do something about it.

At the start of session four, I needed to be canulated because they couldn't find a decent vein, it took five attempts and the whole thing was so distressing that I had to call Sam home from work to pick me up. The Piriton just sent me to sleep, and I felt drowsy for a number of hours afterwards, so I called my boss to explain the situation and she suggested I record the day as sick leave. At the end of this chemo session, they mentioned again that I have a PICC line inserted, which is a peripherally inserted central catheter. The line is inserted into a vein inside your arm and ends up in a large vein in your chest. The drugs are then delivered straight through this line without the need to go through the trauma of trying to find a vein in which to insert the drugs at every visit. It was then that Sam had decided I would not attend another chemotherapy session alone and he scheduled annual leave for all subsequent sessions so that he could be with me.

Later I received a call from my Oncologist to say that she would recommend a Hickman line in my chest, rather than a PICC line. This is more central and is tunnelled under the skin of the chest into a large vein just near the heart, and the end of it, the bit where they inject the drugs, comes out to sit on the chest surface. She thought it would be more manageable for me than the PICC line which would be put in through my arm. The problem with anything that goes in like this is that you leave yourself open to infection, blockages, and perhaps even blood clots. My sister-in-law had to have a Hickman line and had developed a blood clot, so I was a little apprehensive about having one myself, and after speaking with a colleague I decided the PICC line was going to be the better option for me.

At the beginning of December, I met another Oncologist to discuss the next stage of treatments, radiotherapy. I was to have 15 sessions which would reduce my risk of a local recurrence from 15% to just 4%, but because my cancer was on my left breast, it carried a longer-term risk of heart disease.

I had my PICC line fitted on the 14th December and it didn't go well. After the line was inserted, I needed to have X-rays taken to make sure it had gone into the right place. Two attempts sent the tube into my neck, rather than into my chest and after the second attempt I lost it and was uncharacteristically angry with everyone. They called in an IV specialist who was incredibly assertive and not very gentle, but she got the job done whilst somebody else compressed my neck so that the line didn't go back up there. The downside was that due to the placement right in the elbow crease, it wouldn't stop bleeding. It took five hours to complete the insertion of the PICC line, which was a huge chunk of my day and I didn't get much work done.

I picked up another chest infection, my breathing became very laboured, and I was sent for an echocardiogram as a precautionary measure. I also had a massive cold sore and was really feeling the effects on my immune system. It seems I'm rather a sensitive soul because the dressings on my arm also started a flare reaction which was irritating my skin, it was all beginning to get a little too much. At my fifth chemotherapy session I refused the Piriton, believing the only reason I had been given it was because my Oncologist thought it was a reaction to the drug I was given. In my opinion it was because the nurse took my blood pressure whilst administering the drug and I wanted to prove it.

I completed the changes to chapter seven and regained some energy so that I could complete more work on my final chapter, the discussion chapter. My cough had eased off and I was beginning to gain some of my strength. I had spent many days pondering over the decision I was about to take but I knew that if I had to take my corrections through to 2011, I would walk away from it all and finally give in. I had jumped through hoops with this research, I had given in to every request made to me on the changes but felt I couldn't do it any longer. The chemotherapy was taking its toll, my work at Surrey was developing into something really interesting and I was keen to get on with my life. The corrections I felt, were holding me back and I felt that I was drowning without hope of ever resurfacing. I met with Ivor for the final time on 23rd December to gain his feedback on what I had already achieved, and he gave me yet more to complete. I made the decision there and then that I would submit my corrections by the end of December 2010 and if it weren't good enough, so be it. I could not and would not take it any further, so after nine really stressful and challenging years I was finally done.

I had by now completed my chemotherapy sessions and commenced radiotherapy. My right arm was swollen due to thrombosed veins which meant I couldn't hold anything properly. I ached everywhere and had classic symptoms of trochanteric bursitis so when they mentioned I now needed to consider taking a five year course of adjuvant hormone therapy, I set about reading up on it.[17][18] Adding to this, the extravasation (a leakage of fluid from a vessel into the surrounding tissue) from the chemotherapy backflow was now causing a breakdown of the tissue in my right forearm and I was concerned there may be some long term effects, which would not be good for my work as a therapist.[19]

Christmas came and went and for a little while I was able to concentrate on something other than my thesis. I continued to progress my work at Surrey and was starting to get some good data back from those who had taken the survey. I still needed to pay attention to my health as I was struggling with a lot of bone pain, especially at night. It worried me, because I had a friend who had a previous history of breast cancer that had gone to the bone, she had died from the metastasis. I saw my Oncologist again who arranged for me to have a bone scan which revealed major osteoarthritic changes in almost all my joints, but thankfully no metastasis.

On the 4th February, I received a call from Ivor to tell me that they had approved my PhD corrections, and, on the 10th February, it was made official in a letter from the academic registry where they were confirming the award of Doctor of Philosophy. I had finally achieved my PhD after eight years of study, and a year of corrections; quite honestly, I didn't know how to react. I was ecstatic, relieved, elated even, but with everything else that was going on around me, I questioned whether it had actually been worth it. Did we celebrate, hell yes, but the real party would have to wait until after I had completed my cancer treatments and my graduation in July.

I'm thankful for my struggle because without it I wouldn't have stumbled across my strength.

Alex Elle

The issue with the leakage of fluid in my forearm was something that I needed to address, if not for my sake, then for the sake of others going through chemotherapy. I took advice from my colleagues at Surrey before writing a letter to the Chief Executive at the hospital where I had received my treatment. My concern was that there appeared to be a lack in competency. It may have been that because this was the research area I was currently undertaking, I was more focused, but I did feel that I had a duty to report the issue and ensure procedures were set in place to prevent it happening again. After several communications involving the Chief Executive of the hospital trust and the Lead Cancer Nurse at the Haematology and Oncology centre, I received confirmation that procedures were being updated and the nurse practitioner involved in the incident was to undergo further competency-based training. A satisfactory result.

Graduation Day

On the 18th July 2011 I was finally going to graduate. I was both pleased and disappointed. Pleased that I was, after nine years, finally going to receive academic acclaim for all my hard work and endeavours, and disappointed that Sheelagh, with whom I had shared that journey, who had held my hand for so much of it, was not going to be present. It was a bitter-sweet success.

My hair had started to grow back after the chemotherapy but when it did, it was very curly and short, when previously it had been straight and long, so when I put on the graduation Tam, or Tudor bonnet as it is also known, I looked rather ridiculous. I hadn't opted for official photographs of the graduation, maybe my own vanity didn't allow it, I'm not really sure, but my friends and family did take a couple of snaps across the day. In fact, Simone, who had graduated in 2008 with her own PhD, was able to sit on stage and be present for the entire ceremonial procedure. She filmed me marching across the stage to collect my scroll from Dame Sheila Hancock, the then Chancellor of the University of Portsmouth, whilst my husband Sam was cheering extremely loudly and proudly from the audience alongside my parents.

I was only allowed to have three people present within the ceremonial hall, and that was mum, dad and Sam, so my daughter Claire and my friend Sam, watched the ceremony on a big screen that was set up in the Guildhall Square just outside. Despite the fact that Sam, Simone, and I didn't graduate the same year, I still wanted a photograph of the three of us together in our graduation gowns. As Simone had been on stage, she already had her gown, but I remember Sam didn't have one, so she borrowed one from someone else who was considerably taller and wider, just so that we could have the photo taken.

To be perfectly honest, the whole day seemed to be a bit flat. I'm not sure what I was expecting, but it just didn't seem real somehow. I celebrated with my friends and family at home later that day and people came and went, but it was still a 'nothing' kind of day. I was pleased to have finally graduated but I missed Sheelagh, she was supposed to be there, she was supposed to share in the celebration and the achievement, and it just wasn't the same. I think perhaps I had hoped that I might be finally able to sit down with Sheelagh and Ivor and have an adult lunch, an adult conversation where they weren't my mentors but were just friends helping me to celebrate in this momentous title I now had.

My contract at Surrey was due to come to an end in August 2011 and I was keen to get some publications under my belt from the results, especially as I had not yet published from my PhD. The thing is, if you want to progress in academia after completing a PhD, it is really important to publish research papers, the saying goes 'publish or perish' and at the time I thought this path was my future. Sheelagh was always keen for me to publish in scientific journals because it means you stand out from others in your field, but at the same time there is huge competition with academics who may be far more experienced than you. Having something published that is peer-reviewed can influence your future job applications as well as any grants you seek for further research, and I had hoped that I was on track for a future in either academia or research.

I had carried out a large study of qualitative research, a first for me and I learned a lot in the process. It was challenging work alongside my corrections and cancer treatments but such a great learning curve too, particularly as I had gained a very personal insight into cancer and its treatments. At the same time, I was examining the skills and confidences of those who were providing me with those treatments. Right place, right time?

My research brief had been to carry out a qualitative survey to establish how late effects of cancer treatments are managed by both primary and secondary care practitioners. The aim was to establish if they felt ready and confident in managing what are termed 'late adverse effects', something that had not previously been carried out in this field. We were also looking at where there may be gaps in their knowledge and skills, so that the results could be used to propose a framework of competencies in developing educational programmes of the future. Whilst the continuing education strategy of the World Health Organizations[20] for nurses and midwives in cancer care made provision for many other areas, it did not include educational training in the late-adverse effects of treatment on its cancer survivorship programme. This was innovative work, and I was delighted to be a part of it.

The proposed target audience for my research were primary and secondary care staff working in haematology and oncology, but as a complementary practitioner I asked if I might also include a cohort of complementary and alternative medicine practitioners as well as allied health practitioners such as physiotherapists, occupational therapists etc.

Nursing staff at the time were educated mainly on prevention, treatment and palliation so were much less skilled in managing the long-term consequences of treatment.[21,22] We know that cancer patients like to be involved in their own care[23] and the services of CAM practitioners have been used in hospital and hospice care for many years, so involving the CAM community in the survey was important.

Those that work in this area will know that there has been a growing demand for complementary therapies within the cancer service provision. Supporting the knowledge and confidence of primary and secondary care providers so they may be able to refer to these services[24,25,26] is crucial for our future integration. By the same token, the same may be said of complementary therapists who lack knowledge of cancer biology.[27] If a system of integration is to be supported, then it's clear there must be a two-way learning process in all of this. Cancer is now considered a chronic illness and I know from my own personal experience that there is still a vast gap in the unmet needs of many survivors.[28,29] The culmination of my work at the University of Guildford resulted in two reports for Macmillan Cancer Support and two further published papers.[30,31] I was pleased to hear, at a later date, that there was also now a competence framework for nurses caring for patients living with and beyond cancer, and that I had been part of that initial process.

Obviously, I didn't know it at the time, but it was to shape some of what I do now and reminds me that everything has a place in life, even when we are not totally aware of it.

Looking Back

Oftentimes we are unaware of the impact of our actions. I realised that I was under stress on many occasions across the eight years that I studied for my PhD, and yet I didn't fully appreciate how it might put me in a high-risk situation and threaten my life.

One would think that my experiences of the tsunami in 2004 and the subsequent issues I had with post-traumatic stress syndrome, and then finding a lump in my breast, would have set me up for closer monitoring, but that wasn't the case. My vision was always the successful ending of my PhD and yet that success had almost cost me my life.

Cancer impacts many people across the world and like many of these dreadful diseases it has consequences in the long term. Despite this startling reality I genuinely believe that these things happen for a reason. Do we run full steam ahead, engage all our resources just to suffer the consequences, or do we learn from these events? I like to think it is the latter.

I am certain I was put in the right place at the right time and not for the first time either. My life seems to have been guided and yet I didn't really feel the enormity of my success, so I still question, what is success?

For me it was a goal, something that truly motivated me. I started out as a non-academic, without a single qualification to my name, I fought hard battles to get a PhD and there was a tremendous drive in my life whilst I was doing it, but now, now it all felt flat.

CHAPTER 10
What future beckons?

*Don't be afraid of your scars, they are a reminder that you are a survivor.
You are stronger than whatever tried to hurt you.*
Author unknown

After a six-month extension of my original contract, my work at Surrey came to an end. I had completed the research I had been recruited for and as a follow up I had been asked to carry out a literature review on whistleblowing, which I had hoped might lead to another research post. I felt the diversity of the post-doctoral fellowship would provide me with an opportunity to expand my skills further and might even open up research in a new area for me, or perhaps even an entirely new field. Unfortunately, it didn't and my time at Surrey was over. It seems my academic writing was not quite what they were looking for in that role and that really hit my self-confidence again. What was the point of all the research? What had I learned and how was I going to use what I had learnt to progress my future? I beat myself up for a while and then came to realise that much of what I was trying to achieve was happening at a time when I was still healing from my cancer treatments and my levels of concentration were not where they should have been.

There was however a void in my life, and I didn't know what to do. I was empty, my life was empty. I had completed my PhD., I had gone on to do some post-doctoral research in a field that I was unfamiliar with, and now that was over too. I didn't cope well and fell into a deep dark hole, where I remained for several months.

It was now 2012 and Sam and I had so far been unsuccessful in selling our house and so I made the decision to make a fresh start in my clinic. I missed people, that feeling of connecting and I needed to fill that void. I sought help from a counselling friend with whom I would spend many hours just talking, and gradually found enough strength to be able to face clients again. Truth be told I missed working with my clients and I needed to feel that I could make a difference again. It all started out fine, but something didn't feel right. My beautiful clinic at the bottom of the garden was no longer the oasis of peace and tranquillity it had been prior to my research, and I felt trapped. There was a different energy in the room and although I tried moving things around, removing all my research papers and rearranging it so that it had a better flow, it didn't change. I even did some feng shui and sage clearing, but still, it didn't feel right. The immense feeling of belonging there and the grounded connection that I had once had in that space, had gone. A feeling of uselessness started to creep over me again, and I didn't know what to do about it.

I started looking at external complementary therapy centres, places where I could be part of a larger unit and still offer my services as a practitioner, but it was to take a while before I could build up my client base again. I hadn't been a practitioner for almost two years and many of my original clients were now seeing someone else. Some came back, whilst others were happy where they were. Previously I had offered treatments outside of normal hours to accommodate my client base, but I wasn't ready for that this time, and I think not doing so made a difference. My shoulder was still problematic and many of the body work treatments I offered felt as though they were far too labour intensive for me. I persevered for a little over twelve months but struggled to regain sufficient clients to keep me afloat financially. My self-esteem and confidence were on the floor and I felt like I was walking through treacle. It was almost like a bereavement and yet I had so much to offer, I just didn't know how to use it.

I tried to balance my clinic with looking for jobs in academia or research, but there was very little available in the complementary medicine field. I became quite jealous of my colleagues who seemed to have fallen on their feet with work. Why wasn't I doing the same? What was it about me that didn't fit? There was a lot of inner questioning and I guess, self-destruction too. Of course, I understood why they were more easily able to gain work, they were both proper scientists who had come up through undergraduate training, so had the right skillset. And it hit me, I hadn't done any undergraduate training, I had been in the right place, at the right time, for the right reason but I didn't have a science background. I hadn't done any formal undergraduate degree so there was a huge gap in my skill set for the roles I might otherwise have applied for.

I took a step back and realised that many post-doctoral positions were on fixed-term contracts and I wanted something I could get my teeth into again. If you are lucky, you will find a position that leads onto another post-doctoral position within your university, or it can serve as a springboard for your future in academia. For many of us you just seem to be chasing after a new contract in another university that wants your skill set for a particular period of time. You need to think about how far you want to travel for your work and how that might impact on your relationships. If you are happy to move around from one place to another, or keen to progress in research to secure something more fixed, then you will likely fare better than I did. I learned that there is a scarcity of post-doctoral research available in complementary and alternative medicine and many of the teaching posts available at the time were based in London, which would add a further four and half hours in travel time to my day and probably be incredibly stressful. I was scared of putting myself under too much stress, I didn't want to risk my life for research, so whilst I did need a job, I wasn't sure I really wanted a research job. It was time to rethink my future.

I resolved to pick myself up and get off my arse to perhaps do something else for a while. I applied for a job at Southampton University Hospital NHS Trust. It wasn't what I had in mind but at the time I had to get back out amongst people, and I felt it would give me back a little of my confidence. I learned really quickly that there is a danger in having a PhD. When you apply for a non-academic position in industry you appear over-qualified, and so many employers knock you back on that basis without you even getting to the interview stage because they think you won't stay. It is a contest, and you really need to sell the transferrable skills you have developed to fit the job.

I applied because the job role offered a teaching opportunity to healthcare workers and at the same time combined an administrative role supporting educational needs. It was a foot in the door, and I felt it was a step in the right direction. It had been many years since I had done any formal teaching or undertaken office work and I had completely forgotten how bitchy it can be in an office. I struggled to fit in to this particular environment and although they often talked about me teaching neuroanatomy and physiology, it never came to fruition. It wasn't the job I had hoped it would be and after almost 18 months I decided to give my notice. I'm not sure if it was a good thing or a bad thing but there wasn't much work for me to do in that role, and I truly hate boredom. Not having enough to do in a job, is almost as stressful as having too much to do, so I started to work on some ideas for my future and in particular for my own workshops, but I wasn't quite there yet. It had been a while since I had done any real progressive teaching and I was struck once again by a lack of self-confidence.

Who am I?

I was back at square one again. All the time I had been at university I was focussed on what lay ahead, the tasks I needed to get done and the pressures of deadlines. It was an adrenaline fuelled ride, but when suddenly that adrenaline stops, you kind of crave it again.

Whilst I am fully aware that the person responsible for how you progress in life is largely you, when you are presented with opportunities that come knocking at your door, only you can decide whether or not you want to grasp them. I was becoming a victim of my own self-doubt. Berating myself for lack of action and inducing a negativity that went against my entire personality. I couldn't find the things that made me stand out, the strengths I had, and life just frustrated the hell out of me. It was almost like I had given my heart and soul and yet for all of it, I hadn't actually achieved anything.

Finishing a PhD is a major life event like marriage, divorce, moving home etc. but no one tells you about the PhD comedown when you start out, and it takes a while to learn.[1][2] There was no passion in me anymore and my resilience was weakening to the point that I felt that I had lost all control over my life. I think I also felt like a bit of a failure, but I couldn't really tell you why. I was I think frightened of languishing about and of losing all that I had learned. The PhD was the only thing I knew, and it had been a constant source of hope, anxiety, direction, and transformation for the best part of eight years, but life wasn't working out the way I thought it would. It didn't transform my life and I didn't feel as though I had particularly gained a clear destination.

It isn't unusual for a PhD student to go through this kind of self-doubt, and in fact many will feel as though they are always not quite good enough. I went through a huge period of introspection and knew that I needed help, but I wasn't sure where to get it. There was no pastoral role available to me now that I was no longer attached to a university, there was no guidance about my future prospects or what I might be able to offer in either an academic or commercial environment. It was just me, left to my own devices. I had earned my PhD and had a new identity as a 'doctor', but I also felt incredibly abandoned by it too. Where was I going?

There were still things to do at home, in fact we had by now, just sold our house and were in the process of moving, so that gave me a whole new list of things to occupy my mind. It was actually a bit of a lifesaver for me, and I threw myself into all those things you want to change about being in a new home, but it was also stressful because there was a lot to do. It felt like there was a new beginning and I had to grab it with both hands if I were to get myself out of this dreadful hole I felt I was in. There were still the usual stresses of life, the things that you hope to leave behind if you ignore them long enough, but they do eventually come back to bite you on the bum, and my future was one of those things and I craved some direction.

I had learned a lot from my PhD, and there were many life lessons that came with it too. I was hardworking, focussed and certainly tenacious, but I still didn't have that sense of true direction I was searching for.

If you do not change direction, you may end up where you are heading

Lau Tzu

I have found myself at a spiritualist church on more than one occasion across my adult lifetime, and learned how to develop my innate intuitive side, which often served me well with general life observations. It was whilst I was sitting in a psychic development circle that I met Nigel, an ex-policeman turned hypnotherapist. I don't know whether it was my body offloading the long-held stresses and tensions, or whether there was some kind of spiritual awakening going on within me, but every single time that I went into a meditative state I would end up in floods of tears. In fact, our facilitator would put the tissues in front of me as soon as I took my place in the circle. I experienced many profound and life affirming events during this time and started to feel that maybe I was finally going to find my true direction. At the beginning of my journey in complementary medicine I had been a really good reiki practitioner and I felt a real need to get back to that healing environment. What I was learning was that I needed to heal myself before I could take responsibility for and accept that only I could make a difference, that it was my thoughts and feelings that were going to change the direction of the rest of my life and no one else's.

As many do in group environments, you talk, talk about your life, your shared experiences, and your hopes for change. Nigel had recently started to work with clients who, like me, felt lost and directionless. He told me about a programme called 'THRIVE' which is an evidence-based mental health training programme that teaches people the skills they need, to overcome mental health challenges.[3] Now, I didn't see myself as having a mental health issue by definition, so I was a little reluctant at first, but decided to go along and learn more, and I am so glad that I did, as this six-week programme was to change my life forever. Every aspect of the training challenged my thinking, my belief systems, and my comfort zone. It wasn't an easy journey, but then the truth never is. For me it was about taking the control back in my life, about finding the real me and running with it.

Quite naturally, like me, Sam had thought that the PhD would change our lives for the better, that I would get a good job, that I would be very well paid for that job and that we would get our lives back. It didn't turn out that way and although he never once put pressure on me to get a job, staying at home all day was not my idea of fun and I decided to take on a temporary position with Southampton university in administration. The role was easy, but again there wasn't much for me to do and so I started to write up the outline of my first workshop.

In April 2013 I published my first research paper[4] from my thesis and was invited to give an interview about it with the Portsmouth university media team. I was out of the country at the time, and so Ivor gave the interview on my behalf. The interview was published on the university internet and invited a huge amount of attention from both national and international press. It was subsequently published in many of the UK national papers as well as the Nursing Times and as far and wide as America and India. I was absolutely astonished by the attention it had received and it was an enormous boost to my morale which gave me the confidence I needed to move forward with my life.

I had been using Nerve Reflexology for nine years and following my PhD I had supported Nico Pauly, one of the Directors of MNT-NR International (Manual Neurotherapy – Nerve Reflexology) with his UK training programme. After another successful diploma here in the UK, and for the second time, Nico invited me to take over the training, and I now felt ready. As a shadow teacher I regularly found that I needed to be close to wherever Nico was speaking. Many of the rooms we hired had high ceilings, so the noise would bounce and echo around the room making it much more difficult to gain clarity from his speech. It was a major hurdle that I needed to overcome. You may recall from previous chapters that I had already experienced hearing problems, but it seemed that it had got much worse again. At home, Sam was becoming increasingly frustrated at having to repeat himself and for me, it meant that my hopes of teaching might never get off the ground. I was informed that I was experiencing sensorineural hearing loss, which is a condition caused by damage to the auditory nerve that connects your ear to your brain and is unfortunately irreversible. I discovered that it's not unusual for some chemotherapy drugs to affect the hair cells in the ears and it is those hair cells within the cochlea that receive the sound and send it along the auditory nerve to the brain.[5][6][7] I had lost pretty much all body hair both internally and externally following my chemotherapy treatments, so I really shouldn't have been surprised.

I was absolutely terrified that I wouldn't be able to pursue my plans to teach and that any decrease in communication would lead to further social isolation and perhaps in the longer term may even alter my cognitive awareness.[8] I was already actively avoiding any situation where there was a lot of background noise and I even turned down invitations to speak at conferences because I was worried that I wouldn't be able to hear any questions the audience may ask. The psychological impact of hearing loss can, in some people, lead to periods of depression, but for me I think it was embarrassment and the thought that people may think me stupid, and that concerned me, and in turn affected both my self-esteem and confidence.

I have often been perceived as being rude and off-hand when meeting people who don't know that I am hearing impaired. The effect can be very disheartening and so I had a tendency not to speak at all. I would miss out on conference talks and workshops, particularly where there were foreign speakers, when strong accents make clarity untenable for me. I had to really focus on hearing what was being said and would spend so much effort on doing so that it detracted from absorbing what was actually said, so I ended up learning next to nothing.[9] It is such hard work and has given me a real appreciation for those who continue to struggle with communication issues because of hearing loss.

I was offered a pair of NHS hearing aids, but they were basic acoustic levellers and didn't filter out background noise, so I searched the market for other types and discovered that I could get some funding support. I managed to find hearing aids that were far more state of the art and had various filters and channels that I could change or programme according to my environmental needs at the time. That was a real eureka moment, the answer to my dreams and a real game-changer.

Nerve Reflexology

Nerve reflexology originated in Germany through the work of Walter and Ellen Froneberg but has been further developed by the team of professionals at MNT-NR International including Nico Pauly, Griet Rondel and Norbert Gosh. I was honoured to have been invited to teach with such a great team, but it is not for everyone. As you might expect when talking about the nervous system there is a lot of theory involved, much of which is incredibly in-depth and at a level not usually taught to reflexologists here in the UK. The nerve reflexology diploma course involved a lot of rewriting. It had been a long time since I had done my initial training with Nico and it had gone through many new developments over the years, so I needed to do more research, more revision and then work out how I wanted to teach it. I decided to start off by giving an introductory workshop on what I really knew I had a handle on, and that was pain science. Supporting the client in pain with reflexology was my first workshop development but I needed somewhere to teach it, where I would feel comfortable and safe. Nothing too big and not too many people and then a colleague offered me an opportunity to take the workshop to London in a close-knit environment with just six students. I knew my stuff, I had rehearsed the presentation and the scheme of work for the day, but I was still so nervous. I needn't have been, they were a lovely group of practitioners, all keen to learn and all happy with their training. It was just what I needed and was to be the start of my new career in CPD workshops for reflexologists who were supporting clients in pain. It seems I had finally found my new direction.

CHAPTER 10 | WHAT FUTURE BECKONS

The day I found my smile again was when I stood in my own storm and danced with my tribe

Shannon L Alder

Meeting my peer group

I remember meeting Sally Kay back in 2012, at a time when my morale was low and when I was experiencing a lot of lymphoedema in my arm and upper chest. I had finished my post-doctoral research at Surrey and wanted to know more about the research she was doing with reflexology and lymphoedema. I had personally struggled to locate a good Manual Lymphatic Drainage (MLD) practitioner in my area but was lucky enough to receive some funding from my local health authority to access it privately. I knew from the research I had carried out at Surrey that there was a great demand after cancer treatments for lymphoedema management. That need was largely unfulfilled because there was little support within the NHS, so I was extremely interested to know about Sally's progress in this area of research. She had just completed her first round of tests with six participants and the results were promising. She was coming down to my area to teach, I think it was one of her very first workshops, so we agreed to meet midway between my home and the training venue. Sally had just won the Federation of Holistic Therapists (FHT) Excellence in Practice Award and recommended that I apply myself. I didn't know that you had to blow your own trumpet, something I'm not particularly good at, and a bit of anathema to me, so I was forced to step out of my comfort zone so that my research could gain some form of recognition. I was glad that I did because in 2014 I received the Federation of Holistic Therapists Excellence in Practice Award for my research. It felt really good to have that recognition and it was the first time any umbrella organisation had acknowledged my achievement.

I met Judith Whatley, a senior lecturer at Cardiff Metropolitan University and Sally's dissertation supervisor, along with Barbara Scott the author and specialist in 'Reflexology for Fertility' when I gave a talk on my research at the Reflexology in Europe Network (RiEN) conference in Madeira in 2014. I was delighted when I heard that both Sally and Judith were able to attend the FHT presentation dinner later that year. Alongside them was the wonderful Lynne Booth who has been a dear friend and supporter of mine since we met at Nico's first nerve reflexology workshop in 2004.

When we attended the awards ceremony, I still lacked confidence and was visibly shaking when I received the award, I couldn't speak, other than to say thank you and yet inside there seemed to be so much I should have said. Three years later I received the same award from the Association of Reflexologists (AoR) who finally recognised my contribution to the field of reflexology. It was a good feeling. These ladies have featured in my career path ever since. They are my support group, my inspiration, and my go to colleagues. We have a great relationship and support one another in so many different ways, in all aspects of our lives and I am grateful for their friendship and trust.

When I took the nerve reflexology training to Wales for the first time, Sally and Judith both attended the workshop. There were sixteen participants that weekend and I was suffering chronic low back pain after the three-and half-hour drive North. It can be an incredibly labour-intensive workshop when you are trying to ensure that all participants are placing their thumbs in exactly the right place, with the right pressure direction in the correct manner. Judith pointed out to me that I would be unable to sustain this type of teaching over long periods of time, and there were just too many participants for one person alone to manage. So, I decided to reduce the number of participants on each workshop, and I now run with small groups of around twelve at a time. Across the years I have perfected the training and have taught a vast number of practitioners. I like to think that I give everything I can to a workshop and that it is appreciated by those who attend, but I also recognise that we all learn at a different pace. I have changed the workshop so many times to accommodate the many different learning styles but have come to recognise that you cannot meet the needs of everyone, despite your best effort. I would encourage you, if you are a reflexology tutor, to ensure that your students are able to palpate and draw the bones on the feet, rather than simply labelling a sheet of paper with a foot skeleton on it. It is a much better way to learn the bones of the feet and enables practitioners to work from the spinal line in a much more accurate way. We are talking about an anatomical reflection theory, and if you are unable to place the spinal nerves correctly, your anatomy may be way off point. I would also like to encourage you to share more detail on the nervous system, particularly on the different sections of the autonomic nervous system.

Pain in Cancer Survivors

My experience with cancer and the pain that followed provided me with an insight into how it felt, and I was curious as to why it was happening. It would have been easy to put everything down to chemotherapy but I knew better than that and so I set about reviewing the literature, both medical and complementary and built my workshop around it. When I did my research at Surrey, I invited 21,000 CAM practitioners to complete an online survey about skills and confidence in working with the late and long-term consequences of cancer and its treatments. Six hundred and twelve practitioners responded and five hundred and seven said they were working in this area. The things most often treated were either of a psycho-social nature or related to pain and/or lymphoedema.[10] I remember hearing someone somewhere saying that *"there is a terrible irony about cancer and that is, that for someone to survive the onslaught of cancer, they might spend the next decade or more coping with neuropathic pain caused by the very treatment that ensures their survival"*. Indeed, my personal experience of cancer treatment taught me just that.

We are surviving longer but many are living with cancer-related pain and that is proving to be a much more difficult challenge for many survivors. When I attended a CPD cancer pain study day with the British Pain Society, I recall Dr Arun Bhaskar stating that higher doses of opioids increase pain, not decrease it. He said, *"you do not increase the amount of radiotherapy or chemotherapy, so why do medics increase the use of opioids? If it's not working, it's not working!"* Opioid medications don't work in the long term because they mask our own inbuilt warning system, the nociceptive system which tells us that we are in danger. When we receive that initial warning, free nerve endings send a message along the spinal cord to the brain, to tell us that something, somewhere isn't functioning as it should. It then goes into self-protect mode, triggers the fight or flight response, and releases a number of neurochemicals into the bloodstream. Those neurochemicals may include cortisol and endorphins, our body's own natural painkillers. When we take opioid medications, which are much stronger than our own in-built mechanisms, the body can't respond in the same way, so instead of only being on alert when there is real danger, it now senses every touch sensation as a warning and ramps up our pain experience creating a state of hyperalgesia.

At the time I wrote the workshop for 'Pain in Cancer Survivors' I had been eight years post original cancer diagnosis, so I could relate to much of what was written in the literature. I started to review neuropathic pain, and in particular chemotherapy induced peripheral neuropathy (CIPN). I recognised that I had some of the symptoms and chose to look at what might benefit me in the field of CAM. I found lots of research about quality-of-life issues and reflexology, but little, on CIPN.[11][12] I further recognised that there was a need for practitioners to understand the whole plethora of pain-related issues that face cancer survivors and took further CPD and carried out additional research to get to where I am today with my workshop. I have lost many friends and family members to cancer and I have a real desire to make a difference to the lives of those who survive this dreadful disease, so I am truly passionate about the work I do and am keen to get more practitioners to a place of understanding where they feel confident to support their clients in pain after cancer.

Pain, Stress, and the Inflammatory Response

More recently I have been focussed on how I can bring all these things together and there is a huge connection between stress, inflammation, and pain which I have spoken about in my earlier chapters. I want to get it right and to be able to share something insightful and worthwhile with you, so I have delayed this workshop in the light of the pandemic to write about my PhD journey, but will get back to it soon.

I have been asked by many practitioners along the way about how I got into research and where they can do a PhD. PhDs are hard work, as you have read, and not for the faint-hearted. They can come at a huge cost, both personally and professionally but they can also provide you with a massive learning curve and personal insight to your future world. There are still only a very few PhD's in reflexology worldwide, but the research agenda is improving, and a few are now beginning to access funding and support for their research. Certainly, its important too, to recognise that not all research needs to be carried out this way. There are lots of different ways from simple case-studies within your own clinical practice, to case series, surveys, and more. I have not written this book to write about research per se, but I would certainly encourage you to take measurements if you discover that something you are doing for someone with a particular condition, is having a beneficial effect. Write down the treatment you gave, record the results, determine how many people with the same condition respond in the same way, measure the results using validated measurement tools that are appropriate for the outcomes you have seen.

This is how a hypothesis can arise and my peers will tell you, this is how many of them started their own research.

It is however important to remember that research can only answer one question at a time, so pick your question carefully, look at what has already been done in that area and grow from it. My wish is that this book inspires others to do research, to pick up the baton and move research forward for the greater good of the reflexology community worldwide.

My own research though has left me with many questions.

- Does it matter how we do reflexology?
- Does one method perform better than any other and why?
- How do we know for sure?
- Is it the teaching, or the technique?
- How will you know?
- What is the mechanism of reflexology?
- Why is it important?
- How much of what we do is placebo?
- How much do the non-specific effects of reflexology impact the treatment?
- What is the importance of the biopsychosocial element and how do we prove it?

Closing voice

I am generally the type of person who tends to live one day at a time, trying to be in the moment as much as possible and not think too far ahead. The COVID pandemic has given me time to reflect on where I am now and what I want for my future, but ofttimes before you can move forward, you must look back.

At the start of this journey, I was a confident woman with loads of enthusiasm and a real desire to learn. Along the way I lost control of my life and allowed others to dictate its pathway. I sought out those who could and would give me approval, and to a certain extent I still do, but I have come to realise more recently that I don't need the agreement of others to live my life the way I choose. It comes back to control and if you want to make progress in life, that's up to you. Of course, there will always be influencers, and I like to think that in some ways I am one of those people, but by the same token your destiny and your future path is what *you* make it. You don't need to compare yourself with others, with their achievements or with their lifestyle. Life isn't a rehearsal, this is it, and we must make it work the way *we* want it to be, and not how others want it to be.

I feel proud to have been recognised as the leader in my field of research, and although I have carried out some extremely innovative research there are still not many people who have heard about me.

I have struggled to find my voice, to shout about who I am and what I am capable of, because of fear. Fear of being judged, of making mistakes and getting mixed up with what I know and what comes out of my mouth. Chemotherapy has impacted my memory, and although I know a lot, I can't seem to express myself in the right way when I am face-to-face in debate. The obstacles I have faced with my hearing have meant that I easily switch off with accents that don't have clarity. This means that I don't listen well and that I sometimes can't absorb what is being said. Does that make me stupid? No, it just means that I have to find another way around the subject and for me that has been in the written word.

The term 'Imposter Syndrome' is used to represent a psychological issue that affects the way we think and feel about ourselves. I recognise that now and how it was reflected in my belief that I was inadequate, and the feeling that my success may have been a fluke based on a whole host of different things all lining up at the same time. However, and importantly for me, I have also understood that you don't just get 'given' a PhD, you earn it. You earn it because you work hard, because you know your stuff and because you have spent an inordinate amount of time researching your subject. I have learnt that I am very skilled and quite successful in my own right. That I am a bit of a perfectionist, that I often try to be superwoman because I don't want to let anyone down, and that because it takes me such a long time to master something, I'm not what you would call a natural genius.

This book has truly been a cathartic journey and has enabled me to let go of the imposter syndrome that sat with me for so long. I have learned that I know more than I think I do, that I have a lot to offer, not just to the reflexology community, but to life in general. I love sharing my knowledge with you and will continue to teach CPD workshops for as long as I am needed. My focus has always been on supporting clients in pain, and that hasn't changed. I would love to do more research and to be able to find a collaborator and funding for my current research on chemotherapy induced peripheral neuropathy. I am also keen to share more knowledge with reflexologists so that they may fully understand pain from a biopsychosocial perspective. That they may be able to clinically evaluate their treatments and be in a position to share their education on pain with their clients for the greater good.

I'm too inquisitive to stop altogether, and I know that I need to embrace technology more so that I may find a way to adapt my training to reach those across the world who may not have the resources, the convenience, or the ability to join me face to face. More than ever, I would love to see reflexology fully integrated into mainstream medicine and to see research become a vital part of our training, but for that to happen we must all be singing from the same hymn sheet and right now, we are not. Small experimental studies are great and have an added value in research, as does anecdotal evidence and case studies. But for us to truly integrate with orthodox medicine my belief is that we need to speak their language and to use the correct terminology when discussing physiological functioning. We also

CHAPTER 10 | CLOSING VOICE

need to gain much, much, more funding so that we can carry out clinically relevant research that not only matches, but exceeds the needs of conventional medical practice, and we are not there yet.

Finally, I feel that I can write again, so maybe, just maybe, there may be more books in the making!

THE TENACIOUS STUDENT | Dr CAROL A. SAMUEL

Acknowledgements

There are many people to thank when writing a book, so first, I would like to thank those of you who have bought my book. I honestly wasn't sure it would be of interest to anyone and started writing it more for the catharsis than for anything else, so thank YOU! Your interest in me and my PhD journey is what spurred me on during some difficult writing days. Your encouragement made it possible for me to share my knowledge and experience in the hope that it will inspire and garner some new researchers amongst you.

Secondly to my friends who walked the path with me, to my colleagues and peer group, my teachers and family. Because of you I continue to grow, because of your presence in my life I am a better, more focussed person, but more than that, thank you all for sharing life's lessons with me and for helping me to recognise the best in me.

To Dr Sheelagh Campbell and Dr Ivor Ebenezer in particular, without whom the journey would never have happened; for their perseverance and patience, for their guiding hand and for finally trusting that I would deliver what I said I could.

To Karen Williams of Librotas books for introducing me to the 'Smart Author System', which has enabled me to process my thoughts in a methodical and well-structured format. Sam Pearce of SWATT Books for getting me to publication, to my niece Tina Signorelli for your amazing artworks, I know you have an incredible future ahead of you.

There is of course one other person who has walked this path with me and that is Sam, my husband. To him there are no words, but only because I can't seem to shape them out of my heart and onto the page. You have been my rock, my light and my inner voice, my companion, my constant in the stormy seas and the reader of many and varied texts that I have written along the way. I love you now, always, and forever.

About the author

Dr Carol Samuel lives on the South coast of England with her husband Sam and dog, Flint. She has two daughters and six grandchildren. She started her career in complementary medicine in 1994 following ten years as a print buyer and special projects manager and is proud to be able to say that she was the first person in the world, as a non-academic to achieve a PhD in 'Reflexology and Pain Management'.

Her professional acclaim for excellence in the field of research, for pain management, injury prevention and rehabilitation and as a tutor has been recognised by her peers and the public alike.

She has published in both national and international press and in peer reviewed journals and is an invited speaker at conferences worldwide both medical and complementary. Her aim has always been to try and bridge the gap between orthodox medical practices and complementary therapy support through science, clinical reasoning and understanding in pain management.

Now a published author, she seeks to invite understanding of the PhD journey through her story so far.

Glossary of terms

Viva Vocé exam — A viva vocé examination refers to the term used for an oral examination or defence of the written word and is the Latin term for 'with the living voice'. It is sometimes written simply as viva.

Thesis — A written document produced and submitted to an academic institution in support of a professional qualification, and which represents the research carried out and the author's findings.

C.A.M. — Complementary and Alternative Medicine – a branch of medicine that compliments and/or replaces conventional medical practices.

V.R.T. — Vertical Reflex Therapy a technique of applying pressure to the dorsal aspect of the feet or hands. An innovation and advancement of the original classic reflexology techniques by Lynne Booth (reflexologist) in the 1990's.

Morrell Reflexology — A gentle touch reflexology technique developed by Patricia Morrell

Reticular formation — A network of loosely defined neurons within the brainstem that perform a multitude of physiological functions.

Post-partum — The term used for the period following childbirth.

Cytokines	A cellular communication process utilised by the immune system to effect change across a range of cells. They can be either anti-inflammatory or pro-inflammatory in their action and modulate immune and inflammatory responses.
PICC line	A peripherally inserted central catheter or PICC line is a long soft tube inserted into a large vein, usually in the upper arm to infuse drugs that may be required over prolonged periods of time.
Hickman line	A tunnelled central venous catheter which is most often used for the administration of chemotherapy or other medications over prolonged periods, and functions in a similar way to a PICC line.
G-CSF	Granulocyte-colony stimulating factor is a substance used to stimulate the production of a type of white blood cell known as a granulocyte. It helps the bone marrow make more white blood cells and is used to prevent both infection and low white blood cells caused by chemotherapy.
Cruciferous vegetables	A genre of vegetable belonging to the cabbage family, such as kale, cabbage, cauliflower, broccoli, and Brussel sprouts. They are a type of vegetable that is said to have properties that may protect against cancer.
Flavonoids	These are plant chemicals that are found in almost all fruit and vegetables and help provide the vivid colours found in them and are thought to be beneficial anti-inflammatory agents that protect cells from oxidative damage.
Antioxidants	Substances that protect cells from the damage caused by unstable molecules (free radicals) and that may impair cellular health.

CHAPTER 10 | GLOSSARY OF TERMS

Oxidative stress	An imbalance between the production and accumulation of reactive oxygen species (ROS) that may lead to cell and tissue damage.
Neutropenic	Having a low neutrophil count (a type of white blood cell) that helps fight infection.
Extravasation	Refers to a leaking of fluid from a blood vessel or tube into the surrounding tissue. The fluid may be of blood, lymph, or other fluids, such as anticancer drugs.
Stress-induced analgesia	A reduction of the perceived severity of pain due to a conditioned or unconditioned stress stimulus. Also known as hypoalgesia.
HPA	Hypothalamic Pituitary Adrenal Axis is the communication system between the hypothalamus, pituitary and adrenal glands and plays an important role in regulating the physiological mechanisms of stress reactions, immunity, and fertility.
VTCT	Vocational Training Charitable Trust is a specialist awarding and assessment organisation offering vocational and technical qualifications in a range of service sectors across the UK and Ireland.
ITEC	International Therapists Examinations Council is an organisation in the UK that provides international qualifications in the field of health and beauty.
Course validation	A UK quality code for higher education which a degree-awarding body must approve in order for you to gain an award. They are ultimately responsible for the academic standards of any awards granted in its name, and for the quality of the learning programme.

Subjective rating	This is a type of rating used in research enabling a person to give their personal opinion, reaction, or feelings in relation to the topic in question.
PTSD	Post-traumatic stress disorder is classified as a mental health response to a traumatic event.
Action Potential	A sudden, fast, transitory change of the resting membrane potential within the cell that permits the transmission of an electrical signal within the nervous system.
Excitatory signal	A signal that will have an excitatory effect on a neuron which increases its potential to fire an action potential.
Inhibitory signal	A signal that inhibits the potential firing capacity of a neuron, thus decreasing its likelihood of creating an action potential.
Nernst Potential	In the cell membrane of each neurone there is a small difference in electrical charge. The Nernst potential exactly opposes the net diffusion of a particular ion through the membrane.
Nernst Equation	A calculation of the value of the equilibrium potential of a particular cell for a particular ion.

CHAPTER 10 | GLOSSARY OF TERMS

The terms used in this section of the glossary which relate to pain have been categorised by The International Association for the Study of Pain (IASP). The following pain terminology is from "Part III: Pain Terms, A Current List with Definitions and Notes on Usage" (pp 209-214) Classification of Chronic Pain, Second Edition, IASP Task Force on Taxonomy, edited by H. Merskey and N. Bogduk, IASP Press, Seattle, © 1994.

Pain	"Pain is an unpleasant, sensory and emotional experience associated with potential or actual tissue damage or described in terms of such damage".
Pain Threshold	The least experience of pain which a subject can recognize.
Pain Tolerance	The greatest level of pain which a subject is prepared to tolerate.
Noxious Stimulus	A noxious stimulus is one which is damaging to normal tissues.
Analgesia	Absence of pain in response to a stimulus which would normally be painful.
Nociceptor	A receptor preferentially sensitive to a noxious (harmful) stimulus or to a stimulus which would become noxious if prolonged
Nociception	The neural processes of encoding and processing noxious (threatening) stimuli – in simple terms the perception of a painful stimulus.
Anti-nociception	A reduction in the responses to pain.
Receptor	Special places on nerve endings capable of responding to a chemical or physical stimulus from within the body or in the environment.

Endorphins	Endogenous opioid polypeptide hormones synthesised in the areas of the brain and concentrated in areas that modulate nociception. They are referred to as the body's own painkiller because of their resemblance to opiates and their ability to produce analgesia and euphoria.
Dopamine	Dopamine is a chemical messenger found naturally in the brain and is essential for the normal functioning of the central nervous system. It is associated with movement, attention, learning, and the brain's pleasure and reward system. It provides a 'feel good' factor.
Adrenaline	Adrenaline is a neuromodulator of the peripheral nervous system which is also present in the blood. In times of stress, it's activity in the sympathetic nervous system increases the heart rate, contracts the blood vessels, and dilates the air passages so that the body may respond rapidly as in the 'fight of flight' response to stress.
Noradrenaline	Noradrenaline acts as both a hormone and a neurotransmitter. It is released into the blood by the adrenal glands in times of stress. In the brain it acts as a neurotransmitter to produce an anti-inflammatory effect.
Neuromodulator	A hormone or chemical substance released from the neurone or synapse with the ability to regulate neuronal activity.
Neurotransmitter	Conveys electrical signals through hormonal or chemical substances with the ability to change neural activity, either to enhance or modulate such activity.
Acetylcholine	A neurotransmitter which is found in the peripheral and central nervous system.

Histamine	Released from mast cells causing an inflammatory response and vasodilation, causing reddening of the skin.
Neurotag	A pattern of activity within the brain that creates pain perception.
Demyelination	The breakdown of the myelin sheath, the protective coating that surrounds nerves, leading to damage within the nervous system.
EEG	Electroencephalogram is a specialized test or recording which detects the electrical activity within the brain.
Adrenocortical insufficiency	When your adrenal glands produce insufficient amounts of certain hormones, usually cortisol or aldosterone that are used to maintain equilibrium.

THE TENACIOUS STUDENT | Dr CAROL A. SAMUEL

Useful resources

DOCTORAL THESIS

An investigation into the efficacy of reflexology on acute pain in healthy human subjects.
https://researchportal.port.ac.uk/portal/en/theses/an-investigation-into-the-efficacy-of-reflexology-on-acute-pain-in-healthy-human-subjects(be527020-d140-461b-ab17-aad43d62aba0).html

Research Publications

Exploratory study on the efficacy of reflexology for pain threshold and tolerance using an ice pain experiment and sham T.E.N.S. control.
www.sciencedirect.com/science/article/pii/S1744388113000182

Complementary therapy support in cancer survivorship: a survey of complementary and alternative medicine practitioners' provision and perception of skills.
www.ncbi.nlm.nih.gov/pubmed/23855438

Self-reported confidence in long-term care provision for adult cancer survivors: A cross-sectional survey of nursing and allied healthcare professionals.
https://pubmed.ncbi.nlm.nih.gov/26412775/

Reflexmaster is a website hosted by the author, Dr Carol Samuel offering CPD workshops and foot reflexology charts.
https://www.reflexmaster.co.uk/

The Stress Management Society is a non-profit organisation dedicated to helping individuals and companies recognise and reduce stress.
https://www.stress.org.uk/

Rethink Mental Illness work to transform the lives of everyone severely affected by mental illness, and how as a nation we approach mental illness. They provide over 200 services, 140 local support groups and run campaigns that bring about real change.
https://www.rethink.org

Health Talk Online a web-based forum for patients suffering chronic illness that can provide access to a variety of subjects and discussions including chronic pain.
www.healthtalk.org/peoples-experiences/long-term-conditions/chronic-pain/topics

The British Pain Society offers downloadable documents that provide information on how clients may be able to manage their pain.
www.britishpainsociety.org/

The Pain Toolkit is a great resource for self-managing pain and provides a variety of tools including helpful guidebooks, DVD's, CD's, and discussions.
www.paintoolkit.org/resources/for-patients

Arthritis Research UK provide a comprehensive guide to living with arthritis and provide information on the latest research.
www.arthritisresearchuk.org/arthritis-information.aspx

Neuro Orthopaedic Institute offer evidence-based resources and courses for the management of pain for both medical and allied health professionals.
http://www.noigroup.com/en/Home

Body in Mind offers a collection of posts from research influencers that covered human pain studies on the brain and mind in chronic pain.
https://bodyinmind.org/resources/

CHAPTER 10 | USEFUL RESOURCES

MNT-NR International - Manual Neurotherapy and Nerve Reflexology courses for bodywork practitioners including physiotherapists, osteopaths, chiropractors, and Nerve Reflex Therapists (NR) who have attained a Level 3 qualification.
www.mnt-nr.com/English/Home

Booth VRT - Vertical Reflex Therapy (VRT) is an additional method of reflexology used on the hands or feet in a weight bearing position. The technique was developed by Lynne Booth who offers, amongst other things master classes for pain management using the VRT system.
www.boothvrt.com

Adapted Reflex Therapy (AdRx) – Gunnel Berry provides CPD workshops to physiotherapists and reflexologists alike on a technique she has especially developed for musculo-skeletal pain, spinal pain, and whiplash injuries.
https://www.gunnel-berry.com/

For those of you who may be considering writing your first book, I would highly recommend you consider the 'Smart Author System' offered by Karen Williams of Librotas Books.
https://librotas.com/

Self-publication guidance and support from Sam Pearce of SWATT Books.
https://swatt-books.co.uk/

Sensor Products Inc.
Sensor products was the company who hired out the pressure sensitive equipment used for one of my experiments. They are a world leader in the niche field of tactile surface pressure and force sensors.
https://www.sensorprod.com/freeform_devkit.php

Bibliographic references

Introduction

1 Ashton H, Ebenezer I, Golding JF, Thompson JW. Effects of Acupuncture and Transcutaneous Electrical Nerve Stimulation on cold-induced pain in normal subjects. J Psychosom Res. 1984;28(4):301-8.

1 Kemp S, Huffnagel IC, Linthorst GE, Wanders RJ, Engelen M. Adrenoleukodystrophy - neuroendocrine pathogenesis and redefinition of natural history. Nat Rev Endocrinol. 2016;12(10):606-15.

2 Turk BR, Moser AB, Fatemi A. Therapeutic strategies in adrenoleukodystrophy. Wiener medizinische Wochenschrift (1946). 2017;167(9-10):219-26.

3 Berger J, Forss-Petter S, Eichler FS. Pathophysiology of X-linked adrenoleukodystrophy. Biochimie. 2014;98(100):135-42.

4 Engelen M, Kemp S, Poll-The BT. X-linked adrenoleukodystrophy: pathogenesis and treatment. Current neurology and neuroscience reports. 2014;14(10):486.

5 Hexem KR, Mollen CJ, Carroll K, Lanctot D, Feudtner C. How parents of children receiving pediatric care use religion, spirituality, or life philosophy in tough times. J Palliat Med. 2011:39-44.

6   Khalid K, Ku Md Saad S, Abd Ghani NA, Mohamed Abdul Kadher AN. Religious and cultural challenges in paediatrics palliative care: A review of literature. Pediatric Hematology Oncology Journal. 2019;4(3):67-73.

7   Carlino E, Frisaldi E, Benedetti F. Pain and the context. Nature reviews Rheumatology. 2014;10(6):348-55.

8   Meulders A. Fear in the context of pain: Lessons learned from 100 years of fear conditioning research. Behav Res Ther. 2020;131:103635.

CHAPTER 2: How it began

1   Mitchell LA, MacDonalad RAR, Brodie EE. Temperature and the cold pressor test. J of Pain. 2004;5(4):233-8.

2   Elias SO, Ajayi RE. Effect of sympathetic autonomic stress from the cold pressor test on left ventricular function in young healthy adults. Physiol Reports. 2019;7(2 (e13985)).

3   Fagius J, Karhuvaara S, Sundlof G. The cold pressor test: effects on sympathetic nerve activity in human muscle and skin nerve fascicles. Acta Physiol Scand. 1989;137:325-34.

4   Silverthorn DU, Michael J. Cold stress and the cold pressor test. Adv Physiol Educ. 2013;37:93-6.

5   McIntyre MH, Kless A, Hein P, Field M, Tung JY. Validity of cold pressor test and pain sensibility questionnaire via online self-administration. PLoS One [Internet]. 2020; 15(4):[e-0231697 pp.].

6   Black PH. Stress and inflammatory response: A review of neurogenic inflammation. Brain Behav Immun. 2002;16:622-53.

7   Yeager MP, Pioli PA, Guyre PM. Cortisol exerts bi-phasic regulation of inflammation in humans. Dose Response. 2011;9:332-47.

8   Samuel C. Stress Reflex. International Therapist 2017(122):35-7.

9 Lett A. Reflex Zone Therapy for Health Professionals. China: Harcourt Publishers; 2000. 299 p.

10 Younger J, McCue R, Mackey S. Pain Outcomes: A brief review of instruments and techniques. Curr Pain Headache Rep. 2009;13(1):39-43.

11 Bendinger T, Plunkett N. Measurement in pain medicine. BJA Edu. 2016;16(9): 310-5.

12 Backryd E. Pain in the Blood? Envisioning mechanism-based diagnoses and biomarkers in clinical pain medicine. Diagnostics. 2015;5( ):84-95.

13 Ashton H, Ebenezer I, Golding JF, Thompson JW. Effects of Acupuncture and Transcutaneous Electrical Nerve Stimulation on cold-induced pain in normal subjects. J Psychosom Res. 1984;28(4):301-8.

14 Melzack R. From the gate to the neuromatrix. Pain. 1999;Supp 6:S121-S6.

15 Hansson P, Lundeberg T. Transcutaneous electrical nerve stimulation, vibration and acupuncture as pain-relieving measures. In: Wall P, Melzack R, editors. Textbook of Pain. 4th ed. London: Churchill Livingstone; 1999. p. 1588.

16 Brown RE, Basheer R, McKenna JT, Strecker RE, McCarley RW. Control of sleep and wakefulness. Physiol Rev. 2012;92q(3):1087-187.

17 Fechir M, Schlereth T, Kritzmann S, Balon S, Pfeifer N, Geber C, et al. Stress and thermoregulation: Different sympathetic responses and different effects on experimental pain. Eur J Pain. 2008;doi: 10.1016/j.ejpain.2008.11.002.

18 Al Absi M, Petersen KL. Blood pressure but not cortisol mediates stress effects on subsequent pain perception in healthy men and women. Pain. 2003;106: 285-95.

19 Marazatti D, Di Muro A, Castrogiovanni P. Psychological stress and body temperature changes in humans. Physiology & behavior. 1992;52:393-5.

20 Chapman CR, Tuckett RP, Song CW. Pain and stress in a systems perspective: Reciprocal neural, endocrine, and immune interactions. J Pain. 2008;9(2):122-45.

CHAPTER 3: Losing my way

1   Garg R. Methodology for research 1. Indian J Anaesth. 2016;60(9):640-5.

2   Lautenbacher S, Peters JH, Heesen M, Scheel J, Kunz M. Age changes in pain perception: A systematic review and meta-analysis of age effects on pain and tolerance thresholds. Neurosci and Biobehav Rev. 2017;75:104-13.

3   Ditre JW, Brandon TH, Zale EL, Meagher MM. Pain, Nicotine, and Smoking: Research findings and mechanistic considerations. Psychol Bull. 2011;137(6):1065-93.

4   Pulvers K, Hood A, Limas EF, Thomas MD. Female smokers show lower pain tolerance in a physical distress task. Addict Behav. 2012;37(10):1167-70.

5   Page C. Spiritual Alchemy: ; 2005. 288 p.

6   Brannock RG, Litten MJ, Smith J. The impact of doctoral study on marital satisfaction. Journal of College Counselling. 2000;3(2):123-30.

7   Tousignant-Laflamme Y, Rainville P, Marchand S. Establishing a link between heart rate and pain in healthy subjects: a gender effect. J Pain. 2005;6(6):341-7.

8   Charmandari E, Tsigos C, Chrousos G. Endocrinology of the stress response. Annu Rev Physiol. 2005;67:259-84.

9   Kiecolt-Glaser JK. Stress, food, and inflammation: Psychoneuroimmunology and nutrition at the cutting edge. Psychosom Med. 2010;72:365-9.

10 Maduka IC, Neboh. The relationship between serum cortisol, adrenaline, blood glucose and lipid profile of undergraduate students under examination stress. Afr Health Sci. 2015;1:131-6.

11 Black PH, Garbutt LD. Stress, inflammation and cardiovascular disease. J Psycho Res. 2002;52:1-23.

12 Gu Q, Yang H, Shi Q. Macrophages and bone inflammation. J Orthop Transl. 2017;10:86-93.

CHAPTER 10 | BIOBLIOGRAPHIC REFERENCES

13 Porcelli AJ, Cruz D, Wenberg K, Patterson MD, Biswal BB, Rypma B. The effects of acute stress on human prefrontal working memory systems. Physiol & Behav. 2008;95:282-9.

14 Roozendaal B, McEwen BS, Chattarji S. Stress, memory and the amygdala. Nat Rev Neuroscience. 2009;10:423-33.

15 Garg R. Methodology for research 1. Indian J Anaesth. 2016;60(9):640-5.

16 Alexander JK, DeVries AC, Kigerl KA, Dahlman JM, Popovich PG. Stress exacerbates neuropathic pain via glucocorticoid and NMDA receptor activation. Brain, Behav & Immun. 2009;23:851-60.

17 Vierck CJ, Green M, Yezierski RP. Pain as a stressor: Effects of prior nociceptive stimulation on escape responding of rats to thermal stimulation. Eur J Pain. 2009;2009(doi: 10.1016/j.ejpain.2009.01.009):1-6.

CHAPTER 4: Not good enough?

1 MacPherson RD. The pharmacological basis of contemporary pain management. Pharmacol Therapeut. 2000;2000(88):163-85.

2 Enggaard TP, Poulsen L, Arendt-Nielsen L, Hansen SH, Bjornsdottir I, Gram LF, et al. The analgesic effect of codeine as compared to imipramine in different human experimental pain models. Pain. 2001;92:277-82.

3 Lorimer MR, Pedersen K, Lombard W. Optimal dosing interval for epidural pethidine after caesarean section. Acute Pain. 2002;4:27-31.

4 Vonsy JL, Ghandehari J, Dickenson AH. Differential analgesic effects of morphine and gabapentin on behavioural measures of pain and disability in a model of osteoarthritis pain in rats. Eur J Pain. 2009;13:786-93.

5 Ashton H, Ebenezer I, Golding JF, Thompson JW. Effects of Acupuncture and Transcutaneous Electrical Nerve Stimulation on cold-induced pain in normal subjects. J Psychosom Res. 1984;28(4):301-8.

6   Chesterton LS, Foster NE, Wright CC, Baxter GD, P B. Effects of TENS frequency, intensity and stimulation site parameter manipulation on pressure pain thresholds in healthy human subjects. Pain. 2003;106:73-80.

7   Chen CC, Tabasam G, Johnson MI. Does the pulse frequency of transcutaneous electrical nerve stimulation (TENS) influence hypoalgesia? A systematic review of studies using experimental pain and healthy human participants. Physiotherapy. 2008;94:11-20.

8   Claydon LS, Chesterton LS, Barlas P, Sim J. Effects of simultaneous dual-site TENS stimulation on experimental pain. Eur J Pain. 2008;12:696-704.

9   Itoh K, Itoh S, Katsumi Y, Kitakoji H. A pilot study on using acupuncture and transcutaneous electrical nerve stimulation to treat chronic non-specific low back pain. Compl Ther Clin Pract. 2009;15:22-5.

10 Conway BA, Knikou M. The action of plantar pressure on flexion reflex pathways in the isolated human spinal cord. Clin Neurophysiol. 2008;119(4):892-6.

11 Hickey GL, Grant SW, Dunning J, Siepe M. Statistical primer: sample size and power calculations - why, when and how? Eur J of Cardiothorac Surg [Internet]. 2018 08/10/2020; 54:[4-9 pp.].

12 Mendes D, Alves C, Batel-Marques F. Number needed to treat (NNT) in clinical literature: an appraisal. BMC Medicine. 2017;15(1):112.

13 Jackson T, Iezzi T, Chen H, Ebnet S, Eglitis K. Gender, interpersonal transactions and the perception of pain: An experimental analysis. J Pain. 2005;6(4):228-36.

14 Fillingim RB. Individual differences in pain responses. Curr Rheum Rep. 2005;7:342-47.

15 Fillingim RB, Edwards RR, Powell T. The relationship of sex and clinical pain to experimental pain responses. Pain. 1999;83:419-25.

16 Greenspan JD, Craft RM, LeResche L, Arendt-Nielsen L, Berkley KJ, Fillingim RB, et al. Studying sex and gender differences in pain and analgesia: A consesus report. Pain. 2007;132:S26- S45.

17   Gautieri A, Buehler MJ, Radaelli A. Deformation rate controls elasticity and unfolding pathway of single topocollagen models. J Mech Behav Biomed Mat. 2009;2:130-7.

18   Kassolik K, Jaskolska A, Kisiel-Sajewicz K, Marusiak J, Kawczynski A, Kaskolski A. Tensegrity principle in massage demonstrated by electro- and mechanomyography. J Bodyw Mov Ther. 2009;13:164-70.

19   Edsberg LE, Mates RE, Baier RE, Lauren M. Mechanical characteristics of human skin subjected to static versus cyclic normal pressures. JRRD. 1999;36(2):1-8.

20   Kennedy PM, Inglis T. Distribution and behaviour of glabrous cutaneous receptors in the human foot sole. J Physiol. 2002;538(3):995-1002.

21   Nakamaru T, Miura N, Fukushima A, Kawashima R. Somatotopical relationships between corticol activity and reflex areas in reflexology: A functional magnetic resonance imaging study. Neurosci Lett. 2008(doi: 10.1016/j.neulet.2008.10.022).

22   Tiran D, Chummun H. The physiological basis of reflexology and its use as a potential diagnostic tool. Compl Ther Clin Pract. 2005;11(1):58-64.

23   Jones J, Thomson P, Irvine K, J LS. Is there a specific hemodynamic effect in reflexology? A systematic review of randomized controlled trials. J Altern Complement Med. 2013;19(4):319-28.

24   Poole HM. The efficacy of reflexology in the management of chronic low back pain [PhD]. Liverpool: Liverpool; 2001.

25   Evans SL, Nokes LDM, Weaver P, Maheson M, P M. Effect of Reflexology treatment on recovery after total knee replacement. Bone Joint Surg-Brit. 1998;80-B:SUPP II(25):172.

26   Ingham E. Stories the Feet Can Tell Thru Reflexology. USA: Ingham Publishing; 1984.

27   Tay G, Eu Hooi K. The Rwo Shur Health Method: Art Printing Works Sdn, Bhd.; 1988.

28 Marquardt H. Reflex Zone Therapy of the Feet - A textbook for therapists. Vermont: Thorsons 1984. 160 p.

29 Veldhuizen HJR, Pauly NMH. An experimental 'case study' on the effects of nerve reflex points at the foot on the thoracic paraspinal muscles. Eur J Physio. 2001;12(12):33-.

30 Hodgson NA, Andersen S. The clinical efficacy of reflexology in nursing home residents with dementia. J Alt Compl Med. 2008;14(3):000-.

31 Stephenson NLN, Dalton JA, Carlson J. The effect of foot reflexology on pain in patients with metastatic cancer. Appl Nurs Res. 2003;16(4):284-6.

32 Neziri AY, Curatolo M, Bergadano A, Petersen-Felix S, Dickensen AH, Arendt-Nielsen L, et al. New method for quantification and statistical analysis of nociceptive reflex receptive fields in humans. J Neurosci Meth. 2009;178:24-30.

33 Mendes D, Alves C, Batel-Marques F. Number needed to treat (NNT) in clinical literature: an appraisal. BMC Medicine. 2017;15(1):112.

CHAPTER 5: Fighting back – the battle is not yet over.

1 Zuo H, Lu H, Vaupel DB, Zhang Y, Chefer SI, Rea WR, et al. Acute nicotine-Induced tachyphylaxis is differentially manifest in the limbic system. Neuropsychopharmacol. 2011;36:2498-512.

2 Dumas EO, Pollack GM. Opioid tolerance development: A Pharmacokinetic/Pharmacodynamic Perspective. The AAPS J. 2008;10(4):537 - 51.

3 Blackwell Scientific Publications. Blackwell's Dictionary of Nursing. Cambridge: The University Press; 1994. p. 808.

4 LeBlanc J, Potvin P. Studies on habituation to cold pain. Can J Physiol Pharm. 1966;44:287-93.

5   Tipton MJ, Egline CM, Golden F. Habituation of the initial responses to cold water immersion in humans: a central or peripheral mechanism? J Physiol. 1998;512(2):521.-628.

6   Phillips EM, Pugh DS. How to get a PhD: a handbook for students and their supervisors. Third ed. Buckingham: Open University Press; 2000. 235 p.

7   Frediani B, Filippou G, Falsetti P, Lorenzini S, Baldi F, Acciai C, et al. Diagnosis of calcium pyrophosphate dihydrate crystal deposition disease: ultrasonographic criteria proposed. Ann Rheum Dis. 2005;64:638-40.

8   Underwood M. Diagnosis and management of gout. BMJ. 2006;332:1315-9.

9   Ingham E. Stories the Feet Can Tell Thru Reflexology. USA: Ingham Publishing; 1984.

10 Ong C, Banks B. Complementary and Alternative Medicine: the consumer perspective. The Prince of Wales's Foundation for Integrated Health; 2003.

11 Brody H. The placebo response. 1st ed. New York: Harper Collins Publishers Inc.; 2000. 312 p.

12 Heinonen E, Lindfors O, Laaksonen MA, Knekt P. Therapists' professional and personal characteristics as predictors of outcome in short- and long-term psychotherapy. Journal of Affective Disorders. 2012;138(3):301-12.

13 Ferreira PH, Ferreira ML, Maher CG, Refshauge KM, Latimer J, Adams RD. The therapeutic alliance between clinicians and patients predicts outcome in chronic low back pain. Phys Ther. 2013;93:470-8.

14 Bucher MA, Suzuki T, Samuel DB. A meta-analytic review of personality traits and their associations with mental health treatment outcomes. Clinical Psychology Review. 2019;70:51-63.

15 Matthews G, Gilliland K. The personality theories of H J Eysenk and J A Gray: a comparative review. Pers Indiv Differ. 1999;26:583-626.

16 Seminowicz DA, Davis KD. Cortical responses to pain in healthy individuals depends on pain catastrophizing. Pain. 2006; (120):297-306.

17 Banozic A, Miljkovic A, Bras M, Puljak L, Kolcic I, Hayward C, et al. Neuroticism and pain catastrophizing aggravate response to pain in healthy adults: an experimental study. Korean J Pain. 2018;31(1):16-26.

18 Al Absi M, Petersen KL. Blood pressure but not cortisol mediates stress effects on subsequent pain perception in healthy men and women. Pain. 2003;106: 285-95.

19 Marazatti D, Di Muro A, Castrogiovanni P. Psychological stress and body temperature changes in humans. Physiology & behavior. 1992;52:393-5.

20 Vierck CJ, Green M, Yezierski RP. Pain as a stressor: Effects of prior nociceptive stimulation on escape responding of rats to thermal stimulation. Eur J Pain. 2009;2009(doi: 10.1016/j.ejpain.2009.01.009):1-6.

21 Henry JP. Biological basis of the stress response. Integr Phys Beh Sci. 1992;27(1):66-83.

22 Khansari DN, Murgo AJ, Faith RE. Effects of stress on the immune system. Immunol Today. 1990;11(5):170-5.

23 Martenson ME, Cetas JS, Heinricher MM. A possible neural basis for stress-induced hyperalgesia. Pain. 2009;142:236-44.

24 Hodgson NA, Andersen S. The clinical efficacy of reflexology in nursing home residents with dementia. J Alt Compl Med. 2008;14(3):000-.

25 McVicar AJ, Greenwood CR, Fewell F, D'Arcy VD, Chandrasekharan S, Aldridge LC. Evaluation of anxiety, salivary cortisol and melatonin secretion following reflexology treatment: A pilot study in healthy individuals. Compl Ther Clin Pract. 2007;13:137-45.

26 Mackereth P, Booth K, Hillier VS, Caress AL. Reflexology and progressive muscle relaxation training for people with multiple sclerosis: A crossover trial. Compl Ther Clin Med. 2008;Article in Press.

27   Al Absi M, Petersen KL. Blood pressure but not cortisol mediates stress effects on subsequent pain perception in healthy men and women. Pain. 2003;106: 285-95.

28   Marazatti D, Di Muro A, Castrogiovanni P. Psychological stress and body temperature changes in humans. Physiology & behavior. 1992;52:393-5.

29   Chapman CR, Tuckett RP, Song CW. Pain and stress in a systems perspective: Reciprocal neural, endocrine, and immune interactions. J Pain. 2008;9(2):122-45.

30   Esmel-Esmel N, Tomas-Esmel E, Tous-Andreu M, Bove-Ribe A, Jimenez-Herrera M. Reflexology and polysomnography: Changes in cerebral wave activity induced by reflexology promote N1 and N2 sleep stages. Comp Ther Clin Pract. 2017;28:54-64.

31   Sacco M, Meschi M, Regolisti G, Detrenis S, Bianchi L, Bertorelli M, et al. The relationship between blood pressure and pain. The Journal of Clinical Hypertension. 2013;15(8):600-6.

32   Martinez-Gomez M, Whipple B, Oliva-Zarate L, Pacheco P, Komisarukt B. Analgesia produced by vaginal self-stimulation in women is independent of heart rate acceleration. Physiology & behavior. 1988;43(6):849-50.

33   Pocock G, Richards CD. Human Physiology: The basis of medicine. 3rd Ed. ed. Oxford: Oxford University Press; 2006. 638 p.

34   Kurz A. Physiology of thermoregulation. Best Pract Res Cl Anaes. 2008;22(4): 627-44.

35   Black PH. Stress and inflammatory response: A review of neurogenic inflammation. Brain Behav Immun. 2002;16:622-53.

36   Butler RK, Finn DP. Stress-induced analgesia. Prog Neurobiol. 2009;Article in Press(doi:10/1016/j.pneurobio.2009.04.003).

37   Dhabhar FS. Stress-induced augmentation of immune function - The role of stress hormones, leukocyte trafficking, and cytokines. Brain Behav Immun. 2002;16:785-98.

38 Marazatti D, Di Muro A, Castrogiovanni P. Psychological stress and body temperature changes in humans. Physiology & behavior. 1992;52:393-5.

39 Endo Y, Shiraki K. Behaviour and body temperature in rats following chronic foot shock or psychological stress exposure. Physiology & behavior. 2000;71:263-8.

40 Vinkers CH, van Bogaert M, Klanker M, Korte S, Oosting R, Hanania T, et al. Translational aspects of pharmacological research into anxiety disorders: The stress-induced hyperthermia (SIH) paradigm. European journal of pharmacology. 2008;585:407-25.

41 Vickland V, Rogers C, Craig A, Tran Y. Anxiety as a factor influencing physiological effects of acupuncture. Compl Ther Clin Pract. 2009;doi:10.1016/j.ctcp.2009.02.013:1-5.

CHAPTER 6: Throwing everything at it

1 Drescher VM, Horsley Gantt W, Whitehead WE. Heart rate response to touch. Psychosom Med. 1980;42(6):559-65.

2 Gleeson M, Timmins F. A review of the use and clinical effectiveness of touch as a nursing intervention. Clin Effectiveness Nurs. 2005;9:69-77.

3 Cassileth BR, Vickers AJ. Massage therapy for symptom control: Outcome study at a major cancer center. J Pain Symptom Manag. 2004;28(3):244-9.

4 Kyparos A, Feeback DL, Layne CS, Martinez DA, Clarke MS. Mechanical stimulation of the plantar foot surface attenuates soleus muscle atrophy induced by hindlimb unloading in rats. J Appl Physiol. 2005;99:739-46.

5 Green DA, Sumners DP, Hunter SP. Effect of percutaneous electrical stimulation of the sole upon lower limb blood pooling induced by protracted sitting in man: High Tech Health Ltd; 2008 [Electronic article]. Available from: http://www.hthealth.com.

6 Priplata AA, Niemi JB, Lipsitz LA, Collins JJ. Vibrating insoles and balance control in elderly people. The Lancet. 2003;362:1123-4.

7   Proske U, Gandevia SC. The Proprioceptive senses: Their roles in signaling body shape, body position and movement, and muscle force. Physiol Rev. 2012;92:1651-152.

8   Kavounoudias A, Roll R, Roll JP. Foot sole and muscle inputs contribute jointly to human erect posture regulation. J Physiol. 2001;532(3):869-78.

9   Layne CS, Forth KE, Baxter MF, Houser JJ. Voluntary neuromuscular activation is enhanced when paired with a mechanical stimulus to human plantar soles. Neurosci Lett. 2002;334:75-8.

10 Joseph P, Acharya UR, Poo CK, Chee J, Min LC, Iyengar SS, et al. Effect of reflexological stimulation on heart rate variability. ITBM-RBM. 2004;25:40-5.

11 Kessler J, Marchant P, Johnson MI. A study to compare the effects of massage and static touch on experimentally induced pain in healthy volunteers. Physiotherapy. 2006;92:225-32.

12 Degirmen N, Ozerdogan N, Sayiner D, Kosgeroglu N, Ayanci U. Effectiveness of foot and hand massage in post caesarian pain control in a group of Turkish pregnant women. Appl Nurs Res. 2009;doi:10.1016/j.apnr.2008.08.001.

13 Liechti E. Complete Illustrated Guide to Shiatsu: The Japanese healing art of touch for health and fitness. UK: Element Books; 1998.

14 Fishman E, Turkheimer E, DeGood DE. Touch Relieves Stress and Pain. J Behav Med. 1994;18(1):69-79.

15 Malville J, Bowen JE, Bentham G. Effect of healing touch on stress perception and biological correlates. Holistic Nurs Pract. 2008;22(2):103-10.

16 Hertenstein MJ, Keltner D, App B, Bulleit BA, Jaskolka AR. Touch communicates distinct emotions. Emotion. 2006;6 (3):528-33.

17 Bufalari I, Aprile T, Avenanti A, DiRusso F, Agliotti SM. Empathy for pain and touch in the human somatosensory cortex. Cereb Cortex. 2007;2007(17):2553-61.

18   Tombimatsu S, Zhang YM, Suga R, Kato M. Differential temporal coding of the vibratory sense in the hand and foot in man. Clin Neurophysiol. 2000;111: 398-404.

19   Kennedy PM, Inglis T. Distribution and behaviour of glabrous cutaneous receptors in the human foot sole. J Physiol. 2002;538(3):995-1002.

20   Andersen OK, Sonnenborg FA, Arendt-Nielsen L. Reflex receptive fields for human withdrawal reflexes elicited by non-painful electrical stimulation of the foot sole. Clin Neurophysiol. 2001;112:641-9.

21   Whipple B, Komisaruk BR. Elevation of pain threshold by vaginal stimulation in women. Pain. 1985;21(4):357-67.

22   Tay G, Eu Hooi K. The Rwo Shur Health Method: Art Printing Works Sdn, Bhd.; 1988.

23   Issel C. Reflexology: Art. Science and History. Fourth ed. Sacramento, CA: New Frontier Publshing; 1996. 239 p.

24   Lett A. Reflex Zone Therapy for Health Professionals. China: Harcourt Publishers; 2000. 299 p.

25   Marquardt H. Reflex Zone Therapy of the Feet - A textbook for therapists. Vermont: Thorsons 1984. 160 p.

26   Porter AJ. The Practice and Philosophy of Advanced Reflexology Techniques. London: Porter, A J; 1997.

27   Nahin RL, Straus SE. Research into CAM: problems and potential. BMJ. 2001;322:161-4.

28   Senn S. Crossover trials in clinical research. Barnett V, editor. Chichester: John Wiley & Sons; 1993. 266 p.

29   Mackereth P, Booth K, Hillier VS, Caress AL. Reflexology and progressive muscle relaxation training for people with multiple sclerosis: A crossover trial. Compl Ther Clin Med. 2008;Article in Press.

30 Wilkinson ISA, Prigmore S, Rayner CF. A randomised-controlled trial examining the effects of reflexology on patients with chronic obstructive pulmonary disease. Compl Ther Clin Pract. 2006;12:141-7.

31 Pannucci CJ, Wilkins EG. Identifying and avoiding bias in research. Plast Reconstr Surg. 2010;126(2):619-25.

32 Mackereth P, Booth K, Hillier VS, Caress AL. Reflexology and progressive muscle relaxation training for people with multiple sclerosis: A crossover trial. Compl Ther Clin Med. 2008;Article in Press.

33 Wilkinson ISA, Prigmore S, Rayner CF. A randomised-controlled trial examining the effects of reflexology on patients with chronic obstructive pulmonary disease. Compl Ther Clin Pract. 2006;12:141-7.

34 Sharav Y, Tal M. Focused analgesia and generalized relaxation produce differential hypnotic analgesia in response to ascending stimulus intensity. Int J of Psychophysiol. 2004;52:187-96.

35 Field T. Massage therapy research review. Complement Ther Clin Pract. 2014;20(4):224-9.

36 Moyle W, Cooke ML, Beattie E, Shum DHK, O'Dwyer ST, Barrett S, et al. Foot massage and physiological stress in people with dementia: A randomised controlled trial. J Alt and Complement Med. 2014;20(4):305-11.

CHAPTER 7: Writing the Thesis

1 Thomas KJ, Nicholl JP, Coleman P. Use and expenditure on complementary medicine in England: a population based survey. Compl Ther Med. 2001;9:2-11.

2 Eardley S, Bishop FL, Prescott P, Cardini F, Brinkhaus B, Santos-Rey K, et al. A systematic literature review of Complementary and Alternative Medicine prevalence in EU. Forsch Komplementmed. 2012;19 (Suppl 2):18-28.

3   Sharp D, Lorenc A, Morris R, Feder G, Little P, Hollinghurst S, et al. Complementary medicine use, views, and experiences: a national survey in England. BJGP Open. 2018;2(4):bjgpopen18X101614.

4   Dougans I. Reflexology the 5 elements and their 12 meridians: a unique approach. London: Thorsons; 2005. 324 p.

5   Longhurst JC. Defining Meridians: A modern basis of understanding. J Acupunt Meridian Std. 2010;3(2):67-74.

6   Quiroz-Gonzalez S, Torres-Castillo S, Lopez-Gomez RE, Estrada IJ. Acupuncture points and their relationship with multireceptive fields of neurons. J Acupunt Meridian Stud. 2017;10(2):81-9.

7   Head H. On disturbances of sensation with especial reference to the pain of visceral disease. Brain part 1 & 2. 161893.

8   Head H. The afferent nervous system from a new aspect. Brain1905. p. 99-115.

9   Lett A. Reflex Zone Therapy for Health Professionals. China: Harcourt Publishers; 2000. 299 p.

10 Tiran D, Chummun H. The physiological basis of reflexology and its use as a potential diagnostic tool. Compl Ther Clin Pract. 2005;11(1):58-64.

11 Marquardt H. Reflex Zone Therapy of the Feet - A textbook for therapists. Vermont: Thorsons 1984. 160 p.

12 Tiran D, Chummun H. The physiological basis of reflexology and its use as a potential diagnostic tool. Compl Ther Clin Pract. 2005;11(1):58-64.

13 Tiran D. Reviewing theories and origins. In: Mackereth P, Tiran D, editors. Clinical Reflexology: A Guide for Health Professionals, London: Churchill Livingstone; 2002. p. 5-15.

14 Stephenson NLN, Dalton JA. Using reflexology for pain management: A Review. J Holistic Nurs. 2003;21(2):179-91.

15 Melzack R, Wall PD. Pain Mechanisms: A New Theory. Science. 1965;150(3669):971-8.

16 Bear MF, Connors BW, Paradiso MA. Neuroscience: Exploring the Brain. Third ed. Baltimore, USA: Lippincott Williams & Wilkins; 2007. 857 p.

17 Leknes S, Tracey I. A common neurobiology for pain and pleasure. Nature Neurosci. 2008;9:314-20.

18 Froehlich JC. Opioid Peptides. Alcohol Health Res W. 1997;21(2):132-6.

19 Carlsson C. Acupuncture mechanisms for clinically relevant long-term effects - reconsideration and a hypothesis. Acupuncture Med. 2002;20 (2-3):82-99.

20 Claydon LS, Chesterton LS, Barlas P, Sim J. Effects of simultaneous dual-site TENS stimulation on experimental pain. Eur J Pain. 2008;12:696-704.

21 Carlsson C. Acupuncture mechanisms for clinically relevant long-term effects - reconsideration and a hypothesis. Acupuncture Med. 2002;20 (2-3):82-99.

22 Ashton H, Marsh VR, Millman JE, Rawlins MD, Telford R, Thompson JW. Biphasic dose-related responses on the CNV (Contingent Negative Variation) to I.V Nicotine in man. Brit J Clin Pharmaco. 1980;10:579-89.

23 Sandrini G, Milanov I, Malaguti S, Nigrelli MP, Moglia A, Nappi G. Effects of hypnosis on diffuse noxious inhibitory controls. Physiology & behavior. 2000;69:295-300.

24 Koke AJA, Schouten JSAG, Lamerichs-Geelen MJH, Lipsch JSM, Waltje EMH, van Kleef M, et al. Pain reducing effect of three types of transcutaneous electrical nerve stimulation in patients with chronic pain: a randomized crossover trial. Pain. 2004;108:36-42.

25 Jensen M, Patterson DR. Hypnotic Treatment of Chronic Pain. J Behav Med. 2006;29(1):95-124.

26 Wan Y, Wilson SG, Han JS, Mogil JS. The effect of genotype on sensitivity to electroacupuncture analgesia. Pain. 2001;91:5-13.

27   Moore RA, Derry S, McQuay HJ, Straube S, Aldington D, Wiffen P, et al. Clinical effectiveness: An approach to clinical trial design more relevant to clinical practice, acknowledging the importance of individual differences. Pain. 2009;doi:10.1016/j.pain.2009.08.007.

28   Williams DG, Patel A, Howard RF. Pharmacogenetics of codeine metabolism in an urban population of children and its implications for analgesic reliability. Br J Anaesth. 2002;89(6):839-45.

29   Bandolier. Acute Pain - evidenced based healthcare. Bandolier Extra [Internet]. 2003 9/9/09:[1-22 pp.]. Available from: http://www.medicine.ox.ac.uk/bandolier.

30   Adams N, Field L. Pain Management 1: Psychological and social aspects of pain. Brit J Nurs. 2001;10(14):903-11.

31   Apkarian AV, Baliki MN, Gelia PY. Towards a theory of chronic pain. Prog Neurobiol. 2009;87:81-97.

32   Moseley GL, Butler DS. Fifteen years of explaining pain: The past, present, and future. J Pain. 2015;16(9):807-13.

33   Kong J, Fufa DT, Gerber AJ, Rosman IS, Vangel MG, Gracely RH, et al. Psychophysical outcomes from a randomized pilot study of manual, electro and sham acupuncture treatment on experimentally induced thermal pain. J Pain. 2005;6(1):55-64.

34   Chapman CR, Turner JA. Psychological control of acute pain in medical settings. J Pain Symptom Manag. 1986;1(1):9-20.

35   Coghill RC, MacHaffie JG, Yen YF. Neural correlates of interindividual differences in the subjective experience of pain [web page]. 2003 [Available from: www.pnas.org/cgi/doi/10.1073pnas.1430684100.

36   Hodgson NA, Andersen S. The clinical efficacy of reflexology in nursing home residents with dementia. J Alt Compl Med. 2008;14(3):000-.

37   McVicar AJ, Greenwood CR, Fewell F, D'Arcy VD, Chandrasekharan S, Aldridge LC. Evaluation of anxiety, salivary cortisol and melatonin secretion following

reflexology treatment: A pilot study in healthy individuals. Compl Ther Clin Pract. 2007;13:137-45.

38. Stephenson NLN, Weinrich SP, Tavakoli AS. The effect of foot reflexology on anxiety and pain in patients with breast and lung cancer. Oncol Nurs Forum. 2000;27(1):67-72.

39. Stephenson NL, Swanson M, Dalton J, Keefe FJ, Engelke M. Partner delivered reflexology: effects on cancer pain and anxiety. Oncol Nurs Forum. 2007;34(1):127-32.

40. Mackereth P, Booth K, Hillier VS, Caress AL. Reflexology and progressive muscle relaxation training for people with multiple sclerosis: A crossover trial. Compl Ther Clin Med. 2008;Article in Press.

41. Quattrin R, Zanini A, Buchini S, Turello D, Annunziata MA, Vidotti C, et al. Use of reflexology foot massage to reduce anxiety in hospitalized cancer patients in chemotherapy treatment: Methodology and outcomes. J Nurs Manag. 2006;14:96-105.

42. Pud D, Yarnitsky D, Sprecher E, Rogowski Z, Adler R, Eisenberg E. Can personality traits and gender predict the response to morphine? An experimental cold pain study. Eur J of Pain. 2006;10:103-12.

43. Netter P, Hennig J, Munk AJ. Principles and approaches in Hans Eysenck's personality theory: Their renaissance and development in current neurochemical research on individual differences. Personality and Individual Differences. 2021;169:109975.

44. Li CY, Chen SC, Li CY, Gau ML, Huang CM. Randomised controlled trial of the effectiveness of using foot reflexology to improve quality of sleep amongst Taiwanese postpartum women. Midwifery. 2009;doi:10.1016/j.midw.2009.04.005.

45. Tang NKY. Insomnia co-occurring with chronic pain: Clinical features, interaction, assessments and possible interventions. Reviews in Pain. 2008;2(1):2-7.

46 Aggarwal BB, Shishodia S, Sandur SK, Pandey MK, Sethi G. Inflammation and cancer: How hot is the link? Biochem Pharmacol. 2006;72:1605-21.

47 Irwin MR, Miller AH. Depressive disorders and immunity: 20 years of progress and discovery. Brain Behav Immun. 2007;21:374-83.

48 O'Connor MF, Bower JE, Cho HJ, Creswell JD, Dimitrov S, Hamby ME, et al. To assess, to control, to exclude: Effects of biobehavioural factors on circulating inflammatory markers. Brain Behav Immun. 2009;doi:10.1016/j.bbi.2009.04.005.

CHAPTER 8: The final hurdles

1 Gresty MA, Waters S, Bray A, Bunday K, Golding JF. Impairment of spacial cognitive function with preservation of verbal performance during spatial disorientation. Curr Biol. 2003;13(21):R829-30.

2 Denise P, Vouriot A, Normand H, Golding JF, Gresty MA. Effect of temporal relationship between respiration and body motion on motion sickness. Auton Neurosci-Basic. 2009.

3 Williams DC, Golding JF, Phillips K, Towell A. Perceived control, locus of control and preparatory information: Effects on the perception of an acute pain stimulus. Pers Indiv Differ [Internet]. 2004; 36(7):[1681-91 pp.].

4 Ashton H, Ebenezer I, Golding JF, Thompson JW. Effects of Acupuncture and Transcutaneous Electrical Nerve Stimulation on cold-induced pain in normal subjects. J Psychosom Res. 1984;28(4):301-8.

5 Houston AJ, Wong JC, Ebenezer IS. Effects of subcutaneous administration of the gamma-aminobutyric acid(A) receptor agonist muscimol on water intake in water-deprived rats. Physiology & behavior. 2002;77(2-3):445-50.

6 Houston AJ, Wong JC, Ebenezer IS. Effects of the GABA B receptor agonist baclofen on primary drinking in rats. Eur. J. Pharmacol. 2012;674(2-3):327-31.

7 Ludbrook J, Dudley H. Why permutation tests are superior to t and F tests in biomedical research. Am Stat. 1998;52(2):127-32.

8   Duncan N. Adult myeloid leukaemias pathogenesis, clinical features and classification. Clin Pharm. 2010;2:117-21.

9   Patani N, Mokbel K. The clinical significance of sentinel lymph node micrometastasis in breast cancer. Breast Cancer Res Treat. 2009;114:393-402.

10 Mathieu MC, Rouzier R, Llombart-Cussac A, Sideris L, Koscielny S, Travagli JP, et al. The poor responsiveness of infiltrating lobular breast carcinomas to neoadjuvant chemotherapy can be explained by their biological profile. Eur J of Can. 2004;40:342-51.

11 Dillon MF, Hill ADK, Fleming FJ, O'Doherty A, Quinn CM, McDermott EW, et al. Identifying patients at risk of compromised margins following breast conservation for lobular carcinoma. The Am J Surg. 2006;191:201-5.

12 Rakha EA, El-Sayed ME, Powe DG, Green AR, Habashy H, Grainge MJ, et al. Invasive lobular carcinoma of the breast: Response to hormonal therapy and outcomes. Eur J Can. 2008;44:73-83.

13 Anwar IF, Down SK, Rizvi A, Farooq N, Burger A, Morgan A, et al. Invasive lobular carcinoma of the breast: Should this be regarded as a chronic disease? Int J Surg. 2010;8:346-52.

14 Truong PT, Jones SO, Kader HA, Wai ES, Speers CH, Alexander AS, et al. Patients with T1 to T2 breast cancer with one to three positive nodes have higher local and regional recurrence risks compared with node-negative patients after breast-conserving surgery and whole-breast radiotherapy. Int J Radiation Oncology Biol Phys. 2009;73(2):357-64.

15 Apple SK, Moatamed NA, Finck RH, Sullivan PS. Accurate classification of sentinel lymph node metastases in patients with lobular breast carcinoma. The Breast. 2010:1-5.

16 Nielsen I, Gordon S, Selby A. Breast cancer-related lymphoedema risk reduction advice: A challenge for health professionals. Cancer Treat Rev. 2008;34:621-8.

17 Glaser R, Kiecolt-Glaser JK. Stress-induced immune dysfunction: Implications for health. Nat Rev Immunol. 2005;5:243-51.

18 Liu YZ, Wang YX, Jiang CL. Inflammation: The common pathway of stress-related diseases. Front Hum Neurosci. 2017;11:316.

19 Grivennikov SI, Greten FR, Karin M. Immunity, Inflammation and Cancer. Cell. 2010;140:883-99.

20 Gao F, Liang B, Reddy ST, Farias-Eisner R, Su X. Role of inflammation-associated microenvironment in tumorigenesis and metastasis. Curr Cancer Drug Tar. 2014;14:30-45.

21 Patani N, Mokbel K. The clinical significance of sentinel lymph node micrometastasis in breast cancer. Breast Cancer Res Treat. 2009;114:393-402.

22 de Snoo F, Bender R, Glas A, Rutgers E. Gene expression profiling: Decoding breast cancer. Surg Oncol. 2009;18:366-78.

23 Sparano JA, Gray RJ, Makower DF, Pritchard KI, Albain KS, Hayes DF, et al. Adjuvant chemotherapy guided by a 21-Gene expression assay in breast cancer. N Engl J Med. 2018;379:111-21.

24 Raphael MJ, Biagi JJ, Kong W, Mates M, Booth CM, Mackillop WJ. The relationships between time to initiation of adjuvant chemotherapy and survival in breast cancer: a systematic review and meta-analysis. Breast Cancer Res Treat [Internet]. 2016 05.01.2020; 160(1):[17-28 pp.].

CHAPTER 9: A hopeful road

1 Sandelowski M. Combining qualitative sampling, data collection, and analysis techniques in mixed-method studies. Res Nurs Health. 2000;23:246-55.

2 Ostlund U, Kidd L, Wengstrom Y, Rowa-Dewar N. Combining qualitative and quantitative research within mixed method research designs: A methodological review. Int J Nursing Studies. 2011;48:369-83.

3   Molassiotis A, Helin AM, Dabbour R, Hummerston S. The effects of P6 acupuressure in the prophylaxis of chemotherapy-related nausea and vomiting in breast cancer patients. Comp Ther Med. 2007;15:3-12.

4   Ashton H, Marsh VR, Millman JE, Rawlins MD, Telford R, Thompson JW. Biphasic dose-related responses on the CNV (Contingent Negative Variation) to I.V Nicotine in man. Brit J Clin Pharmaco. 1980;10:579-89.

5   Gresty MA, Waters S, Bray A, Bunday K, Golding JF. Impairment of spacial cognitive function with preservation of verbal performance during spatial disorientation. Curr Biol. 2003;13(21):R829-30.

6   Pitman EJG. A note on normal correlation. Biometrika [Internet]. 1939 19.5.10; 31(1/2):[9-12 pp.]. Available from: http://www.jstor.org/staable/2334971.

7   Bland M. An introduction to medical statistics. 3rd Edition ed. Guildford: Oxford University Press; 2000. 405 p.

8   Good P, Xie F. Analysis of a crossover trial by permutation methods. Contemp Clin Trials. 2008;29:565-8.

9   Carlsson C. Acupuncture mechanisms for clinically relevant long-term effects - reconsideration and a hypothesis. Acupuncture Med. 2002;20 (2-3):82-99.

10 Sandrini G, Milanov I, Malaguti S, Nigrelli MP, Moglia A, Nappi G. Effects of hypnosis on diffuse noxious inhibitory controls. Physiology & behavior. 2000;69:295-300.

11 Jensen M, Patterson DR. Hypnotic treatment of chronic pain. J Behav Med. 2006;29(1):95-124.

12 Montgomery GH, DuHamel KN, Redd WH. A meta-analysis of hypnotically induced analgesia: how effective is hypnosis? Int J Clin Exp Hypn. 2000;48(2):138-53.

13 Milling LS. Is high hypnotic suggestibility necessary for successful hypnotic pain intervention? Curr Pain Headache Rep. 2008;12(2):98-102.

14 Tilg H. Cruciferous vegetables: prototypic anti-inflammatory food components. Clinical Phytoscience [Internet]. 2015;[1-10 pp.].

15 Majewska-Wierzbicka M, Czeczot H. Flavonoids in the prevention and treatment of cardiovascular diseases. Pol Merkur Lekarski. 2012;32(187):50-4.

16 Borstad JD, Szucs KA. Three-dimensional scapula kinematics and shoulder function examined before and after surgical treatment for breast cancer. Human Movement Science. 2011.

17 Freedman RA, Winer EP. Adjuvant therapy for postmenopausal women with endocrine-sensitive breast cancer. The Breast. 2010;19:69-75.

18 Josefsson ML, Leinster SJ. Aromatase inhibitors versus tamoxifen as adjuvant hormonal therapy for oestrogen sensitive early breast cancer in post-menopausal women: Meta-analysis of monotherapy, sequenced therapy and extended therapy. The Breast. 2010;19:76-83.

19 Hale O, Deutsch PG, Lahiri A. Epirubicin extravasation: consequences of delayed management. BMJ Case Rep. 2017;2017:bcr2016218012.

20 World Health Organization. WHO Europe Cancer Nursing Curriculum: WHO European strategy for continuing education for nurses and midwives. Denmark: WHO Regional Office; 2003. Report No.: E81551 Contract No.: EUR/03/5043918b.

21 Kelly D, Gould D, White I, Berridge EJ. Modernising cancer and palliative care education in the UK: Insights from one cancer network. Eur J Oncol Nurs. 2006;10:187-97.

22 Griffiths J, Willard C, Burgess A, Amir Z, Luker K. Meeting the ongoing needs of survivors of rarer cancers. Eur J Oncol Nurs. 2007;11:434-41.

23 Jefford M, Tattersall MHN. Informing and involving cancer patients in their own care. The Lancet Oncol [Internet]. 2002 19.11.2010; 3:[629-37 pp.]. Available from: http://oncology.thelancet.com.

24. Roberts D, McNulty A, Caress AL. Current issue in the delivery of complementary therapies in cancer care - policy, perceptions and expectations: An overview. Eur J Oncol Nurs. 2005;9:115-23.

25. Schofield P, Diggens J, Charleson C, Marigliani R, Jefford M. Effectively discussing complementary and alternative medicine in a conventional oncology setting: Communication recommendations for clinicians. Patient Educ Couns. 2010;79:143-51.

26. van der Riet P, Francis L, Levett-Jones T. Complementary therapies in healthcare: Design, implementation and evaluation of an elective course for undergraduate students. Nurse Educ Practice. 2010;doi:10.1016/j.nepr.2010.10.002.

27. Mackereth P, Carter A, Parkin S, Stringer J, Caress A, Todd C, et al. Complementary therapists' training and cancer care: A multi-site study. Eur J Oncol Nurs. 2009;13:330-5.

28. Richardson A. Creating a culture of compassion: developing supportive care for people with cancer. Eur J Oncol Nurs. 2004;8:293-305.

29. Ream E, Wilson-Barnett J, Faithfull S, FIncham L, Khoo V, Richardson A. Working patterns and perceived contribution of prostate cancer clinical nurse specialists: A mixed method investigation. Int J Nurs Stud. 2009;46:1345-54.

30. Samuel CA, Faithfull S. Complementary therapy support in cancer survivorship: a survey of complementary and alternative medicine practitioners' provision and perception of skills. Eur J Cancer Care (Engl). 2014;23(2):180-8.

31. Faithfull S, Samuel C, Lemanska A, Warnock C, Greenfield D. Self-reported competence in long term care provision for adult cancer survivors: A cross sectional survey of nursing and allied health care professionals. Int J Nurs Stud. 2016 53:85-94.

CHAPTER 10: What future beckons?

1. Schmidt M, Hansson E. Doctoral students' well-being: a literature review. International Journal of Qualitative Studies on Health and Well-being. 2018;13(1):1508171.

2. Wang X, Wang C, Wang J. Towards the contributing factors for stress confronting Chinese PhD students. International Journal of Qualitative Studies on Health and Well-being. 2019;14(1):1598722.

3. Kelly R. Thrive. Cambridge: Rob Kelly Publishing; 2011. 226 p.

4. Samuel CA, Ebenezer IS. Exploratory study on the efficacy of reflexology for pain threshold and tolerance using an ice-pain experiment and sham TENS control. Comp Ther Clin Pract. 2013;19:57-62.

5. Miaskowski C, Paul SM, Mastick J, Schumacher M, Conley YP, Smoot B, et al. Hearing loss and tinnitus in survivors with chemotherapy-induced neuropathy. European Journal of Oncology Nursing. 2018;32:1-11.

6. Miaskowski C, Paul SM, Mastick J, Abrams G, Topp K, Smoot B, et al. Associations between perceived stress and chemotherapy-induced peripheral neuropathy and otoxicity in adult cancer survivors. Journal of Pain and Symptom Management. 2018;56(1):88-97.

7. Ma Y, Wise AK, Shepherd RK, Richardson RT. New molecular therapies for the treatment of hearing loss. Pharmacology & therapeutics. 2019;200:190-209.

8. Fortunato S, Forli F, Guglielmi V, De Corso E, Paludetti G, Berrettini S, et al. A review of new insights on the association between hearing loss and cognitive decline in ageing. Acta otorhinolaryngologica Italica : organo ufficiale della Societa italiana di otorinolaringologia e chirurgia cervico-facciale. 2016;36(3):155-66.

9. Bost TJM, Versfeld NJ, Goverts ST. Effect of audibility and suprathreshold deficits on speech recognition for listeners with unilateral hearing loss. Ear and hearing. 2019;40(4):1025-34.

10 Samuel CA, Faithfull S. Complementary therapy support in cancer survivorship: a survey of complementary and alternative medicine practitioners' provision and perception of skills. Eur J Cancer Care (Engl). 2014;23(2):180-8.

11 Kurt S, Can G. Reflexology in the management of chemotherapy induced peripheral neuropathy: A pilot randomized controlled trial. Eur J Oncol Nurs. 2018;32:12-9.

12 Ben-Horin I, Kahan P, Ryvo L, Inbar M, Lev-Ari S, Geva R. Acupuncture and reflexology for chemotherapy-induced peripheral neuropathy in breast cancer. Integr Cancer Ther. 2017;16(3):258-62.

THE TENACIOUS STUDENT | Dr CAROL A. SAMUEL